A Place Called Grand Canyon

SOCIETY, ENVIRONMENT, AND PLACE

Series Editors Andrew Kirby and Janice Monk

A Place Called

GRAND

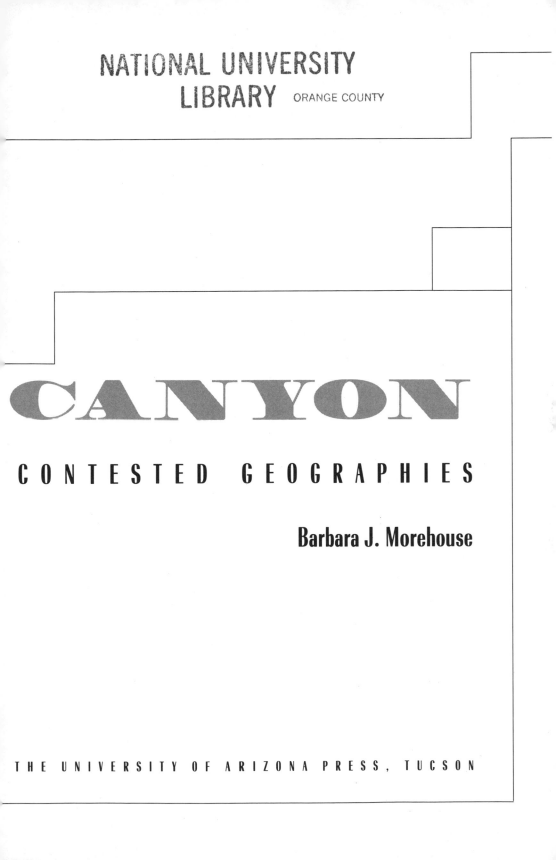

CANYON

CONTESTED GEOGRAPHIES

Barbara J. Morehouse

THE UNIVERSITY OF ARIZONA PRESS, TUCSON

The University of Arizona Press
Copyright ©1996
The Arizona Board of Regents
All Rights Reserved
⊗This book is printed on acid-free, archival-quality paper.
Manufactured in the United States of America
01 00 99 98 97 96 6 5 4 3 2 1
Library of Congress Cataloging-in-Publication Data

Morehouse, Barbara J. (Barbara Jo), 1945–
    A place called Grand Canyon : contested geographies / Barbara J. Morehouse.
        p.   cm. — (Society, environment, and place series)
    Includes bibliographical references and index.
    ISBN 0-8165-1603-0 (cloth : alk. paper). —
    ISBN 0-8165-1628-6 (paper : alk. paper)
        1. Human geography—Arizona—Grand Canyon Region—History.
    2. Land use—Arizona—Grand Canyon Region—History.   3. Landscape
    changes—Arizona—Grand Canyon Region—History.   4. Grand Canyon
    National Park (Ariz.)—History.   5. Grand Canyon Region (Ariz.)—
    History.   6. Grand Canyon Region (Ariz.)—Environmental conditions.
    I. Title.   II. Series.
    GF504.A6M67   1996   95-32495
    333.73'09791'32 — dc20   CIP

British Library Cataloguing-in-Publication Data
A catalogue record for this book is available from the British Library.

CONTENTS

ACKNOWLEDGMENTS

This book is the product of five years of research and thought and would never have reached its final form without the advice, assistance, and support of many people. The staff at Grand Canyon National Park generously gave of their all-too-limited time and provided invaluable information and insights, as well as access to park documents. Particular thanks go to Kim Crumbo, whose assistance and cooperation made my research trips to the canyon incredibly efficient and productive. Thanks also to Jan Balsom, Doug Brown, Frank Buono, Mark Law, John Ray, John Reed, Brad Travers, and former park superintendent Robert Chandler for granting me interviews. At the U.S. Forest Service offices in Williams and Tusayan, special thanks go to Dennis Lund and George Gibbons for the information and materials they generously provided. Leigh Jenkins of the Hopi Tribe and Herbert Yazhe of the Navajo Nation provided insights I could have obtained nowhere else. Jim Ruch, Roger Clark, and Tony Skrelunas filled me in on the work being done by the Grand Canyon Trust.

To Robert Keller I extend a world of appreciation for not only sharing knowledge, literary references, and interview transcripts with me in areas where our research overlapped, but for extending a kind of friendship and interest that is all the more precious for its rarity. His comments on an earlier version of this book not only provided much needed linkages to the larger context within which events at the Grand Canyon transpired, but also pointed out to me where I had gotten lost in the labyrinths of academese. Thanks also to the anonymous reviewer who provided ideas and references that have assuredly improved not only this book, but my understanding of how it all fits together.

I want to extend profound gratitude and friendship to the people who were there from the beginning of this project: to Marvin Waterstone, without whose generous gifts of time, intellectual exchange, patience, encouragement, and support this project would never have gotten off the ground; to Ervin Zube, for facilitating the permit process, which allowed me to do my research at Grand Canyon National Park, as well as for the irreplaceable knowledge I gained about environmental perception and heritage resource management; to Sallie Marston, for hitting the nail on the thumb at crucial junctures; and to Andrew Kirby, for the excursions into political and social geography. Thanks also to Christine Szuter of the University of Arizona Press for her un-flagging enthusiasm, to Chuck Sternberg for his excellent map, and to Sally Bennett for the subtle copyediting.

This list would be woefully incomplete without acknowledging my deep appreciation to my son, Jeffrey Morehouse, for remaining, through it all, the light of my life. To my parents, George and Donna Salmon, immense gratitude for their steadfast belief, support, and en-couragement. And last, but certainly not least, I am forever indebted to my husband, Philip Johnson, for understanding the need to march to one's own strummer.

A Place Called Grand Canyon

Introduction

Grand Canyon . . . the very words have become immersed in our everyday language. We speak of things being as deep as the Grand Canyon, or of gaps that are as wide. We see it as a wilderness, a spectacle, an antidote to urban stresses, a brief stop on the way to somewhere else. It speaks of our national heritage and lends its identity to Arizona, the Grand Canyon State.

Yet this Grand Canyon as most people conceptualize it includes only Grand Canyon National Park. Beyond the boundaries of the park exists a much larger region: the greater Grand Canyon. It includes five Indian reservations, lands managed by three federal land management agencies and by the states of Arizona and Utah, and numerous settlements; it provides a setting for a variety of economic activities. It stretches from southern Utah on the north to Flagstaff and Williams on the south. From east to west, it stretches from the western half of the Navajo Reservation to the California and Nevada state lines. The region is united, rather than divided, by the Grand Canyon itself.

Yet it is also divided along lines of difference regarding how its resources are valued and used in any given context and is further divided by the particular historical experiences, traditions, cultural identities, practices, and aspirations of its inhabitants and protectors. The result is a mosaic of spaces that represent different kinds of knowledge, different values, different goals.

This geographical mosaic is fascinating, for its landscapes vary over time in response to interactions between physical processes and human activities. Likewise, the political boundaries that give definition to the jurisdictional units of the greater Grand Canyon are dynamic, changing

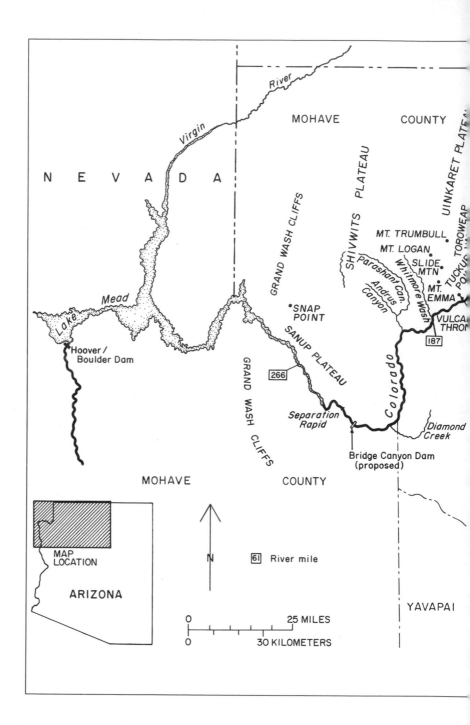

MOHAVE   COUNTY

NEVADA

Virgin *River*

SHIVWITS PLATEAU

UINKARET PLATEAU

MT. TRUMBULL
MT. LOGAN
SLIDE MTN
MT. EMMA

TUCKUP TOROWEAP

POINT

Parashant Can.

Whitmore Wash

Andrus Canyon

GRAND WASH CLIFFS

Lake Mead

•SNAP POINT

VULCAN THRONE

•Hoover / Boulder Dam

SANUP PLATEAU

266

Colorado

187

GRAND WASH CLIFFS

Separation Rapid

Diamond Creek

Bridge Canyon Dam
(proposed)

MOHAVE   COUNTY

MAP LOCATION

ARIZONA

N

61 River mile

YAVAPAI

0   25 MILES

0   30 KILOMETERS

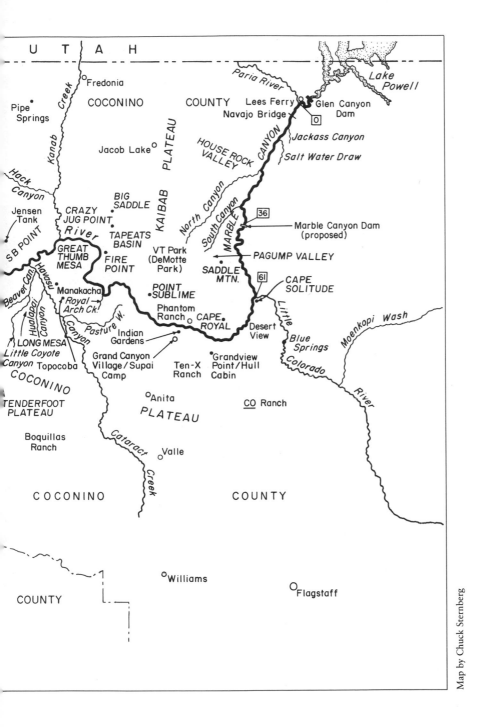

U T A H

COCONINO   COUNTY

Fredonia

Pipe
Springs

Lake
Powell

Paria River

Lees Ferry   Glen Canyon
Navajo Bridge   Dam

0

Jackass Canyon

Salt Water Draw

HOUSE ROCK
VALLEY

Jacob Lake

KAIBAB PLATEAU

Kanab Creek

Hack
Canyon

Jensen
Tank

CRAZY
JUG POINT

BIG
SADDLE

TAPEATS
BASIN

River

North Canyon

South Canyon

MARBLE CANYON

36

Marble Canyon Dam
(proposed)

SB POINT

GREAT
THUMB
MESA

FIRE
POINT

VT Park
(DeMotte
Park)

SADDLE
MTN.

PAGUMP VALLEY

61

CAPE
SOLITUDE

Beaver Can.

Havasu

Manakacha
Royal
Arch Ck!

POINT
SUBLIME

Phantom
Ranch

CAPE
ROYAL

Desert
View

Blue
Springs

Little

Moenkopi Wash

Colorado River

Hualapai Canyon

Pasture W.

Indian
Gardens

Canyon

LONG MESA
Little Coyote
Canyon Topocoba

Grand Canyon
Village/Supai
Camp

Ten-X
Ranch

Grandview
Point/Hull
Cabin

COCONINO

TENDERFOOT
PLATEAU

Anita

PLATEAU

CO Ranch

Boquillas
Ranch

Cataract Creek

Valle

C O C O N I N O   COUNTY

COUNTY

Williams

Flagstaff

Map by Chuck Sternberg

in response to human demands, expectations, and power relationships.

With visitation to Grand Canyon National Park approaching five million people per year (Kreutz 1994), pressures on the lands and resources of the park are intense. When the larger domain of the greater Grand Canyon is considered, the problems become significantly more complex: grazing, timber cutting, recreation, wilderness designation, mining, a growing population base, and the activities occurring on the five Indian reservations in the area create a web of demands, contests, and interactions that vastly complicate broad-scale environmental management.

Contests over the lands, waters, and other resources of the greater Grand Canyon date back to prehistory, as we can clearly discern from the defensive positioning of the cliff dwellings that were built by early inhabitants and that still dot the landscape today. Yet the imposition of mapped boundaries occurred only with the expansion of the United States into the area in the mid-nineteenth century. At that point, the story became one of recurrent contests among different interests, all seeking to divide and control the land and its resources according to their own needs or desires and all trying to influence how the area was mapped. The story reveals how the spaces within the mosaic have reinforced—or destabilized—social, political, and economic relationships among the various individuals and interest groups.

But who were these individuals and groups? What did they want, and how effective were they in achieving their goals? How did they define Grand Canyon? Answers to these questions reveal how society and space have interacted to make and remake the place called "Grand Canyon."

This book is a meditation on how the mosaic of the greater Grand Canyon has changed over time and what brought about the changes. It is a story of the contests that have taken place regarding how the area should be shared, inhabited, protected, and used.

Although the greater Grand Canyon is the subject of this book, the story is neither singular nor unique. Rather, it is representative of one of the most fundamental processes of human existence: society's organization of geographical space (Soja 1989, 79). The use of boundaries to delineate the edges or limits to those spaces is an ancient practice (Jones 1959; Prescott 1987; see also Sahlins 1989). However, the more formal and complex methods that we use today for partitioning territory (and water and air, for that matter) and for inscribing the boundaries of those territories on maps date back to the seventeenth century, when the nation-state system began forming.

The present system of spatial partitioning and boundary drawing is not the only way to allocate territory and resources, of course, but within the context of our contemporary national (and global) political and economic systems, it remains—for all its failure to permanently resolve disputes over territory and resources—the best one available. Yet drawing lines in the sand (so to speak) and on maps to resolve contests over territory and resources is only the beginning. Even giving the domain a new interpretation, and establishing new rules and practices for how it should be used, is insufficient. For the domain to take on a particular identity and be used in the prescribed ways, the people and organizations that control it must reiterate and defend their spaces. To the extent that they are successful, they reaffirm their domain and its boundaries. To the extent that others are able to assert different ideas, the space and its boundaries become unstable, susceptible to change.

Three geographical concepts are especially useful for understanding how and why these changes occur. Absolute space, relative space, and representational space are important catalysts in contests over the spaces of places like the greater Grand Canyon.

Absolute space (and its boundaries) functions as a container, as a defined area within which certain ideas and ways of behaving dominate (Gattrell 1983). We need only think of the spaces within the four walls of our homes, or of a wilderness area where few are allowed in— and then only for a brief time and for strictly specified purposes—to conceptualize an absolute space.

Relative space, by contrast, refers to an area that supports multiple definitions and uses, either simultaneously or at different times. For example, a forest may be at the same time a place to cut timber, graze cattle, and mine for ore. All of these activities may take place simultaneously or at different times, but each defines the space relative to particular attributes: trees, grass, minerals. The boundaries of that space change depending on the characteristics of the space and the expectations of those giving it definition (Gattrell 1983).

Unlike either of the other two concepts, *representational space* (LeFebvre 1991) enfolds symbols, values, experiences, histories, and traditions—many of which are intangible and unquantifiable—that give someone (or some group) a sense of attachment to that location.

Often people refer to this feeling as a "sense of place," of being in their proper place, of being rooted. These spaces and places may be as small as a roadside shrine or as large as the sweeping vistas of the Great Plains. Such places, especially when they are of deep-seated importance to sustaining cultures and lifeways, may fuel long-standing and intensely fought contests when other people begin to assert their own values over the area.

The history of our national parks provides an excellent example of how contests over spaces unfold. How people such as ranchers, miners, loggers, recreationists, environmentalists, American Indians, and others define contested territory and resources makes a big difference in the language they use and the actions they take. The particular type of knowledge they draw upon (whether it is scientific, legal, bureaucratic, economic, cultural, or religious) plays an important role in how they understand an area such as a large national park in their midst, and what they want to do with it. These definitions and types of knowledge, in turn, are important influences in how territory and resources come to be redefined and repartitioned.[1]

As the story of the spaces of the greater Grand Canyon reveals, the boundaries were in each case proposed, and drawn, to serve particular functions. These functions were crucial factors in the determination of the size and configuration of the spaces being contested. Once inscribed, the boundaries and their functions provided valuable inputs to the conduct of subsequent contests. The human story of the spaces and boundaries of the greater Grand Canyon is one of both persistence and change. The story speaks through the words and actions of the participants, for it is the individuals—and the social, political, economic, cultural, and bureaucratic contexts within which they have operated—that have created Grand Canyon as we know it.

It is a story of dreams, given substance by the National Park Service, to protect scenic portions of the canyon for the benefit of the American public. It is also a story of the agency's voracious appetite for land, even at considerable expense to others. Similarly, efforts by the U.S. Bureau of Land Management and the U.S. Forest Service to introduce rationality into the management of the timber, ore, and grazing resources of the area are paralleled by the agencies' long history of blindness to the recreational and wilderness values that have long been held by broad segments of the population.

Residents of the Colorado River Basin, particularly in California and Arizona, manifested an insatiable appetite for water and electric power. Their demands produced legislation at the state and federal levels that authorized the construction of a series of dams on the Colorado River. Though understandably reflecting the nation's fascination with progress and growth, with creating gardens in the desert and more leisure time for millions, legislators remained stubbornly myopic when it came to understanding the depth of opposition to interfering with the natural conditions of the Grand Canyon.

So, too, local residents, most of whom have been either directly or indirectly dependent on the exploitation of natural resources for their livelihoods, refused (and in some cases continue to refuse) to acknowledge fundamental changes in the way most people in the United States live. The industrialization and urbanization of the nation—from which local resource users benefit every day—have given rise to a variety of interest groups representing hikers, campers, tourists, preservationists, and others who not only want but have a right to a share of those remnants of scenic nature that still remain.

Arguments can be made for and against all sides. Perhaps the lesson to be learned from the stories of places like Grand Canyon is that there is no longer "someplace else" to which undesirable uses can be relocated. The frontier closed more than a hundred years ago. What is left is to learn how to share the spaces that we have created, to learn how to make decisions and manage resources in such a way that the maximum number of future options remain open, at the least possible cost.

To accomplish this task, we must look beyond the boundaries drawn on maps to discover the location, size, and configuration of the spaces that are important to different people. We need to understand the values, goals, and practices of all people who have an interest in the area—including those whose voices tend to be occluded—and to guard against causing irreparable harm to them.

The learning process also requires becoming more responsive to the (entirely voiceless) physical environment so that we not only minimize irreversible impacts on landscapes, communities, and ecosystems, but also actively work to ensure that natural processes continue to operate as freely as possible. It means remembering that democratic decision making and the spaces in which those decisions take form are never simple. Boundaries drawn on maps never tell the whole story, for beyond every boundary lies "something different." And it is the differences that we must constantly negotiate.

CHAPTER ONE

Physical and Cultural Background

The greater Grand Canyon, encompassing the plateau lands and canyons of northern Arizona and southern Utah, presents a breathtaking microcosm of natural processes. The topography of volcanic peaks, high plateaus, mesas, and deeply incised arroyos is sharply defined by the Grand Canyon itself, a great east-west-trending chasm that is 277 miles long, 10 miles wide (on average, but 15 miles across at its greatest width), and 4,000 feet deep. Here granite, sandstone, and limestone provide an unparalleled lesson in the geological processes that have formed the home we know as Earth.

The landscape of the greater Grand Canyon is one of contrast; depending primarily on local elevation, climate, and weather, the surrounding desert gives way to islands of grassland, chaparral, and forest. Grand Canyon National Park alone contains five of the seven life zones (the Colorado Plateau, within which the park lies, contains six of the seven zones) and three of the four North American deserts (Grand Canyon National Park 1993b). Pine and fir forests thrive on the eastern portions of the North and South Rims. Yet with relatively small changes in elevation these forests fade quickly, in all directions, into landscapes of scrublands, grasslands, and desert.

A characteristically wide range of temperatures contributes strongly to this landscape. On the North Rim, temperatures range from 37.8 degrees Fahrenheit in January to 77.0 degrees in July. On the South Rim, January temperatures reach an average of 46.4 degrees and July temperatures, 84.7 degrees. At Phantom Ranch, on the Colorado River at the bottom of the Grand Canyon, January temperatures average

56.3 degrees and July temperatures may easily reach or exceed 106 degrees (Whitney 1982).

Climate also plays a strong role. Over time the greater Grand Canyon has been a land of strong climatic variation, especially with regard to precipitation. Drought lurks always just over the horizon, abundance is seldom more than a dream. Insufficient water has long been a major factor influencing the landscape and one that continues to affect the human uses of the land and its resources even today. Agriculture has traditionally been limited to areas of perennial (or at least periodically dependable) water supplies. Elsewhere, the lack of dependable water constrains resource users to less water-dependent activities such as grazing, logging, mining, and recreation.

The human history behind the partitioning of the spaces and resources of the greater Grand Canyon is a long and fascinating one, linking human values and activities with the ever-present realities of the physical landscape. Radiocarbon dating of split twig figurines found in the greater Grand Canyon region has revealed that hunter-gatherer groups roamed the area between 5,000 and 3,200 years ago (Hughes 1978). Southeast of the canyon proper, in Hopi country, occupancy may well date back at least 10,000 years (Brew 1979).

Going back in time, we do not know the extent to which the early inhabitants of the greater Grand Canyon engaged in disputes or hostilities over space and resources, but the climatic history of the area clearly indicates that the ability of the land to support human populations has varied radically, depending especially upon the amount and timing of precipitation. Precipitation was a particularly important factor in the earliest days of prehistory, for periodic droughts diminished the availability of wild and cultivated foods. If the droughts persisted over a series of growing seasons, residents abandoned their settlements and moved on, leaving in their wake the dwellings and artifacts from which we have learned of their existence.

The Spanish entry into the American Southwest changed old ways forever, especially—though largely indirectly—for the Hopi and Navajo. The first Spaniards to appear in the area were the members of an exploration party searching for gold. Led by Friar Marcos de Niza, they traveled northward in 1539 under the orders of Antonio de Mendoza, the viceroy of New Spain. The group traveled as far north as the Zuni pueblos, in what is today New Mexico, but apparently had no contact with any of the five peoples of the greater Grand Canyon. Yet the Spaniards had an indirect influence on these peoples by introducing into trade networks such items as red flannel cloth, horses, sheep, cattle, and a variety of agricultural products, including peaches that came to be cultivated by all four groups living south of the Colorado River. The Hualapai, Havasupai, Hopi, and Navajo all (to a greater or lesser extent) began growing new types of crops, and all adopted horses, but only the Hopi and the Navajo seem to have engaged in sheep herding to any large extent at this early date, and of these peoples only the Navajos used their newly acquired equestrian skills to raid their neighbors on a regular basis. These practices had major impacts on how the land and its resources were shared and used.

Herding, being more extensive and nomadic than agricultural activity, gave rise to a redefinition of geographical space and to intensified contests over the control and uses of that space. In time, the resident group's sheep herd became a symbol of social organization, and the group's social standing within the larger community came to be judged in terms of the size and well-being of their herd (Witherspoon 1986).

By 1540, when Don Pedro de Tovar and his party first made contact with residents of the easternmost of the four Hopi mesas, the Hopis were already almost entirely surrounded by the Navajos, themselves relative newcomers to the area (Brugge 1986). One hundred years later, local land disputes gave way to a remarkable episode of cooperation when the Navajo joined with the Hopi and other Puebloans to drive the Spanish, whose increasing military and missionary encroachments had become insupportable, out of their homelands. Their resistance culminated in the Pueblo Revolt of 1680. The allied peoples expelled all missionaries from their midst and forced a major Spanish retreat to the Rio Grande near present-day El Paso.

After the Pueblo Revolt of 1680, Hopi tribal members moved the First and Second Mesa towns from the lower terraces they had occupied for many years to more defensible locations on the top of the mesas, locations the towns continue to occupy today. The Spaniards fought to reconquer the area from 1692 to 1695 and occupied it until the end of the century, reintroducing pressures that rippled far beyond their New Mexico base.

The Navajos took advantage of destabilized conditions to challenge their neighbors through territorial expansion, demographic growth, and cultural adaptation (Ellis 1974). Pressure on the Hopis' land base increased, and the stage was set for an ongoing and bitter struggle over lands and resources to the east of the Grand Canyon proper, a contest that has continued to the present day. By the mid-eighteenth century, the Navajos had enlarged their territorial base, though apparently not without hostilities, even into the eastern range of the Havasupai people (Brugge 1986).

At this time the Navajos, like their northern neighbors, the Utes, were also preying on the weaker Southern Paiute bands, taking slaves for themselves and for the New Mexican slave market. The Paiutes' vulnerability to predation became even greater when, in the 1830s, Euro-American traders opened the Old Spanish Trail across northern Arizona (Kelly and Fowler 1986).

The Geographies of Local Knowledge

The peoples of the greater Grand Canyon lacked maps of their geographical spaces, but they did have a very detailed and intimate knowledge of the land and its resources. Their definition and use of geographical space was somewhat fluid, in that some types of areas were governed more explicitly than others. In general, valuable agricultural lands and water sources were subject to stricter rules of usufruct[1] than were the lands used for hunting and gathering. Even on nonagricultural lands, however, some power was exerted, for outsiders had to obtain permission from the local group before entering into those areas.

The absence of sharply delineated boundaries, while not posing a problem in interactions among the local indigenous groups, became a serious drawback when the United States began laying claim to the same lands and resources. The lack of clear, indisputable evidence that the indigenous peoples were actually using many of the lands being claimed by incoming settlers did not help their cause either. The settlers operated from the assumption that a property right was established through clear evidence of possession, such as proof of permanent agriculture or residence (Rose 1985). Because in many cases the indigenous peoples' main uses were hunting and gathering—uses that left no permanent mark or symbol of possession on the landscape—these lands became defined as "unoccupied" and therefore available for permanent appropriation by others.

The indigenous peoples' lack of political organization above the level of the band (or clan in the case of the Hopi and Navajo) caused them further problems. Whereas the peoples of the greater Grand Canyon did not recognize a single leader, much less any Western concept of hierarchy, officials of the United States expected to negotiate with a single spokesperson for each of the cultural groups. In the end, the government created the Indian "tribes" as we know them today, and spokespersons emerged to mediate between the federal bureaucracy and traditional political structures. These innovations brought their own problems, because agreements made by tribal leaders outside traditional consensus-building proceedings often generated dissent within the tribes and eroded tribal cohesiveness. Despite being largely a matter of governmental expediency, however, the creation of the tribes has proved to be a boon for the indigenous peoples, for through their acceptance of tribal identities they have been able to claim land. By possessing even a small portion of their traditional lands, they have been able to ensure a territorial anchor for their cultural identities and to sustain (in varying degrees) the unity necessary to preserve their unique language, socioeconomic institutions, and cultural traditions.

Possessing a territorial anchor is crucial to Indian cultures, for native peoples' definitions of space often have their foundation in Nature itself. In Western Apache culture, for example, landscape features play a prominent role in stories tribal members tell each other to sustain their cultural traditions and to address personal or communal problems. Thus, specific landscapes serve as both moral guides and reminders of tribal connections (Basso 1990).

So, too, are geographically specific places indispensable to the cultures of the Grand Canyon peoples. The division of the spaces of the greater Grand Canyon among the resident peoples traditionally relied on identification of specific natural features either to mark the outer extent of their territory or to designate localities they associated with specific traditions, beliefs, or practices. For example, the Havasupais say that originally they occupied "all of the mountains you can see" from a vantage point near present-day Valle, Arizona (Wray 1990). Indeed, one need only inquire into the long fight of the Navajos and Hopis to prevent recreational developments on the San Francisco Peaks to fully realize the importance of geographical places to the local peoples. In this case, the long-standing claims of the Hopis and Navajos to the peaks (today managed by the U.S. Forest Service) rest on religious claims: the peaks are the home of the Hopi kachinas and the locus for Navajo origin stories and myths.[2] On a broader scale, Hopi filmmaker Victor Masayesva's video, *Itam Hakim Hopiit*, reveals through Hopi storytelling his people's deeply rooted and intimate relationship with their ancestral lands and landscapes.

Discovering the Abyss

The expansion of the frontier into the greater Grand Canyon began with the arrival of trappers in the late 1820s but did not take on its own momentum until the 1860s. Speculation and greed went hand in hand with hearty assertions that opening the western lands would provide a safety valve for the teeming masses of landless city dwellers in the East. The masses would become armies sent out to subdue the "virgin lands" (Smith 1970), to turn the West into a garden. And they were to divide and conquer: the map and the boundary marker were as much the weapons of conquest as were the gun and the plow. Inscribing ownership on paper and on the land made the arrangements seem permanent, indelible, inevitable. Yet for the greater Grand Canyon, as elsewhere, it was precisely these arrangements that set the stage for ongoing contests over the control and use of the land and its resources.

The Mormons and Their Dreams of Deseret

The Mormons (members of the Church of Jesus Christ of Latter-day Saints) were the first Anglo-Americans to settle the area, extending their activities into territories occupied by the Hopi, Havasupai, Hualapai, and Paiute peoples. Though their religion was different from that of mainstream society, they brought with them many of the country's ways of life and of dividing and controlling land and resources.

Having been hounded in the East and Midwest for their nonconformist religious practices, the Mormons sought to protect their religious freedom by moving to a new place, one far from Bible-thumping zealots and other self-appointed guardians of morality. Even though they believed that all of North and South America was their "Zion," they began moving westward in 1846 to find a core—a territorial heart—that would sustain life the way they wanted to live it. Utah Territory was vast and desolate, but it also had streams and farmlands. Along the Virgin River, Kanab Creek, Moccasin Creek, Escalante River, Paria River, and Sevier River they saw the Paiutes' simple floodplain farms and knew that with their more sophisticated knowledge, these same lands could be made to yield much more.

The Mormons called their new home Deseret and set about creating a self-sufficient society (Smith 1972). They expanded southward into the greater Grand Canyon, appropriating Indian lands and, more important, water sources (Stoffle and Evans 1978). Where they could not farm the land, they grazed livestock, especially cattle.

One of the most important practices that the Mormons brought to Deseret was that of dividing the land into individual parcels marked off by boundaries. The native peoples in the area had apportioned farmland among band members, but "ownership" was based on usufruct: if the land was not used over a specified period of time, the band reallocated it to another family. The Mormons set about establishing permanent ownership of all the lands they wanted, for whatever reason. And ownership meant no Indians allowed—except as hired labor.

Congress, in the Compromise of 1850, affirmed Mormon control over the area the religious group had settled. But the Mormons wanted more. In 1864, Brigham Young called on the United States to allow the Mormons the lands extending two degrees of latitude on one side or the other of the Colorado River (Smith 1972, 281, 283). His motive was to give the Mormons jurisdiction over a route to the Pacific Ocean and to give them the lands they had been cultivating along the Muddy and Virgin Rivers in Utah.

Territorial delegates from Nevada and Arizona blocked the idea in Congress, aided by the Mormons' very bad timing: the gold rush had drawn vast numbers of people to California, the Civil War still raged, and the federal government was becoming increasingly concerned about what to do with the immense territory ceded by Mexico. Thus, in the end, national politics overrode the Mormons' territorial designs, which at their most ambitious would have incorporated all of Utah, Arizona north of the Gila River (including the Grand Canyon), most of Nevada, and parts of California, New Mexico, Colorado, Wyoming, and Idaho (Walker and Bufkin 1986). What they ended up with was present-day Utah and Nevada and parts of Wyoming and Colorado. The new boundary was the 37th parallel, which to this day separates Utah from Arizona.

Not satisfied with the territory allotted them by Congress, the Mormons continued their efforts to add territory to the Mormon state and to control strategic transportation routes. In the meantime, they did not ignore the native peoples. Believing Indians to be descendants of peoples described in the Book of Mormon (Smith 1972, 248), the Mormons devoted considerable time and energy to proselytizing among them. But a considerable amount of pragmatism was involved too: they wanted to generate strategic alliances among the native peoples, such as the Paiutes and the Hopis, who controlled important parcels of territory.

Jacob Hamblin, a Mormon missionary, was the first permanent Anglo-American settler to set eyes on the Grand Canyon (Verkamp 1940). He was even more notable for his ability to speak to the native peoples in their own languages and for his success in winning their confidence. However amicable relations between indigenous people and individual Mormons like Hamblin might have been, though, an uneven contest over territory in the greater Grand Canyon ensued. Mormon settlers increasingly encroached on Indian lands, especially those inhabited by the Southern Paiute bands on the North Rim and by the Hopi and Havasupai (who had farms in the Moenkopi Wash area) east of the Grand Canyon proper.

The Arizona Strip, between the North Rim of the Grand Canyon and the Utah-Arizona boundary, was one of the places where Mormon activity was—and is—strongest. The reason lies in the geography of the region. Until the late 1920s, this patch of land remained relatively inaccessible, especially from the south where travelers had to travel miles out of their way to cross the wide chasm of the Grand Canyon. The closest crossing was on the east side at Lees Ferry, near where Marble Canyon joins the Grand Canyon. Access was much easier from the north, the heart of Mormon country. Mormon livestock raisers could operate from ranches on the Arizona Strip or from homesteads in southern Utah and thus control much of the grazing land and timber of the wider area.

The Birth of Arizona Territory

The Compromise of 1850 had, among its other provisions, given the Mormons a land base. It also created the Territory of New Mexico, which included all of Arizona as well as New Mexico within its borders. More lines were drawn on maps, more efforts made to establish control over the last frontier of the American West. Yet the arrangement proved ephemeral. By 1855, Texans who had settled in southern New Mexico were agitating to split the territory in half along an east-west line. By 1860, ten such bills had been introduced into Congress. The outbreak of the Civil War in 1861 put a halt to the idea, though, because any line dividing north from south in New Mexico Territory would have resulted in a concentration of Confederate sympathizers in the southern portion—a result Congress would not accept. Instead, in 1863, President Abraham Lincoln signed a bill creating a separate Arizona Territory based on a north-south line, drawn approximately along the 109th meridian, that divided Confederate sympathizers between the two territories (Walker and Bufkin 1986).

Things stayed fairly quiet until the Civil War ended. With a return to a civilian economy, large numbers of adventurers and entrepreneurs such as speculators, prospective farmers, miners, loggers, and small-businesspeople began looking west for new opportunities: a piece of land, a share of the resources, a new beginning. They divided up the land, drew property lines, turned their cattle and sheep loose on those rangelands for which they saw no value in appropriating as private property, and chopped down trees at a furious rate. Miners poked and prodded the earth, though they never came up with the kind of gold, silver, or copper they needed to make their work profitable over the long (or even medium) term.

The arrival of civilization to Arizona Territory brought not only ranches and towns but a further partitioning of the greater Grand Canyon into counties. County boundary lines, drawn and redrawn in the years between 1864 and 1909 (and again in 1983 when another county, La Paz, was created), gave rise to new political positions and entities, such as mayors and town councils, who did not hesitate to enter into the fray whenever issues over territory and resources arose.

The creation of Arizona Territory and its counties was not accomplished without challenge, however, for Utah continued to look southward for expansion, targeting the Arizona Strip. Brigham Young had been trying for years to have the Arizona Strip transferred from Arizona Territory to Utah, but the process took on a new momentum in 1896 when Utah attained statehood—Utah politicians immediately set about having bills introduced in both houses of Congress to sever the Strip from Arizona Territory. The Utah politicians complained that the area had become a haven for outlaws and was too remote for effective policing from the Arizona side (Hughes 1967).

What the Utah politicians did not mention was that the Arizona Strip was at that time a haven for polygamous Mormons who refused to abide by the prohibition of the practice by both the state of Utah and the Mormon Church (Hughes 1967). If the area were annexed to Utah, the miscreants could be more easily brought to heel. Needless to say, the settlers on the Strip were opposed to being incorporated into Utah, probably considering their isolation from the rest of Arizona better protection than having to adhere to the rules issued from Salt Lake City.

In 1902 Utah's congressional representatives introduced another bill in Congress to annex the Strip and, in accordance with rules requiring that any such transfer be done only with the consent of the state giving up the territory, sent a delegation to confer with the legislators of Arizona Territory. The Arizonans squelched the bid straightaway by simply refusing to meet with the Utah delegation. Undeterred, Utah's senators introduced a bill in the U.S. Senate in 1904 to annex the Strip. This time Mohave County protested, and the effort failed. The project finally died when Arizona became a state in 1912 (Hughes 1967).

The Early Explorers

Though the Mormons were the first non-Indians to overlay their own designs on the greater Grand Canyon, it was explorers, surveyors, scientists, and adventurers such as Edward Fitzgerald Beale, Joseph Christmas Ives, John Wesley Powell, and the men who accompanied them who initiated the most far-reaching changes. Their incursions into the Indian country of the greater Grand Canyon were, in the end, devastating to the native peoples.

At the forefront of the westward expansion was the U.S. Army Corps of Topographical Engineers. The engineers were men educated in the latest scientific advances. In the West, they brought their training to bear in ways that produced profound cultural as well as political change (Pyne 1982). In the greater Grand Canyon area, the corps used firsthand knowledge of the canyon and its environs to produce remarkable maps, drawings, photographs, written narratives, and scientific measurements. Between 1859 and 1906, mapmakers associated with the survey parties (and with the U.S. Geological Survey after its creation) answered the basic questions about the Grand Canyon: precisely where it was located, how it was configured, how it related to its context (Seavey 1994).

Yet the early explorers were not just randomly wandering over the land. They had a mission: finding land and water routes to the West Coast. The United States needed these routes to consolidate control over its West Coast possessions and to keep the Mormons and the Indians in line (Pyne 1982). The first of the surveyor-explorers to enter

Grand Canyon country were Amiel Weeks Whipple, who from 1853 to 1856 surveyed for the best railroad route to California, and Edward Fitzgerald Beale, who from 1857 to 1858 surveyed a wagon road across the plateau lands south of the canyon.[3] Their efforts mark the beginning of a new era in which science was increasingly put to the task of partitioning, and controlling, geographical space.

Extension of control over the waterways also began at this time, with Lieutenant Joseph Christmas Ives leading a War Department–sponsored exploration of the Colorado River aimed at quelling the so-called Mormon wars. The "wars" were really no more than a series of skirmishes between Mormons and other settlers over land and resources in the Southwest, but the federal government was worried that the growing possibility of a split between North and South would be mirrored by a division between East and West—a nightmare that would surely destroy the country. In the end, the Colorado River defeated Ives, but his expedition provided valuable new information about the area.

Ives published an account of his adventure, *Report upon the Colorado River of the West*, in 1861. The book, the first of many accounts published in the years after the war, gave the American public one of its first views of Grand Canyon (Ives 1861, cited in Pyne 1982), though certainly not a very prescient one: Ives saw absolutely no value in the landscape!

The Civil War brought exploration to a temporary halt. At the close of the war, interest in exploring and conquering the West intensified. Undoubtedly the most famous of the explorers of this era, and one of the first to redefine Grand Canyon in favorable terms, was Major John Wesley Powell. Powell's explorations of the Colorado River in 1869 and 1872, as well as of the plateaus north of the canyon, contributed immeasurably to knowledge of the region. And with knowledge came control.

Much of the early mapping—always a highly political action—was undertaken by Almon H. Thompson, Powell's intrepid brother-in-law, and subsequently by cartographer François Emile Matthes. Trained in his native Europe and at the Massachusetts Institute of Technology, Matthes was best known for the artistry and precision of his topographic renderings of the Grand Canyon. These maps, along with the photographs of, for example, John K. Hillers (whose photographs also provided information for famous Grand Canyon painters Thomas

Moran and William Holmes), codified public knowledge of the canyon and provided the basis for further research and exploration.

The Indians

Until 1868, federal Indian policy focused on civilian or military pressure to force Indians off their lands and to sign treaties.[4] Most of the treaties specified the relationship that would exist between the tribe and the government and in many cases specified a division of territory. By 1868, the Indians retained only 240 million acres of their aboriginal lands and had lost almost two billion acres.

With the demise of formal treaty signing and congressional approval, arrangements with Indians, especially the creation of reservations, came to be done by presidential proclamation—a process that did not require congressional approval. The proclamations, while introducing some stability to relations between Indians and non-Indians, were far from ideal, however, because they proved relatively easy to reverse or modify.

In the greater Grand Canyon region, the earliest conflicts between the federal government and the Indians involved the Navajos. The contest was a long one, lasting from 1848 to 1864. The outcome was devastating for the Navajos, whom the U.S. Army forced to move to a dismal, disease-ridden camp in Bosque Redondo, New Mexico. Withstanding profound hardships, they struggled for four years to survive[5] before persuading federal officials to send them back to the heart of their homeland.

In 1868, the United States delineated a reservation for the Navajos that encompassed 3.5 million acres in the northeastern corner of Arizona and in northwestern New Mexico.[6] This was the first instance in which Indian lands in the greater Grand Canyon were given new identity and substance through the drawing of boundaries. It was also the first instance in which the federal government set aside lands in the greater Grand Canyon region for political purposes, in this case, to protect them (by putting them in trust status) for the Navajo.

The nascent territorial government and its constituents saw the federal government's move as a decidedly unfair loss of rights to those lands and their potential income and tax revenues. For the Navajos, however, it meant official recognition that they were culturally different from other groups occupying the area and that they had a right to their own base of land and resources. Creation of the reservation institutionalized that difference and gave it a geographical expression. Though far short of encompassing the whole of their representational space, the new reservation gave the Navajos a defined, absolute space. Even these arrangements were contingent, however: the federal government, as trustee, ultimately controlled their domain.

No other Indian reservations were established in the greater Grand Canyon region during the 1870s, but the entry of explorers and early settlers during this decade set the stage for conflicts in the heart of Grand Canyon land. Paiutes killed members of Powell's first exploration party and attacked Mormon settlers. At about the same time, the Hualapais began challenging people who were encroaching on their lands and resources on the southwestern side of the canyon; they ended by losing a series of battles with the U.S. military during the Hualapai War, which lasted from 1866 until 1869. In 1874, U.S. soldiers uprooted most of the Hualapais and moved them to a reservation (already occupied by several other tribes) on the lower Colorado River. Unable to survive the diseases and heat of the lowlands, the Hualapais resisted by surreptitiously filtering back to their ancestral lands on the south side of the Grand Canyon. The U.S. Army, faced with a fait accompli, extended an offer to the Hualapais that if they would no longer fight, they would be allowed to remain on their lands. The Hualapais agreed. President Chester A. Arthur signed the presidential proclamation on January 4, 1883, that established a reservation encompassing the heart of the Hualapais' ancestral lands. This reservation, measuring nearly one million acres, is the same one that the Hualapais continue to hold today (Hughes 1978).

Less than a month earlier, on December 16, 1882, President Arthur had signed an executive order establishing a reservation of 2.5 million acres for the Hopi and for other Indians as determined by the secretary of the interior. The reservation cut deeply into the Hopis' domain, for it encompassed only the residential and agricultural lands surrounding their villages. The Hopis regained control of important agricultural lands within the new reservation boundaries that had been appropriated by Mormon settlers. Unfortunately, the government officials who had drawn the boundaries had failed to recognize that even though the Hopis were an agricultural people, they had hunted and gathered over a much larger portion of the lands on the eastern side of the Grand Canyon to supplement their diet.[7] More important, the new boundaries excluded important religious sites, some of the most significant of which were located in the Colorado and Little Colorado River canyons.

The Havasupai, like the Hopi, had refrained from battling the U.S. military. The tribe did not participate in the Hualapai War and did not take the aggressive stand of the Paiute and the Navajo. Like the Hopi, the Havasupai lost substantially in the processes that established the reservations. Living and farming in Havasu Canyon during the summer and hunting and gathering on the plateau above during the winter, the Havasupais continued to consider the wide area south of the Colorado River and eastward as far as Moenkopi Wash (near present-day Tuba City, Arizona) as their home even though Mormons had already appropriated their agricultural lands in the Moenkopi Wash area. As encroachment intensified, the land base of the Havasupais shrank to an area directly south of the Colorado River and east of the Hualapai Reservation.

Distressed by the pressures exerted by settlers and clearly losing control over their territory, the Havasupais petitioned Territorial Governor John C. Frémont for relief; the governor responded by providing them with a letter that characterized them as a peaceful people and asked non-Indian visitors to respect their rights (Frémont 1878, cited in Hughes 1967). The gesture was an empty one, however, for the Havasupais saw their original territory shrink almost to nothing as settlers continued to appropriate their lands and—most importantly— water sources on the South Rim.

President Rutherford B. Hayes tried to resolve conflicts between the settlers and the Havasupais by setting aside a reservation for the tribe by proclamation in 1880. The original reservation, measuring five miles wide and twelve miles long, comprised approximately 40,000 acres and encompassed the cultivated portion of Havasu Canyon, as well as important portions of rimland (Dobyns and Euler 1971). Unfortunately, only two years later, ostensibly due to pressures from mining interests and difficulties in surveying the area, President Chester A. Arthur signed a new proclamation that allowed the Havasupais to keep only 518.6 acres of their agricultural lands located at the bottom of Havasu Canyon. In a grave omission, the proclamation deprived tribal members of control over the rimlands where they had traditionally hunted, gathered, and lived during the winter months (Hirst 1976).

As with the Hopis, the federal government recognized only those lands that the Havasupais had continuously occupied and farmed. This was a convenient interpretation, for it cleared away any potential

obstacles to non-Indian takeover of the area. By 1900 the Havasupais
had lost 90 percent of their winter hunting and gathering area, which
previously may have provided as much as 75 percent of their subsistence, and had thereby lost almost 70 percent of their total economic
base (Bureau of Indian Affairs 1979, h–9). With the exception of a
small (but noncontiguous) addition to the reservation in 1944, the Havasupais had to make do with this scrap of land until 1975, when,
after years of effort, they finally managed to regain an important part
of their rimland domain.

The Southern Paiutes fared even more poorly. After repeated efforts
to move them to a combined reservation with the Utes (whom the Paiutes feared), President Ulysses S. Grant signed a proclamation in 1872
that gave the Southern Paiutes their own reservation in an area north-
west of St. George, Utah. Grant expanded the reservation in 1874, but
full relocation of the Paiutes was never successfully accomplished, and
in 1875 the reservation was reduced to 1,000 acres. Named the Moapa
Reservation, this small tract of land continues to be held in trust for
the Paiutes. The Shivwits band of Paiutes, located to the south, was
not even this fortunate, for in the 1880s a successful rancher from
southern Utah named Anthony W. Ivans obtained a federal appropriation that allowed him to remove them from their home on the Arizona
Strip and relocate them to a reservation along the Santa Clara River
in southern Utah, later named the Shivwits Reservation (Kelly and
Fowler 1986).[8]

Not until 1907 did the remaining Kaibab Paiutes, decimated by disease and poverty, gain a small reservation at Pipe Springs, one of the
few areas with substantial quantities of dependable water on the Arizona Strip, and an area they had previously lost to Mormon settlers.[9]
Though their reservation was subsequently enlarged twice, they retained little of their ancestral lands between Pipe Springs and the
Grand Canyon. The San Juan Paiutes had an even harder time being
recognized: the government has only formally recognized them within
the past decade. The band had established deep roots on lands north
and west of the Hopi lands but eventually was surrounded by the expanding Navajo reservation (Bunte and Franklin 1987). With no separately recognized land base and with no official recognition as a separate and distinct people, the San Juan Paiutes found themselves with
the fewest resources to sustain their culture of any of the indigenous
peoples of the area.

New Spaces, New Lives

By the early 1880s the greater Grand Canyon had been radically transformed from a space shared by a few indigenous peoples since "time immemorial" to an active place of cash-economy production and consumption. Loggers razed large swaths of forest, huge numbers of livestock roamed the area, settlers built towns, and entrepreneurs introduced new modes of transportation.

Surveyors committed the area to paper, and men like Clarence Dutton and François Matthes gave names to the physical features. Thus Indian names like Kaibab Plateau (in Paiute, "mountain-lying-down") and Havasu Canyon ("blue-green water") appear alongside Mount Emma (named for John Wesley Powell's wife) and Vulcan's Throne (Hughes 1967).

The partitioning of space was a major strategy on the part of the United States not only to exert social and geographical control, but also to change the terms of contest from armed force to legalistic negotiation. This new space of negotiation was one of coexistence, mixed with a strong element of paternalism—a more subtle but no less corrosive form of power.

The native peoples found themselves encircled not only by a new culture, but also by geographical lines that were used to dictate where they could live and what they could do (Jenkins 1992). Individualism and private property replaced the traditional rights and privileges of band, tribe, and usufruct. Contests over how the geographical spaces of the greater Grand Canyon would be defined occurred no longer just between Indians and non-Indians but also among the non-Indians themselves. Repartitioning of the greater Grand Canyon into smaller spaces, and according to different uses, began. For the indigenous peoples, the spaces of subsistence had become the places of resistance. For the newcomers, the spaces of the unknown became places where familiar social, cultural, political, and economic ideas and practices could be reaffirmed.

CHAPTER TWO

Westward Expansion: 1870 to 1908

The U.S. government accomplished little with regard to the lands it had acquired from Mexico until the end of the Civil War. Yet in the East and Midwest, the 1860s were a time of growing concern about the rampant exploitation of timber resources. Scientists such as George Perkins Marsh strove to introduce European ideas of scientific forestry to America, and preservationists such as John Muir sought protection of wilderness areas to ensure the spiritual uplift and renewal of humankind. All in their own way worried that rampant exploitation of natural resources was threatening the very foundations of the nation's wealth and cultural identity. For each, the solution was assertion of federal ownership and control over natural resources.

After the Civil War, contests over who was to own and exploit the nation's lands and resources became especially heated in the West, prompting a spate of new laws. One of the most important of these was the General Allotment Act of 1887 (the Dawes Act), which aimed to break up the reservations and turn the Indians into yeoman farmers, each household tending its own 160-acre parcel. The vast amounts of "surplus" lands left over after all tribal members had received their allotments would be purchased by the federal government—at minimal cost—and then offered to non-Indians (Deloria and Lytle 1984). Before the act was terminated in 1933, Indians throughout the United States lost 90 million acres of their ancestral lands.

Meanwhile, in the greater Grand Canyon region, exploitation of natural resources grew at an alarming rate. Logging, mining, and ranching became the dominant activities on the landscape.

Perhaps the most successful of the new exploiters in the greater

Grand Canyon region were the timber operators. Seeing wealth in the stands of Ponderosa pine that grew on the North and South Rims, loggers moved onto the plateau with their saws and axes in the 1870s. Flagstaff and Williams, today two of the largest communities in northern Arizona, emerged as a result. Not coincidentally, both towns were built using the trees of the South Rim forests. Likewise, the North Rim forests provided lumber to build the Mormon settlements of Kanab and St. George, Utah (Hughes 1978).

The Atlantic and Pacific Railroad, with its voracious appetite for railroad ties, fuel, and construction materials, increased the pressure on the forests in the region (Perlin 1989; Putt 1991, 80). So did the penchant of the early timber operators and ranchers to underestimate Nature, for in the late 1880s and early 1890s, the entire Southwest underwent several years of drought. Throughout the Grand Canyon region, the drought ravaged the vegetation that still remained after years of intensive logging and grazing. Ranchers lost thousands of head of livestock for lack of water and forage. When a series of unusually wet winters followed, much of the exposed soil washed down into the Arizona lowlands. Cattle and sheep compacted what soil remained (Putt 1991, 22). Yet with renewal of the rains, overexploitation returned, eventually prompting the creation of federal laws and land management agencies to bring some semblance of order to the area.

Prospectors began exploring the canyon and its environs as early as 1874 and began mining in earnest around 1885. William H. Ashurst, father of future Arizona senator Henry Ashurst, and Ralph Cameron, who later became perhaps the most controversial U.S. senator ever to represent Arizona, were among those who believed wealth was hidden in the canyon formations (Verkamp 1940). The miners registered many claims, built trails, and actually managed to extract some ore—mainly copper and asbestos—from a few of the mines. But for all the effusive optimism of the would-be miners, the canyon area never fulfilled early expectations. Some gave up and moved on; others began catering to the tourists.

Whereas timber operators and miners often made no effort to establish ownership of much of the land they exploited, ranchers needed to establish some degree of private property ownership to conduct their operations. However, given the large amount of land available and the relatively small demand for private land ownership in the area, a rancher could get away with owning outright only a relatively small amount of land—often acquired through the government's homestead laws—and parlaying that resource base into a much larger operation by expanding into the surrounding public lands. In some cases, ranchers simply fenced scarce water sources. By controlling the water, they were effectively able to control vast tracts of surrounding (but waterless) land. They gained in another way, too, for they could not be taxed by local government for the lands they did not "own." It was a perfect example of what Garrett Hardin (1968) called the tragedy of the commons: everyone stood to gain from running as many livestock as possible (in fact it was their loss if they did not, for someone else would use any open-range forage they left unconsumed), and no one had to pay the costs of overexploitation of the resource base—at least not right away.

Among those who began to amass a grazing empire on lands south of the Grand Canyon were the Babbitt brothers. Arriving from Cincinnati in 1886, David and William (Billy) Babbitt spent $17,640 to buy a cattle ranch they promptly dubbed the CO Bar (CO being a sentimental reminder of their origins in Cincinnati, Ohio). Their holdings grew steadily, eventually covering much of the grazing lands of the Coconino Plateau (unlike many western ranchers but in common with other local stock raisers, they operated both sheep and cattle operations, though their cattle business remained dominant).[1] By 1915, the peak year for the Babbitts' ranching enterprise, they controlled an empire that included land in Kansas and California as well as substantial holdings in Arizona and generated an income of some $1.5 million (Smith 1989).

Mormon ranchers dominated activity on the North Rim (Hughes 1967). The United Order of Orderville, Utah, in fact, controlled the North Kaibab range for the years between 1877 and 1887 (Hughes 1978). Sheep ranchers on the North Rim (some of whom were Mormons themselves) challenged the cattle growers' domination over the range. The cattle ranchers saw in this situation a case of overexploitation: the sheep, they said, cropped the forage too short and ruined the grazing for everyone. Armed conflict eventually broke out between cattle ranchers and sheep ranchers.

Transportation at the Grand Canyon

The arrival of miners, ranchers, and loggers set the stage for new ways to carve up space: the building of roads capable of accommodating wagons, stagecoaches, and later, automobiles and trucks. The first roads were primitive and rough, doing little to reduce the remoteness and primitiveness of the area. Railroads were a different story.

Miners and loggers needed cheap and efficient transportation to move their timber and ore to market, so they began early on to push for railroad service to the area. The arrival of the Atlantic and Pacific Railroad to the plateau lands south of the Grand Canyon in 1883 opened new possibilities for profit by linking the area, in an east-west direction, to the national economy.

Yet, while the railroad was immensely important in accelerating settlement, commerce, industry, and tourism in the area, it also intensified conflicts between Indians and non-Indians by bringing them into more frequent contact with each other and by bringing into the area ever more people who appropriated the land, depleted the game, and took over the water sources. Here again, the division of the spaces of the greater Grand Canyon played a prominent role in the politics of the times: part of the bargain struck between the Atlantic and Pacific Railroad Company (later the Santa Fe Railroad) and the U.S. government was that the railroad would receive every odd-numbered section of land for forty miles on either side of the tracks. Never mind that much of that land was Indian land. The threat to the Hualapais was especially ominous, for Mohave County requested the U.S. government to abolish their reservation (Hughes 1978). Fortunately for the tribe, the county's request was denied. But the Indians' control over their reservation lands remained tenuous for more than half a century as the railroad persisted in claiming every other section of land within the Hualapai (and Havasupai) domains.

While generally connecting the region with the rest of the United States, the new railroad line did nothing to facilitate north-south travel, including easier access to the Grand Canyon itself. Flagstaff and Williams began trying to remedy the situation as early as 1886 by seeking backers for a rail line to the South Rim of the canyon (Hughes 1978). Flagstaff residents dangled the lure of profits from tourism, but to no avail. Boosters from the town of Williams, by contrast, stressing that there were profits to be made from mining, persuaded the Santa Fe and Grand Canyon Railway Company to build a line from Williams to the mining camp of Anita. Rails reached Anita in 1900 and the South Rim of the Grand Canyon in 1901.

Ironically, it was tourism as promoted by the Santa Fe Railroad and

its concessioner (the Fred Harvey Company)—rather than mining—
that ultimately made the railway profitable. Many of the early miners
turned to tourism when they could not find wealth from the mines,
and the railroads elevated the enterprise to a grand scale.

Tourists and Tourism

The growth of tourism (and the development of a sense of nationalism
based on the scenic splendors of the country) was probably the most
influential factor in changing the ways in which the spaces of the
greater Grand Canyon would be defined. Although tourism had grown
with the wide dissemination of words and pictures celebrating the
beauties of the area, the number of tourists who actually visited the
area remained modest until the completion of the railroad made it possible to comfortably travel to the South Rim in a single day. Visitation
to the North Rim remained minuscule for much longer, due to the
length of the trip and the difficult road conditions.

The railroads, seeing possibilities for profits, launched advertising
and promotional campaigns to lure people to their hotels, restaurants,
and tourist services throughout the West. The Fred Harvey Company,
in conjunction with the Santa Fe Railroad, was especially successful in
making nature tourism a distinctly national pastime. With its hotels
and restaurants at every train station (where service was provided by
the equally famous Harvey Girls), the company did much to define
what a tour of the West meant. The company's El Tovar Hotel, built
on the South Rim of the Grand Canyon, for example, introduced lux-
ury in the midst of rough Nature. Although ruder accommodations
and opportunities for primitive packing and camping were available,
the construction of the El Tovar Hotel and, later, the construction of a
commodious lodge on the North Rim by the Union Pacific Railroad
redefined the representational space of Grand Canyon from one of remote grandeur to one of easily accessible scenic pleasure.

The Resource Managers

As the nineteenth century waned, concern steadily escalated over the
rampant despoliation of the natural resources of the West. From 1891
to 1920, the country's first conservation movement brought together
resource management professionals with people representing outdoor

recreation organizations, scenic preservation organizations, garden clubs, civic betterment associations, and even some resource extraction enterprises in a quest to make resource exploitation practices more compatible with nature preservation and enjoyment. These conservationists, who derived much of their inspiration from the Progressive movement, ultimately saw more than 150 million acres of the public domain transformed into national forests, parks (the first was Yellowstone National Park, created in 1872), and monuments (Foresta 1984; Schrepfer 1983).

Management of the newly defined lands required the creation of new bureaucratic arrangements at the federal level. Conservationist Gifford Pinchot led the way, introducing many important innovations in the process of founding and leading a new government agency, the U.S. Forest Service. His concepts of wise use and sustained yield continue to guide forest management on public lands. The Forest Service, established in 1905 within the Department of Agriculture, was soon sending trained foresters into the field, educating users about proper methods of exploiting forest resources, and enforcing the agency's rules for exploiting public land resources.

On the preservationist side, an important new voice emerged at the federal level in 1914 when Stephen T. Mather, a longtime aficionado of the outdoors, wrote a letter to Woodrow Wilson's secretary of the interior, Franklin K. Lane, complaining about how poorly the parks were being managed. Lane retorted that if Mather did not like the way things were being run, he should come to Washington and do it himself (Shankland 1951). Mather did just that.

Mather, a California native, was a philanthropist, mountain climber, and millionaire who had made his fortune in borax. Not needing a large salary, he was in a position to accept Lane's challenge—and a meager stipend—to create a national park system. He began by hiring a particularly able assistant: Horace Albright. Albright, an excellent administrator, complemented Mather's strengths as promoter, persuader, and fund-raiser. In time, he went on to become the superintendent of Yosemite National Park, then the director of the Park Service, before retiring to private life (Albright 1985).

Mather achieved his first goal within only two years: in 1916, Congress established the National Park Service, within the Department of the Interior, to administer the federal government's parklands. Thereafter, Mather immediately embarked on what turned out to be a three-year crusade to have a national park created at Grand Canyon. In the meantime, management of the area—such as there was—remained in the hands of the Forest Service.

Preservation and the Grand Canyon

Between 1882 and 1919, a variety of interests and individuals entered the contest over how—and whether—to "protect" Grand Canyon. This contest, reflective of larger contests within the United States over how the nation's natural heritage was to be defined and managed, pitted conservation- and preservation-minded activists who advocated government control against local citizens and eastern capitalists who sought local jurisdiction. Because each group valued different resources, each had a different conception of the location, size, and configuration of the space they wanted devoted to their interests.

In the end, no group was either totally victorious or entirely defeated. By the end of the second decade of the twentieth century, the railroads had achieved a considerable amount of control over tourist facilities in the area, the contest between sheep ranchers and cattle ranchers was defused, and timber operators and miners had accommodated themselves to some government regulation of their operations. Even the livestock raisers came to find the idea of a modicum of government regulation to be desirable, when faced with the alternatives of having to buy and pay taxes on all the land they had been using at no cost or of seeing their operations bankrupted as a result of overgrazing the commons.

The preservationists had a harder fight: protection of Grand Canyon proceeded only slowly and incrementally, due to powerful, entrenched opposition from livestock raisers, timber operators, other entrepreneurs, and tight-fisted congressmen bent on pinching the government's pennies. Continued dissemination of information about the wonders of the Grand Canyon, however, continued to breathe life into the fight for its protection.

John Wesley Powell, a geologist and ethnographer, had been instrumental in giving many people their first introduction to the Grand Canyon as a unique and awe-inspiring representation of the forces of nature. Powell's dramatic accounts of his trips down the Colorado River and his exploration of the rimlands were the first to capture the public's imagination. His 1878 *Report on the Lands of the Arid Region of the United States* (Powell 1962) provided detailed information about the physical geography and land uses in Utah, western Colorado, and northern Arizona; geologist Grove Karl Gilbert's chapter on water in the region was equally comprehensive. Most important, the report spelled out a program for changing the ways in which land and water would be administered in these arid lands that lay beyond the hundredth meridian. Powell's recommendation for partitioning land according to watershed boundaries was a revolutionary attempt to introduce forms of land and resource use based on explicit recognition of the constraints posed by water scarcity. Unfortunately, in a society where adequate water supplies had never been an issue, his ideas fell on deaf ears. Although the ideas held by this one-armed Civil War veteran found little support among decision makers at the time, his book remains among the most important and prophetic books ever written about the West (Stegner 1954).[2]

Visual images also provided important information about the Grand Canyon area. William Henry Holmes, among the best of the image makers, produced illustrations for Clarence Dutton's monumental *Tertiary History of the Grand Canyon,* which depicted the canyon with an accuracy and artistry that remains unsurpassed (Stegner 1954). More romantic but no less stunning were the paintings by Thomas Moran. His scenes of the Grand Canyon, vividly colored and dramatically portrayed (if not always accurate), provided a sense of immediacy and went a long way toward dispelling the "forbidding wilderness" descriptions of earlier explorers such as Ives.

Among the most skillful of the writers to communicate the wonders of Grand Canyon was essayist and wilderness preservation advocate John Muir. Muir is today best known for his works on the Sierra Nevada mountains in California, for his efforts to save Yosemite Valley from exploitation (in which he was successful) and Hetch Hetchy Valley from dam building (certainly his greatest defeat), and for his activities on behalf of preservation of the California redwoods. Yet the venerable writer and founder of the Sierra Club, having visited Grand Canyon many times, was also an eloquent advocate for its preservation. He called for a national park at Grand Canyon as early as 1898 and wrote an article published in *Atlantic Monthly* in which he described the Grand Canyon as "unearthly in the color and grandeur and quantity of its architecture, as if you had found it after death, on some other star" (Muir 1898, 28, quoted in Hughes 1978).

The Early Days of Grand Canyon National Forests

Initially the contest over how best to manage the timber resources of the greater Grand Canyon region remained between local users and urban (mainly eastern) idealists. As long as the conservationists' agenda was resisted by Congress as well as by locals, the exploiters were able to continue their customary practices unimpeded. Even the establishment of a series of protective reserves did little beyond halting outright settlement in the protected areas.

In terms of absolute space, the contest was a strangely mixed one, with assertions of private property rights commingled with equally vociferous demands for unlimited rights to access and use of all resources in the public domain. Thus, boundaries were drawn to defend private property, but at the same time, campaigns were waged to ensure that no boundaries were drawn in the public domain that impeded resource exploitation.

Having seen large tracts of forest decimated within ten years, and fearing that tourism entrepreneurs would irretrievably destroy the primitive quality of Grand Canyon, a few individuals persisted in calling for preservation of the area. In the beginning the activists were outsiders: few in Arizona were interested in or dared to support protection. Even at the national level many influential people remained uncertain about the purpose of national parks and about the advisability of permanently removing large tracts of the federal domain from potential development.

Each new increment of protection arose from a change at the federal level: a new piece of legislation, a new agency, or a new president with a commitment to changing the way the public domain was managed and used. Though in time support for more effective conservation and preservation efforts arose at the local level, it was the federal government that imposed each new measure of protection—always in the face of strenuous objection from local interests.

Efforts to manage the forests of the greater Grand Canyon had begun with an 1890 report published by John Wesley Powell on conditions in the area (U.S. House of Representatives 1906, cited in Putt 1991). Solely on the basis of the Powell report, Secretary of the Interior John W. Noble recommended to President Benjamin Harrison that he take advantage of a rider, which had been attached to the 1891 Appropriations Bill, to create a forest reserve surrounding the Grand Canyon (Putt 1991). In 1893, President Harrison signed a proclamation creating a new reserve that encompassed one degree of latitude and longitude, containing 29,000 square miles (nearly 20 million acres) of public domain, including the odd-numbered sections of railroad grant lands (Putt 1991). Arizona timber operators, ranchers, and businesspeople, believing they were a safe distance from federal government interference, dismissed the reserve as a fad (Putt 1991, 2–3). The creation of the reserve was seen to be so meaningless, in fact, that at the time, neither the *Williams News* nor the *Coconino Weekly Sun* of Flagstaff bothered to report on it (Putt 1991, 23). The new reserve was not even included on most maps of Arizona Territory.

Even on paper, the designation of the Grand Canyon Forest Reserve did little beyond closing the area to homesteading. The proclamation gave lumber companies that held leases on the railroad's odd-numbered sections grandfathered rights to work those sections. The Mining Law of 1872 protected existing mining operations within the new reserve (Putt 1991, 24–25). Grazing continued unabated, in flagrant violation of the intent of the proclamation.

Though the reserve might have been ineffective for protecting the resources of the area, in time its very existence bred opposition. The Coconino County Board of Supervisors unanimously passed a resolution on June 11, 1898, calling for the restoration of all or part of the reserve to the "public domain" (Minutes of the Coconino County Board of Supervisors, vol. 2, 105, quoted in Verkamp 1940). During that same year, when other local interests began an effort to gain a national park at Grand Canyon, opposition rose so strongly that the project had to be abandoned (*Coconino Sun* 24 September 1898, cited in Verkamp 1940).

Still determined to assert effective federal control over western public lands, Secretary Noble established, in 1896, a commission from the National Academy of Sciences to study and make recommendations for the management of public lands. Among the commission members were Gifford Pinchot and John Muir, who visited the Grand Canyon area that same year (Putt 1991). Although their visit generated no immediate changes, their report and the subsequent passage of federal legislation tightening federal control over forest reserves had a direct impact on northern Arizonans. No longer would locals be able to follow their own ways with impunity; the country was gaining too much knowledge about the area.

Residents of the greater Grand Canyon region soon found themselves in the midst of a second forest reserve, for on August 17, 1898,

President William McKinley signed an executive order establishing the San Francisco Mountain Forest Reserve. The reserve, which encompassed more than 975,000 acres of land on even-numbered sections, was located southeast of the Grand Canyon Forest Reserve and was established in response to complaints from settlers downstream that deforestation was causing an increase in flooding in the Salt River Valley. The action almost led to open rebellion in northern Arizona, and federal agents quickly set out to reassure local residents; they even suggested that sheep might be allowed to continue grazing the area during part of the year even though that activity was banned by the forest reserve designation (Putt 1991).

The mosaic produced by the partitioning of space into even-numbered sections of federal forest land and odd-numbered sections of private (largely railroad) lands proved impossible for forest managers to administer and regulate. The biggest winners were the livestock growers and timber operators. Requiring ranchers to fence their lands, for example, was legally and economically unfeasible. The upshot was that instead of implementing scientific forest management as they had been intended to do, federal agents spent most of their time simply trying to prevent trespass. In the end, forest managers were able to convince Congress that acquisition of the sections of private land was essential to rational forest management. In the Sundry Civil Appropriation Act of 1897, Congress obliged: private owners were allowed to sell their holdings in the forest reserves to the government or exchange them for equal amounts of federal land elsewhere (Putt 1991).[3] In time, the Forest Service succeeded in consolidating a considerable portion of its lands, though even today private inholdings continue to dot the forest.

In 1903, President Theodore Roosevelt visited Grand Canyon (Hughes 1978). Though inspired by its scenery, he was struck by the number of quarrels that were raging over who should be using which resources for what reasons (Verkamp 1940). Discerning that considerable damage was being done in the greater Grand Canyon region by the combination of untrammeled use and ferocious competition, he came out in support of stronger controls over the area and on June 29, 1906, signed into law a bill sponsored by Senator Reed Smoot of Utah (a conservation sympathizer who had visited the North Rim) to protect the wildlife of the reserve. Roosevelt reinforced that protection by issuing a proclamation on November 28, 1906, designating the area as the Grand Canyon Game Preserve.[4] A limit to protection seemed to have been reached, however, for attempts made in 1908, 1910, 1911, and

1913 to enlarge and revise the game preserve all failed (Hinchliffe 1976).

In 1907, as part of his project to institutionalize federal forest management, Gifford Pinchot changed the designation of the forest reserves to national forests. The national forests, according to Pinchot, were to be managed for continuing development and use for purposes such as hunting, mining, logging, and grazing.

Together, the legislation and the proclamations establishing the forest reserve, the wildlife reserve, and the national forest units provided boundaries that spread a net over the forests and over some species of animals, drawing them into a common protective legal and administrative structure. The boundaries did not, however, function to preserve the area in its ecological, sociological, or political entirety. Such preservation had to await the enactment of new legislation.

National Monument Designation

Control over grazing, logging, and mining in the Grand Canyon national forests struck many, including Roosevelt, as inadequate, given the unique qualities of the area. Fortunately for the conservationists, Congress passed the Act for the Preservation of American Antiquities in 1906. Under the act, the president, by proclamation, may withdraw areas that contain objects of historic or scientific interest. Roosevelt elected to give the law a broad interpretation that covered protection of natural features, a choice that over the years facilitated the protection of many scenic areas when Congress refused to protect them through legislation. In one of his last acts as president, and supported even by Forest Service officials, who believed that it was the best way to protect the area from further damage, he established Grand Canyon National Monument by presidential proclamation on January 11, 1908 (Presidential Proclamation No. 794).[5] Roosevelt justified issuing the proclamation by citing the existence of prehistoric archeological ruins and the scientific (primarily geological) value of the Grand Canyon. The proclamation, though challenged, was upheld in the United States Supreme Court.

The Grand Canyon National Monument that Roosevelt created was smaller than the reserves established earlier in the Grand Canyon area and encompassed only the scenic eastern portion of the canyon. It was administered by the Forest Service until 1919, when the lands were transferred to the Park Service. Roosevelt's action proved pivotal, for the lands encompassed in the original Grand Canyon National Monument were the same ones that became Grand Canyon National Park (Hinchliffe 1976).

In 1908, as a result of the spatial divisions in the national forest brought about by the creation of the monument, Pinchot combined portions of the San Francisco Mountain Forest Reserve and the southern portion of the Grand Canyon Forest Reserve into a single, more efficient unit: Coconino National Forest, headquartered in Flagstaff. Tusayan National Forest, headquartered in Williams, was designated as a separate unit in 1910. Because of the barrier posed by the Grand Canyon abyss, the Forest Service continued to treat the North Rim forest as a separate unit, renaming it Kaibab National Forest (Putt 1991). Later, the forests adjacent to the Grand Canyon acquired their present-day names: North Kaibab and South Kaibab National Forests.

Again, though boundaries were drawn and intentions were good, protection of the canyon environs was minimal due to inadequate administrative capacity and a lack of resources (Verkamp 1940). To make matters worse, although prospecting and mining activity could not be initiated after the proclamation, already validated claims could still be worked (Hughes 1967).

In 1909, President William Howard Taft visited Grand Canyon and soon thereafter moved to include Grand Canyon National Monument in the Grand Canyon Game Reserve (Verkamp 1940). In doing so, he fixed a serious flaw in the national monument declaration: it had failed to provide for game preservation. Taft's action reinstated, at least on paper, protection for desirable species such as deer and bighorn sheep. It also reinforced the prevailing view that varmints—especially the ones that flashed teeth and claws (mountain lions and coyotes, among others)—had no value and should be actively hunted (Worster 1979).[6]

The Contest Goes On

Designation of a part of the greater Grand Canyon as a national monument did little to appease those who believed nothing less than national park designation was appropriate. Led by Park Service Director Stephen Mather, the contest to preserve the area intensified. Eventually, a combination of economic forces, a series of strategies carefully designed to take advantage of scheduled events, and increased support from Arizonans converged to create the necessary conditions for establishing a national park at Grand Canyon.

CHAPTER THREE

The National Park: 1909 to 1919

I n 1909, only a year after President Theodore Roosevelt had created Grand Canyon National Monument by proclamation, Secretary of the Interior Richard A. Ballinger recommended in his annual report that Grand Canyon be designated a national park (Hughes 1967; *Coconino Sun* November 26, 1909, cited in Verkamp 1940). Clearly, considerable concern persisted that the area could not be adequately protected under national monument status.

Yet creation of the park proved stubbornly difficult to achieve. Between 1882 and 1886, Senator (later President) Benjamin Harrison of Indiana had introduced three bills to create a national park at Grand Canyon. As with other efforts to protect the area, Harrison's actions prompted a storm of protest on the part of ranchers, hunters, and loggers, as well as among entrepreneurs interested in water power, mining, and tourism (Tillotson and Taylor 1935). Lack of support from sufficient numbers of the general public did not help matters. Under these circumstances, it is not surprising that Congress had little incentive to increase federal control over the area.

Senator Frank P. Flint of California introduced another bill (S. 5938), supported by President Taft, to create a national park at Grand Canyon in 1910 (Verkamp 1940). Grazing interests rose in opposition, prompting Flint to recommend to the president that the matter be referred to the Departments of Interior and Agriculture (Kauffman 1954). Ultimately, E. C. Finney, representing the Department of the Interior, and Henry S. Graves, representing the Department of Agriculture, studied the issue and recommended not scrapping the park idea entirely but revising the boundaries of the proposed park.

Only a year earlier, a bill had been introduced to permit the construction of a railway along the rim (H.R. 225, March 8, 1909), a proposal that prompted the American Scenic and Historic Preservation Society to urge the president to avert such a catastrophe by enlarging Grand Canyon National Monument from 1,279 square miles to 7,154 square miles (from less than a million acres to nearly five million acres). The enlargement would have extended the monument boundaries westward to the 114th meridian—almost to the Arizona-Nevada border—and would have included almost the entire 277 miles of the canyon as well as its tributary canyons and most of the three adjacent national forests (Coconino—including Tusayan—and Kaibab in northern Arizona, and Dixie in Utah). The U.S. Geological Survey, to which the proposal had been referred, disagreed with the recommendations, noting that the society's proposal included much land that was needed for grazing. Instead, the Geological Survey recommended to the secretary of the interior that the national park should encompass only 1,012 square miles (647,680 acres). The secretary transmitted the recommendation to the president on December 10, 1910, along with the observation that the national forest lands surrounding the canyon would protect the non-park lands from undesirable uses (Kauffman 1954).

In response to the proposal by the Geological Survey, Senator Flint introduced a revised version of his park bill (S. 10138) on January 11, 1911. Though this revised bill had the support of President Taft (Hughes 1967), it met with no more success than had previous bills. Shortly thereafter, Congressman E. A. Hayes of California introduced a second bill (H.R. 6331), which would have named the park in honor of Andrew Carnegie in recognition of his work for world peace.[1] This bill died also (Hinchliffe 1976; Kauffman 1954).

Later in the year, Chief Forester Henry S. Graves spelled out his opinion on what the boundaries of a national park at Grand Canyon should be. He described himself as being "inclined to recommend that the Cataract Canyon [the location of the Havasupai reservation] and perhaps the entire north division of Tusayan National Forest be included in the Park." Subsequently, he recommended that the park include "all of the Canyon from below the mouth of Cataract Creek to above the mouth of the Little Colorado River," that being the portion of "greatest scenic value." On the North Rim, he recommended that the boundary be one to four miles away from the canyon rim to include all the scenic points; the boundary on the South Rim should extend back from the canyon edge, in some places even farther than on the North Rim to include all of the area needed for national park roads and to incorporate a portion of the forest (Graves November 29, 1911, quoted in Kauffman 1954, 2). The park has never encompassed within its boundaries all of the lands Graves recommended, but to the present day, these remain among the areas preservationists most desire to protect.

Arizona statehood, achieved in 1912, changed the context within which the contest over national park establishment was played out. One of the key players was Congressman Carl Hayden of Arizona. Hayden, who eventually served fifty-seven years in Congress (eight terms in the House of Representatives followed by seven terms in the Senate), came to be a well-known and very effective advocate of national road building and water projects. In an era when national parks were seen less as inviolate wildernesses than as public playgrounds, it was not at all contradictory that he should also promote—within limits—the expansion of Grand Canyon National Park within his own state. Along with Congressman Henry F. Ashurst and a growing number of Arizona residents, Hayden saw the creation of a national park at Grand Canyon as a valuable means for promoting the state (Hughes 1978).

By then, cracks had begun to appear even in the armor of northern Arizona opposition, as a few Flagstaff businessmen—though they remained in the minority and were criticized as only wanting to profit from growth in the tourist trade (Hinchliffe 1976)—began to urge their congressional representatives to work toward establishment of a national park.

Meanwhile, at the national level, the American Scenic and Historic Preservation Society, in a letter to President Taft dated February 26, 1913, recommended that the existing western boundary of the monument be extended downstream along the Colorado River, incorporating fifteen miles on each side of the river, to a point five miles below the end of the Grand Canyon geologic formation (Kauffman 1954). Not until sixty years later was the canyon protected in its entirety; even then the eastern and western boundaries of the park were limited by Glen Canyon Dam on the northeast and Hoover Dam on the west.

The 1915 San Francisco World's Fair prompted a large influx of tourists into Arizona. Grand Canyon was one of their primary destinations. Aware of the opportunities this situation provided for promoting the state, the Phoenix Chamber of Commerce passed a resolution that same year urging park establishment (Verkamp 1940), as did the Chamber of Commerce of Yavapai County and the Arizona State Legislature.

By this time, tourism had increased so much that the Forest Service began inviting people to open livery establishments. Unfortunately, however, intensified competition for the tourist's dollars was rapidly approaching chaos. The Santa Fe Railroad, unhappy about the conditions under which it had to operate, refused to spend any more money at the canyon until the government asserted more control (Verkamp 1940). Even the secretaries of agriculture and interior, usually opponents on any issue involving public lands or resources, found themselves in agreement with each other—and with private groups such as the Sierra Club—that a national park was needed at Grand Canyon (Hughes 1967).

Eventually even many of the more recalcitrant residents of northern Arizona—except hunters and miners, who remained implacably opposed (Tillotson and Taylor 1935)—came to realize that the canyon, as a tourist mecca, was indispensable to economic growth and prosperity. Resistance began to take on a different form: rather than opposing the park altogether, local interests concentrated on making sure that as much grazing land was kept out of the park as possible (*Coconino Sun* November 17, 1916, cited in Verkamp 1940).[2]

Chief Forester Graves and National Park Service Director Stephen T. Mather discussed acceptable boundaries for the park in 1915 and 1916. In a long letter to Mather (January 3, 1915, cited in Kauffman 1954), Graves reiterated long-standing—and justifiable—arguments against boundaries that incorporated range- and timberlands adjacent to the canyon rims: they were too important to local livelihoods to be included in the park. The Park Service, nevertheless, continued to press for inclusion of substantial portions of the forests on the North and South Rims, which provided a dramatic setting for the canyon itself.

The creation of the National Park Service in 1916 turned out to be crucial to the effort to gain national park status for Grand Canyon. The singularly effective guidance of Mather, its first director, provided the necessary momentum and resources to overcome the still-powerful opposition of both congressmen and local interests.

The early days of the National Park Service were a heady time. Advertising techniques began to be perfected late in the nineteenth century, and Director Mather was adept at their use, having earlier masterminded the advertising and marketing of Twenty Mule Team Borax before going on to make a fortune with his own borax company. Having influential contacts in the publishing field helped, as did the support of famous writers such as Mary Roberts Rinehart and Emerson Hough. One of his most influential supporters was George Horace Lorimer, editor of the *Saturday Evening Post* (Shankland 1951, 85), who proved invaluable to Mather's campaigns to add significant new territories to the park system.

Although Mather devoted much of his energy to the creation of a national park to protect stands of redwood trees in California (Schrepfer 1983), he also very much wanted to add Grand Canyon to the lands under the jurisdiction of the National Park Service. He devised a high-profile campaign to generate increased support for the park system among the wealthy and the powerful. His strategy—and a successful one it was—was to publish the *National Parks Portfolio*, a handsome commentary on the national parks that was bound in leather and was mailed, free of charge, to a carefully selected list of important people (Shankland 1951). Grand Canyon was at the top of Mather's list of areas to be added to the system. By including it in the portfolio, he hoped to convince his audience that its uniqueness and beauty warranted their support for its preservation. Equally important, by including it among the existing national parks, he suffused his project with an aura of indisputability, of inevitability.

Meanwhile, on February 26, 1916, Secretary of the Interior Franklin K. Lane forwarded drafts of a new bill to create a park at Grand Canyon to Congressman Hayden and Senator Marcus A. Smith of Arizona (Kauffman 1954). Unfortunately for the Park Service's goals, grazing interests found an advocate in Hayden, who opposed excessive federal "land grabs." Hayden drafted a competing bill creating a national park with boundaries located much closer to the canyon rims (Verkamp 1940) and that encompassed only the more spectacularly scenic east end of the canyon. Hayden introduced his bill (H.R. 20447) into Congress on January 24, 1917.

On February 14, 1917, Senator Ashurst introduced an identical bill in the Senate (S. 8250), but he soon recanted and introduced a different bill (S. 390) that eliminated still more of the South Rim lands from the park. The bill protected valid land claims within the proposed park and, in a bow to a powerful private interest, prohibited the construction of any structures between lands owned by newspaper magnate William Randolph Hearst and the rim of the Grand Canyon (Kauffman 1954). Among the amendments made to Ashurst's bill as it made its way through Congress was a precedent-setting provision that explicitly allowed the Havasupais to use park lands for traditional purposes.[3] This bill became law (P.L. 277) in 1919.

When President Woodrow Wilson signed the legislation on February 26, 1919, Grand Canyon became the seventeenth national park. It encompassed an area of a little over 1,000 square miles (645,000 acres), including 56 miles of the canyon itself. The vast majority of the contested, resource-rich plateau lands remained outside the park boundaries.

In retrospect, it is astounding that the park was created when it was, given that the United States had just emerged from World War I, the country had just suffered the ravages of a deadly influenza outbreak, and private commerce was turning from the production of war material to the creation of consumer products. Nevertheless, a great pent-up demand for travel existed—especially for those who could afford the latest in transportation technology: automobiles. Likewise, the isolationism that overtook the country after the war may have played into the "See America First" campaign invented by park advocates.

Also influential were the works of well-known writers such as Charles Lummis and John C. Van Dyke, photographers Emery and Ellsworth Kolb, and painters Thomas Moran and William Holmes, whose works helped convince Congress and the general public of the value of preserving at least portions of Grand Canyon as a national park. In no small part their arguments were compelling because they stressed the primitive wilderness quality of the canyon: limitless views, boundless expanses of land, and borderless landscapes. Yet only the "worthless" land ended up being incorporated into the park (Runte 1979), for the language of the legislation stressed the values of the geological formations and the monumental qualities, not the protection of ecological values, which would have impinged considerably upon the continued exploitation of the natural resources of the region (Sutphen 1991).

Also at odds with the ideals of strict preservation were the calculated efforts to increase travel to the canyon, to portray it as a focus—and locus—of consumption. Promoters of Grand Canyon, including Stephen Mather, extolled the area for the "diversity of its pleasures, the joy of exploring its depths, its extraordinary monuments, its diversified viewpoints and its altogether fascinating rim forests" (Yard 1919, 4). Travelers were exhorted to stay more than one day so that they could truly come to know the canyon in all its diversity. In fact, Grand Canyon in subsequent years became a prime example of the contradiction built into the National Park Organic Act: how to preserve the land and its resources for future generations while making them available to present-day visitors.

The Havasupai Land Quest

The Havasupais were by far the most vocal of the tribes during this era (though they won few concessions), for they were the ones most directly and heavily affected by changes in land management in the greater Grand Canyon region. The creation of the park and the establishment of Tusayan National Forest from the remnants of forest not subsumed into the park meant that the tribe's small reservation was completely surrounded by Park Service and Forest Service lands.[4] Members of the small tribe, confined within the narrow walls of Havasu Canyon and pressured by restrictions on their use of the rimlands, struggled to add more lands to their tiny reservation. Arizona Territorial Delegate C. C. Bean visited the reservation in 1885 and, perceiving that the reservation was woefully inadequate to meet the people's needs, wrote a letter to the federal government calling for assistance for the Havasupais. Nothing came of his request. In 1888, Lieutenant Colonel B. N. Brayton reported to General Nelson Miles that the reservation was too small and requested that it be enlarged. Miles agreed and referred the report to Washington. Nothing happened.

The tribe's agent, Henry P. Ewing, recommended new and enlarged boundaries for the reservation to the commissioner of Indian Affairs in 1896. Perhaps hoping to make his proposal more attractive, he stressed the worthlessness of the lands for other purposes. Even though the requested lands were the ones that the Havasupais had been using for some years, the government's unsympathetic answer was to propose relocating tribal members from Havasu Canyon to land on the Colorado River near Parker (Havasupai Tribe 1973).

The Indian Rights Association then got into the act, recommending that the reservation be enlarged. The federal government ignored that organization's recommendation. Indeed, from 1893 to 1908, the Forest Service tried to drive the Havasupai off the plateau lands above the reservation. Not succeeding in removing the Havasupai, the Forest Service began issuing the tribe annual grazing permits in 1908, concurrent with the creation of the Coconino (ironically, the Hopi word for Havasupai) National Forest. But even then the Indians did not obtain exclusive rights to their traditional rimlands, for in 1917 and 1918, the Forest Service started letting non-Indian ranchers graze their cattle in the Pasture Wash area, arguing that the Havasupais were not developing it sufficiently, even though the area clearly continued to be important to the tribe for residential and farming activities (Hirst 1976). The Havasupais complained, but as with previous efforts, nothing was done (Havasupai Tribe 1973).

In 1914, the tribe's Indian Affairs agent, J. J. Taylor, wrote to the commissioner of Indian Affairs in yet another attempt to expand the reservation. Again nothing came of the effort. Likewise, the 1916 effort of A. M. Young, supervisor of the Havasupai Agency, fell on deaf ears. By 1917, when it appeared certain that a park would be established at Grand Canyon, the superintendent in charge of irrigation, H. F. Robinson, as well as the tribe's agent, C. H. Gensler, wrote to Congressman Hayden that the tribe needed its reservation enlarged. In response, Hayden added section 3 to S. 390, Ashurst's park establishment bill. Ultimately, the legislation, enacted as P. L. 277, ensured the tribe's continued use and occupancy of the bottomlands along Cataract Creek and authorized the secretary of the interior to permit members of the tribe to use and occupy other tracts of land within the park for agricultural purposes. It was a very small victory for the Havasupais, for they still lacked control over important portions of their ancestral lands. Park officials soon acted to restrict the activities of the Havasupais within Grand Canyon National Park when it interpreted the provisions of the act to prohibit their use of park lands for residence and hunting (Martin 1985). These were two of the most important needs of the Havasupais, for they had lived in and hunted on the lands encompassed by the park for centuries. Worse, besides being at the mercy of park officials with regard to how the provisions of P. L. 277 were to be interpreted, their rights outside their reservation boundaries remained severely limited by the Forest Service.

Until the creation of the national park, the Havasupais had managed to remain self-sufficient, even under extraordinary pressures (including devastation from the 1919 influenza epidemic, which had produced particularly high death rates among the women of the tribe). With the advent of the park, however, their condition began deteriorating. That they were able to survive as a cultural entity at all may well be due to two factors. First, an important precedent had been established in the park organic act, which recognized the Havasupais' rights to use park lands in their traditional ways. This precedent served them well fifty-six years later when they fought yet again for enlargement of their reservation. Second, even after the creation of the park, lack of enforcement power enabled them to defy Park Service (and Forest Service) rules to some extent. In fact, some Havasupais were still spending the winters on South Rim plateau lands as recently as the 1950s (Hirst 1976).[5]

Implications of the New Boundaries

With the incremental changes in power relationships between local users, Phoenix-area activists, the state of Arizona, and the federal government came changes in the definition of the spaces of the greater Grand Canyon. On paper, absolute spaces were delineated that, in addition to defining Indian reservations, divided the area into national forests, private lands, railroad lands, a game preserve, a national monument, and ultimately, a national park. Each of these spaces had its own set of rules and everyday practices. But while such boundaries existed on paper, in practice, relative space remained the primary way these spaces were defined: the timber operators, miners, ranchers, and government bureaucrats defined the spaces according to their own goals and needs.

The delineated boundaries did not agree with the various representational spaces of the area either. The Havasupais and the Paiutes were in possession of only small portions of the lands that formed their cultural heritage; the Hopis lacked complete control over their religious sites in and near the canyon. For many park advocates, the park boundaries failed to encompass scenic forestlands on both rims that they believed gave special meaning and significance to Grand Canyon.

While the changes in the definition and use of the spaces of the greater Grand Canyon looked strong on paper, lack of enforcement power and lack of local acceptance of the new rules translated into "business as usual." Resistance ranged from continuing customary practices in outright defiance of rules to pressuring and influencing politicians, local newspaper editors, and civic organizations such as the chamber of commerce to support particular stands. To the extent that local resource users were able to assert their power, the boundaries drawn to define and set apart the areas under federal management were, in practical terms, nonexistent.

The establishment of the park in 1919 (due to the efforts of Stephen Mather and Horace Albright[6] and their supporters, and of magazines such as *Good Housekeeping*) provided a jurisdictional framework for exerting greater power over the definition and uses of the spaces and resources of the eastern Grand Canyon. In this area, and in this area alone, the boundaries formed a shell that gave tangible form and substance to the long-held idea of a national park. The new entity, the national park, came into being in large part because of the earlier boundaries that had established the federal government as a legitimate presence in the area. In turn, the establishment of the park, far from resolving the problem of how to apportion the lands of the greater Grand Canyon among competing uses, provided the foundation for renewed efforts to withdraw from exploitation even more lands and resources.

CHAPTER FOUR

Park Consolidation and Expansion: 1920 to 1927

he years between 1919 and 1927 encompassed the end of World War I, the free-wheeling Roaring Twenties, and a deep recession, especially in agriculture and timber. The recession was particularly difficult for the West, because many of the western states (including Arizona) that were late in being admitted to the Union lacked large urban populations and strong industrial bases. Their best recourse for participation in the U.S. economy was full exploitation of their natural resources.

The extent to which these resources were controlled by the federal government, by the state, or by private owners was an important factor in the unfolding of relationships between the states and their citizens and the federal government and its agencies. In Arizona, vast amounts of land were—and continue to be—held by the federal government. These holdings, today totaling 51,393,000 acres or 70 percent of the lands in the state (Walker and Bufkin 1986),[1] played an important role in defining the terms and outcomes of the contests over territory and resources.

The Early Park Years

Although compromise had been reached on the boundaries of the new Grand Canyon National Park at the time it was created in 1919, preservation advocates were dissatisfied with the results and immediately began working to acquire more territory for the park. Entrepreneurs, like the Babbitts, took advantage of the existence of the park to open up businesses: Babbitt Brothers Trading Company opened in Grand Canyon Village in 1921 (Smith 1989).

In response to efforts to enlarge the park, many of the same interests that had resisted the creation of Grand Canyon National Park in the previous decades became active once again. Ranchers, timber interests, and citizens of the communities of Flagstaff and Williams, already feeling the effects of the post–World War I agricultural recession, pressed the Forest Service to defend the lands and resources they thought they had permanently protected from Park Service control. Even the Babbitts were not immune from economic hardship: they were forced to turn their enterprises over to bank management when they found themselves at the edge of bankruptcy (Smith 1989). Combined with legitimate fears of financial failure engendered by the periodic and unpredictable droughts of the region and the constant potential for an outbreak of livestock disease, the ranchers' resistance to further loss of pasturage was not only understandable, but eminently rational.

Perhaps most problematical was park officials' plan to expand the park charter. Although the creation of the park, like most others in the National Park System, had been sold to Congress and the public on the grounds of the scenic uniqueness and economic worthlessness of the Grand Canyon—not for its value as a haven for wildlife (Runte 1979)—park administrators undertook a herculean effort to redefine the mission of the park to include wildlife management and to acquire the additional territory that such a mission required.

In the meantime, exploration of the greater Grand Canyon continued. Perhaps the most important project undertaken at this time, in terms of its impact on negotiations over the spaces of Grand Canyon, was a trip made by the U.S. Geological Survey to survey for dam sites. This survey, a portent of the future battles over the water resources of the canyon that reached their height in the 1960s, not only added considerably to the specialized knowledge about the hydrology and geomorphology of the canyon, but also provided a basis for the designation of specific portions of the canyon that, because of their value as dam sites, would be ineligible for incorporation into the park. The issue became more acute when, in 1922, all of the Colorado River Basin states—except Arizona, which disputed the water allotment granted to California—signed the Colorado River Compact. An important document that apportioned the waters of the river among the basin states, the agreement heavily stressed the construction of dams—

several of which were to be built within the Grand Canyon—and irrigation and hydroelectric projects.

Fascination with the possibilities offered by science and technology affected Grand Canyon in other ways as well, for the Park Service was quite interested in applying modern advances in engineering and technology to park management problems. At Grand Canyon National Park, the person to fulfill these aspirations was a civil engineer himself.

Park Superintendent Minor Raymond Tillotson, a graduate of Purdue University and a former employee of the Forest Service, moved from Yosemite National Park to Grand Canyon in 1922, hoping to find a better climate for his son's severe respiratory ailments. He held the job of park engineer at Grand Canyon National park from the time he arrived until he took over as the first permanent superintendent of the park in 1927. As superintendent, his most lasting legacy may well be the engineering projects over which he presided: the construction of a suspension bridge over the Colorado River, a water recycling plant, and a system to pipe fresh water up from the canyon to the visitor area on the South Rim (Hughes 1978).

One of the biggest projects to land on his desk was never built, however. During the 1920s, the Park Service seriously entertained a suggestion to build a road across the Grand Canyon that would connect the South Rim directly to the North Rim (Tillotson and Taylor 1935, 61). Though never realized, the proposal did highlight an ongoing problem peculiar to Grand Canyon National Park: the difficulty of administering a deeply bisected landscape. Even today, access to the remote northern portion requires a 217-mile trip around the east end of the canyon by automobile—or a trip across the canyon on foot or muleback via the Kaibab Trail and Tillotson's suspension bridge.

Developments in Forest Management

World War I brought more federal control over loggers' operations on public lands nationwide, as well as increased competition among timber operators. The situation worsened after the war, when sagging markets for forest products and labor unrest threw the lumber industry into a depression (Putt 1991, 107). Even the more accessible timber operations, such as those in northern Minnesota, suffered during this time (Searle 1977).

At Grand Canyon, problems initially arose from a wartime policy governing the pricing and sale of railroad ties—a big business in the region. The railroads were required to buy the ties from local lumber companies, but prices were tightly controlled. The arrangement was a boon for the railroads but put a serious cap on the amount of profits the timber operators could earn. The end of the war did not solve the problem, however, for in the 1920s, while local lumber companies stubbornly clung to the belief that local timber supplies were inexhaustible, local Forest Service officials began warning (even in the face of slumping markets) of impending shortages of commercial timber in the area: timber resources in the Tusayan area, on the South Rim, were near exhaustion, they said, and timber resources throughout the forest would not last more than twenty years at the existing rate of cutting. After this, there would be a gap of fifty years in which there would be little or no timber to be cut. To address these problems, the agency implemented an innovative policy in 1923 that defined where and when logging would be allowed and what types of revegetation should be undertaken (Putt 1991).

Interestingly, even given this bleak scenario, the timber planners did not anticipate that they would immediately need to open the forested area nearest Grand Canyon National Park to logging. Timber operators thought differently. Having quickly exhausted other supplies and knowing that the segment of forest south of the Grand Canyon remained unlogged (having been bypassed earlier due to poor access and distance from local sawmills), the influential Saginaw and Manistee Company persuaded local Forest Service officials to open the area to harvesting ahead of schedule. The Forest Service issued the company a contract in 1927 to harvest more than 142,000 board feet of timber. Cutting in the Moqui-Anita area began in the fall of 1929 (Putt 1991).

The logging in turn stimulated concern about threats to the park and its resources. It did not take much imagination to envision the park reduced to an island in a sea of ugliness. Thus, concern over destruction of the forest provided the immediate stimulus for an intensive campaign to incorporate at least portions of the remaining forest into the park.

On another front, the park was embattled by hydroelectric power interests. The history of water projects undertaken by the Bureau of Reclamation in the West echoes the story of the exploitation of the forests of the region, with resource users making vociferous demands for water and energy development, and their congressional representatives working to ensure that their demands were met. Carl Hayden of

Arizona was in the forefront of these efforts, beginning with his success in inserting language into the 1919 Grand Canyon National Park organic act that specifically allowed for the construction of dams in the Grand Canyon. Throughout his years in Congress, Hayden continued to play an instrumental role in promoting water resource development along the Colorado River. In the end, he succeeded all too well: the Colorado became "a river no more" (Fradkin 1981).

Efforts to Expand the Park

In the midst of dealing with concerns about the destruction of the South Rim forest and plans for dam building, Park Superintendent Tillotson found himself facing the issue of how to administer a game management program. The issue was a complicated one, given that the wording of the 1916 National Park Service organic act stipulated that the parks were to provide for visitors' pleasure while preserving natural conditions, and the 1919 Grand Canyon National Park organic act stressed that the purpose of the park was to protect geological formations and scenic views. The boundaries of the park, carefully negotiated by Arizona congressmen Carl Hayden and Henry Ashurst, had been drawn close to the canyon rims to preserve only the geologic formations and the most scenic vista points. The configuration rendered park administrators' efforts to preserve biotic resources untenable.

The Park Service intensified its campaign to expand Grand Canyon National Park, arguing—among other reasons—that the existing boundaries did not protect sufficient wildlife habitat. Meanwhile, the National Parks Association added fuel to the controversy in its first publication by observing that the newly created park did not encompass nearly enough territory to provide visitors with access to "the diversity of its pleasures" (Yard 1919, 4). Movies, photographs, paintings, and magazine articles continued to pique public interest, but advocates of park expansion recognized that it was the up-close-and-personal experience of the area that attracted people most to their cause. Therefore, the park needed more visitors (and more facilities to accommodate them), more territory, and a wider diversity of recreational opportunities.

The path ahead, however, was rocky. The rapid increase, then disastrous decline, of the Kaibab deer herd on the North Rim prompted ferocious criticism of the park for administrators' policies of predator extermination and no hunting. These policies had enabled the deer population to grow from 4,000 in 1906 to nearly 100,000 in 1924. Their numbers vastly exceeded the forage available, leading to such severe overgrazing that 60 percent of the herd perished in the winters of 1924–25 and 1925–26 (Russo 1964). The disaster became a celebrated case study in game management and haunted the park as administrators attempted to expand their control over the entire range of the herd throughout the 1930s.

Meanwhile, local ranchers, loggers, and miners found common ground on another front: what they saw as the increasingly intrusive policies and practices of the federal land management agencies—especially the Park Service and to a lesser extent the Forest Service. Early harbingers of the Sagebrush Rebellion and Wise Use movement of the 1980s and 1990s, resource users mobilized political support at the local and state level by vilifying the federal agencies for operating against local experience and outside of the local context.

The Park Service failed to respond to the criticisms and, over the years, repeatedly found itself embattled in its attempts to preserve representative portions of the nation's biotic resources. In contrast, the Forest Service—by allowing resource exploitation and by heeding the demand that the agency work within the local context—succeeded more thoroughly in building and sustaining credibility with its constituents. Its successes, in turn, were bolstered by the fact that companies and individual operators derived considerable benefit from cooperation: they could continue to exploit the resource base without being responsible for husbanding the resource or for paying local taxes. Not surprisingly, at Grand Canyon and elsewhere, many people saw the Forest Service as the lesser of two evils.

Indeed, local preference for management by the Forest Service rather than the Park Service was widespread during these years. In the Boundary Waters Canoe Area along the border of Canada and Minnesota, for example, opponents prevented the establishment of a national park until 1971. Even then, the national park was created by executive order—not by congressional legislation—and did not include any of the lands or waters of the adjacent Superior National Forest. Because the Forest Service had succeeded for more than thirty years (though not without controversy) in managing a substantial portion of its lands for multiple use while reserving the most valued portions of its waterways and the adjacent forest for wilderness protection and primitive recreation, it was able to keep its territorial base intact (Witzig 1983).

In California, analogous efforts were aimed at keeping the Park Service out of the struggle to protect the redwoods (Schrepfer 1983).

A very different story emerged, however, with regard to Olympic National Park in Washington state. Here, the Forest Service intransigently ignored the demands of recreationists and ended up losing thousands of acres of valuable timber lands to the Park Service (Twight 1983).

At Grand Canyon, while the Forest Service was consolidating support from local users, the Park Service sought support from nonlocal constituencies. Writers, artists, editors and publishers, environmentalists, recreationists, social organizations, politicians, and some scientists worked for park expansion. The results of their efforts were mixed.

The Quest for Efficiency

Ranchers on the North Rim, many of whom lived in Utah and ran herds on the Arizona side of the boundary,[2] continued to be particularly influential in the contests over modification of the park boundaries. In 1923, Park Service Director Stephen Mather visited Grand Canyon National Park to confer with Park Superintendent Walter W. Crosby and with Charles McCormick, a sheep rancher on the Arizona Strip (Kauffman 1954; Mather 1923). In response to the recommendations he received from Crosby and McCormick, Mather requested that Topographic Engineer R. T. Evans of the Geological Survey, at that time engaged in mapping the park, recommend a more "natural" boundary on the North Rim: one that followed natural features which could be identified on the ground and that facilitated control (presumably of livestock) across park boundaries (Kauffman 1954).

Mather's request is interesting, for it highlights a recurrent issue: what criteria should be used to determine placement of boundaries. Any number of boundaries may be drawn on maps, but unless they can be marked on the landscape as well, enforcement is difficult. Therefore, natural features have long been preferred as boundary markers—especially ones, like mountain crests, that do not change location (rivers and streams, though popular boundary markers, can be remarkably undependable in this regard).

Evans contradicted Mather's ideas that the best boundaries would follow recognizable physical features such as the canyon rims. Instead, having reconnoitered the area, he recommended boundaries that followed the section lines of the U.S survey system, reasoning that the ravines and ridges made the definition of a natural boundary line difficult and vague, whereas a land line "is definite to a foot and can be easily marked through woods by blazing and posting notices" (Evans 1923, 2).

In the same report, Evans recommended several areas for incorporation into the park. Two of these tracts were highly contested for years to come: the beautiful woodland-and-meadow area on the North Rim known at the time as VT Park (now called DeMotte Park) and Long Mesa, which lay between the southwestern boundary of the park and the Hualapai Reservation. The Long Mesa tract included five square miles of good grassland and was even then supporting a herd of twenty-four antelopes. This tract of land, Evans noted, could be converted into pasture for game animals simply by building a fence one mile long on the landward side. Besides, Evans commented, the south end of the lobe was a "canyon of rare beauty possessing curious and fantastic recesses and a large group of pinnacles" (Evans 1923, 3). Long Mesa was among the lands that the Havasupais had been trying to add to their reservation. Clearly, Evans deemed neither the Havasupais' need for the resources contained within the relative space of the area nor their attachment to the larger representational space of their former domain to be important enough even to be incorporated into his evaluation.

Not all boundary adjustment proposals threatened tribal lands, however. In fact, in a letter to Park Service Director Mather, the new (temporary) park superintendent, John R. Eakin, called for the return of territory located along the eastern boundary of the park to the Navajos,[3] noting that the area, lying north of the Little Colorado River and east of the Colorado River, was of no interest to the park and was difficult to administer.[4] Evans's predilection for surveyed boundaries notwithstanding, Eakin suggested that the change could be justified "from the standpoint of a natural boundary" (Eakin 1924a).[5]

That Eakin wanted the park expanded in other areas, however, is abundantly clear from a memo he wrote on August 6, 1924, to Mather recommending that the northern boundary of the park be moved northward to at least 36 degrees, 30 minutes. He acknowledged that the forested land, then managed by the Forest Service, might prove difficult to acquire, but he rationalized the adjustment based on another form of efficiency: the need to provide winter range for deer within the park boundaries (Eakin 1924b).

Mather fired another salvo in the battle to revise the park boundaries when he wrote a letter to Congressman Carl Hayden complaining that the north boundary line of the park had never been satisfactory. He reiterated the Park Service's position that the boundary interfered with proper road development, excluded water sources needed for hotels and camps, and generally restricted opportunities for recreational development on the North Rim. Mather stressed the necessity of incorporating into the park a portion of VT Park (emphasizing its importance as an administrative and transportation hub), as well as lands in Kanab Canyon and South Canyon—both considered to provide important winter habitat for deer (Kauffman 1954, 4).

Predictably, the Park Service proposals ran into opposition from the Forest Service (Kauffman 1954). As a result of this dispute, as well as ones involving boundaries at other national parks, the President's Committee on Outdoor Recreation set up a Coordinating Commission on National Parks and Forests. The participants, all of whom had a record of park activism or had worked on public lands issues at the national level, included Henry W. Temple (congressman from Pennsylvania), Charles Sheldon (noted naturalist, hunter, explorer, and personal friend of Theodore Roosevelt), Major W. A. Welch (general manager of Palisades Interstate Park), Colonel William B. Greeley (Chief Forester, U.S. Forest Service), Barrington Moore (member of the Council on National Parks, Forests, and Wildlife), and Stephen Mather. Their recommendations played an important role in resolving issues of control over the spaces and resources of the greater Grand Canyon.

Among those making recommendations to the commission on behalf of the Park Service was Topographical Engineer Evans, who reiterated and elaborated upon the recommendations he had made in his report to Mather. The North Rim boundary, he said, should be drawn to encompass Tapeats Basin and the Big Saddle country, lands for winter deer pasture and for a road to Big Saddle, all of VT Park, lands on the East Rim and in Pagump Valley, and approximately thirteen miles of the Marble Canyon gorge. On the South Rim the Long Mesa area should be added, as well as Little Coyote Canyon, and small tracts of land near the south entrance to the park, at Grandview Point, and along the road to Desert View (Evans 1925).

Eakin took issue with some of Evans's recommendations, noting that the proposed addition on the southeastern side of the park was an area used by the Navajo Indians and that, "as it is the intention of the Service to eventually stop grazing at the canyon, we should be in a very

embarrassing position if we attempted to stop Navajos grazing their
sheep and goats where they had been for a good many years. Furthermore, on lands that are grazed by Navajos, it would be absolutely impossible to protect the wildlife." Eakin also noted that if all of the lands
designated by Evans were incorporated, the boundaries as outlined
would have included private property, the owners of which, being uni-
formly antagonistic to the Park Service, would fight any loss of territory (Eakin 1925a).

In a subsequent letter to Mather, Park Superintendent Eakin expressed his misgivings about the Forest Service's forthrightness regarding its plans for the Kaibab Forest. In discussions with the Forest
Service on the subject, he said, local agency officials had invariably
protested that they never had any intention of logging the Kaibab Forest. He went on to cite a 1924 circular from the U.S. Department of
Agriculture (number 318) that made it quite clear that the Forest Service planned to allow the area to be logged whenever appropriate
transportation became available. Eakin suggested that this was one
more reason why certain areas of the forest should be added to the
park as soon as possible. Furthermore, he warned, "An ex–Forest Service employee some time ago stated to me that in his opinion, the Forest Service wished to get rid of the deer in the Kaibab and the conservationists would never permit the Kaibab to be logged while this fine
herd of deer were on it. I thought perhaps he was mistaken, but since
reading this circular, I begin to suspect he is quite right in the matter"
(Eakin 1925b).

The controversy became even more heated when, during the spring
of 1925, Chief Forester Greeley, accompanied by District Forester
Frank Pooler of Albuquerque and Supervisor George Kimball of the
Tusayan National Forest, visited Eakin at the Grand Canyon to discuss
boundary issues. Among the biggest points of contention was a proposal to transfer a key tract of pine forest on the South Rim to the
park. Eakin said the park wanted to incorporate the tract to develop
bridle paths and to protect the local wildlife. Greeley asserted that the
Forest Service not only had plans to log all the way up to the park
boundary, but planned to designate the entire area as a game preserve,
a contradiction of missions that prompted Eakin to retort, "Any game
refuge subject to logging operations could never be a game preserve in
any sense of the word" (Eakin 1925c).

On another topic, Eakin invoked administrative efficiency to argue
for adjustments that would straighten out jogs in the boundary: the

existing boundary required almost twice as much material to fence and obliged park rangers to travel almost twice the distance on their patrols. Greeley, not surprisingly, disagreed with even these small adjustments to their common boundary, since what was viewed as efficiency from the Park Service's perspective was seen as loss of territory by the Forest Service. Under these conditions, the debate could only escalate—and it did.

Mather wrote to Temple, chairman of the commission, to reiterate yet again Evans's recommendations for a new North Rim boundary and to promote modified boundary changes for the South Rim that would have entailed only minor additions to the park—including the tract of yellow pine forest south of headquarters over which Greeley and Eakin had argued just the week before (Mather 1925).

The Forest Service did not object to the addition of approximately 43,160 acres of forestland on the North Rim; however, it remained implacably opposed to the other proposed changes, branding them as "not . . . in accord with the principles governing the establishment or enlargement of national parks, or with good public policy" (Kneipp, quoted in Kauffman 1954, 6). In direct contradiction to efforts aimed at giving the park biologically based boundaries, the Forest Service insisted that the geological Grand Canyon was the "single natural phenomenon of national importance within the limits of either the present or proposed Park boundaries. . . . The lands back from the rims can function only as settings for the Canyon itself and their inclusion within the Park is justified only so far as is necessary to adequately provide for public use and enjoyment of the Canyon and its tributaries through the construction of roads, trails, water supply etc." (Kneipp, quoted in Kauffman 1954, 7). By comparison, the value of local timber cutting was estimated at more than one million dollars a year and would cause only a "slight sacrifice of any recreational values." Furthermore, splitting jurisdiction over the national game preserve and the deer herd that inhabited the area would actually make management more difficult, given the wide difference in game management policies between the Forest Service and the Park Service. Finally, the inclusion of water sources within the park would impede the use and development of areas outside the park (Kauffman 1954).

Congressman Hayden, leaping into the fray, asserted that no material additions, other than minor ones needed for road building and administrative purposes, should be made to the south boundaries of the park because the present boundary reflected the agreement struck with local resource users. Revealing a reluctance to engage in a fight he was not likely to win, Eakin retreated, commenting to Assistant Forester L. F. Kneipp that the southern boundary was relatively unimportant but that the members of the commission, due to arrive at Grand Canyon for a public hearing on September 2, should agree on boundaries before the hearing began.

The ensuing behind-the-scenes negotiation ultimately limited the available options in several ways. First, it restricted participation to those who were recognized as legitimate players: appointees to the commission, an influential Arizona politician, and local land management supervisors from the affected federal agencies. Second, it restricted to this group the privilege of defining the problem and the alternative solutions that would qualify for consideration. Third, it served to control access to knowledge about the various positions and viewpoints of the participants, limiting such access to those participating in the closed-door sessions. That the boundary changes ultimately enacted by Congress were limited in scope traces back, in part, to this meeting.

On the morning of September 2, members of the commission, representatives of the Forest Service and Park Service, and Congressman Hayden held the agreed-upon meeting in Eakin's office. For the South Rim, the group agreed to a boundary proposed by Hayden that would allow for the construction of a new road. Eakin declared his satisfaction with this agreement, since this boundary would also allow game resources to be improved. Except for some additional scattered parcels of land, including eight sections for construction of a road to Cape Solitude, the group added no other areas to the South Rim sector of the park; however, there was a tradeoff, as the Forest Service agreed that lumbering operations in the yellow pine tract would not be allowed to extend to the park boundary and that a considerable belt of timber along the boundary would be left untouched. Not surprisingly, the Forest Service was not receptive to giving up any more land; the commission's secretary reinforced the agency's intransigence by pointing out that any lands added on the South Rim would raise enough objections in Congress to jeopardize the more important additions (45,000 acres) on the North Rim.

The commission presented the agreed-upon South Rim boundaries at a public hearing that same evening. Remarkably, given the intensity of earlier opposition, once the conferees explained the boundaries to the public, no objections were raised (Eakin 1925d).

Soon thereafter, the Department of the Interior announced in a press release that the commission had completed its field investigations and had made its recommendations for adjustments to the boundaries of Grand Canyon National Park. For the North Rim, the commission's recommendations took into account the forest and other economic resources of the Kaibab Plateau, the respective needs of the Forest Service and Park Service for central administration sites that had available water, and the need to protect the approaches to the rim of the canyon and to provide for necessary development of roads in the park. For the South Rim, the commission considered the desirability of following natural boundaries in Havasupai country, the need for road development, and the exclusion of private holdings. Having taken these factors into account, the commission concluded that 45,000 acres on the North Rim and approximately 2,000 acres on the South Rim should be transferred to the park from the adjacent national forests (Coordinating Commission on National Parks and Forests 1925; U.S. Department of the Interior 1925).

Revision of the park boundaries was not yet accomplished, however, for the changes required congressional approval. Mather moved quickly to get the written boundary description approved by Congress, but local resistance again arose when the Flagstaff Chamber of Commerce announced that any transfer of lands to the park represented a loss of resources to the community, even in the case where those resources were already under the jurisdiction of another federal land management agency—in this case, the Forest Service. Aware that local interests had the power to derail the proposed boundary adjustments, Eakin wrote a letter to the chamber of commerce defending park administrators' position—a position that had been significantly revised by this time to focus only on the efficiency argument. The additions to the South Rim, he said, were essential to the road-building program for the park. Less than one-and-a-half sections of merchantable timber were being added to the South Rim portion of the park, he argued, and besides, the Buggeln and Babbitt cattle interests (the affected parties in the area) had agreed to the changes.

As for the North Rim, Eakin stressed the need for enough territory to allow roads to be built to Cape Royal and Point Sublime (areas having spectacular views that are popular with tourists to the present day) to include a representative tract of the Kaibab Forest, and to provide summer and winter range for "a small portion" of the deer herd. Eakin also stressed that the addition was not then under grazing permit, since the Forest Service had reserved it entirely for the deer. Besides, he argued, the "citizens of Kanab, Utah, have, by resolution, indorsed [sic] the proposed new boundaries." He concluded by arguing that "the proposed addition is not a 'grab' in any sense but is a sincere effort to weld the park into a compact administrative unit . . . and make the park as interesting as possible to visitors" (Eakin 1926a).

Soon thereafter, Eakin received support from Alfred Skeels of Williams (Eakin had sent him a carbon copy of his letter): "Upon receipt of your letter, yesterday, I run [sic] in to Flagstaff and took the matter up with Fred Breen. The boys apper [sic] to have gotten off on the wrong foot, as this matter was all settled, long ago to the satisfaction of all concerned. I believe that if Fred [probably Fred Breen, editor of the *Coconino Sun*] had attended the last meeting of the Flagstaff Chamber, it would not have happened. As I recall it, I had the County Board indorse [sic] the proposed changes in boundry [sic] line, but our Clerk was slow about notifying Carl Hayden" (Skeels 1926).

Meanwhile, the Department of the Interior requested the incorporation into legislation of the commission's recommended boundaries for Grand Canyon National Park. Senator Robert N. Stanfield of Oregon (chairman of the Senate Public Lands Committee) responded by introducing S. 3433 on March 3, 1926, and Congressman Nicholas J. Sinnott (chairman of the House Public Lands Committee), also of Oregon, introduced an identical bill, H.R. 9916, on May 3, 1926. Even Senator Ashurst, while visiting the park, commented to Chief Ranger Eivind T. Scoyen that he had written to "all big tax payers and other citizens" and had found no one who objected to the proposed boundary revisions (Eakin 1926b).

All objections having apparently been resolved, Congress enacted H.R. 9916 on February 25, 1927 (Kauffman 1954). The new boundaries incorporated a representative sample of the Kaibab Forest on the North Rim; on the South Rim, the bill added enough land to allow construction of a road to Desert View entirely within park boundaries. In total, the bill, though deleting a few isolated parcels, added 32,000 acres (51 square miles) to the park—a far smaller sum than park advocates had desired (Hughes 1978).

Implications of the New Boundaries for the Tribes

The repartitioning of the spaces of the Grand Canyon neither enhanced nor damaged the status of Indian lands, and Indian voices were ob-

scured or remained silent during the contests over how the repartitioning would be accomplished. Suggestions to include in the park a
portion of Navajo Reservation land, for game management reasons,
were rejected out of concern that such inclusions would be strongly
resisted by the tribe. The outcome suggests the considerable extent to
which the reservations, with their absolute spaces marked by clearly
defined boundaries, had invested the tribes with some degree of latent,
territorially based power. Combined with the fact that they had finally
been accorded formal status as U.S. citizens in 1924 (the Fourteenth
Amendment had excluded Indians from citizenship), their possession
of a territorial anchor constituted an important base of power. Yet the
fact that no lands were transferred to the tribe from the park (as Eakin
had originally recommended) suggests a strong inertia inherent in the
boundaries and absolute spaces of the park.

The Havasupai continued trying, through their Bureau of Indian
Affairs representative, to acquire the plateau lands they needed and
had been using for centuries. As mentioned in the previous chapter, the
1919 enabling legislation for the park allowed the tribe to use the plateau lands located within the park; however, lack of trust title made
their position tenuous at best. Most important for them, the new
boundaries enacted by Congress did not incorporate into the park the
Forest Service's Long Mesa and Beaver Canyon areas that Evans had
recommended for inclusion. The retention of existing Forest Service
jurisdiction over the contested terrain allowed the Havasupais greater
latitude with regard to their use of these lands. Over the course of the
next fifty years this situation not only worked to the Havasupais' benefit, but also kept alive their claim that the contested spaces were part
of their ancestral lands.

The Park Enlargement Process in Retrospect

Though Grand Canyon National Park gained new lands by relying on
efficiency arguments, the park failed to acquire substantial portions of
the territory deemed essential to carrying out its self-defined mission
of biological preservation. Ranchers on the North and South Rims justified their efforts to maintain the status quo by using arguments based
on economic necessity and the lack of other viable options. Their strategy proved successful once again, for they lost little of their relative
spaces of resource exploitation. The Forest Service and its logging constituency also fared well, since they lost little of the timber resource

base. The Forest Service also succeeded in retaining control over valuable deer habitat areas and thus over the management of the deer herds. The local communities and the county fared well, for a time, because the wealth accompanying timber cutting in the Kaibab National Forest continued to contribute to county and city revenues.

The greatest success of the Park Service was linked to affirmation of the legitimacy of Grand Canyon National Park as both a national treasure and a source of local revenue and wealth: despite strong resistance to any sort of expansion, there were no significant efforts to dismantle the park. After all, wealth was accruing to the local communities from increased tourism associated with the park, just as the Park Service had predicted. The contest was not yet over, however, for powerful forces continued to advocate further expansion of the park boundaries.

CHAPTER FIVE

Park Expansion Versus a New
National Monument: 1927 to 1940

I n the 1930s the Great Depression dominated social, political, and economic life in the United States. The social and political reforms of President Franklin D. Roosevelt's New Deal created, among other innovations, the Civilian Conservation Corps. Workers in the Civilian Conservation Corps did much to improve facilities (such as trails and campgrounds) in the national parks, including Grand Canyon National Park. Roosevelt's federal reforms also included the transfer from the War Department to the National Park Service of two national parks, eleven military parks, ten battlefield sites, ten national monuments, three miscellaneous memorials, and eleven national cemeteries (Executive Order 6166; Olsen 1985).

As the holdings of the Park Service grew in number, its jobs became more specialized. By 1938, due to massive additions to the national park system (including Great Smoky Mountains, Acadia, and Everglades National Parks), field administration had become so complex that the Park Service created a new layer of management: four regional offices, located in Richmond, Virginia; Santa Fe, New Mexico; San Francisco, California; and Omaha, Nebraska (Olsen 1985).

Concurrently, a pronounced shift occurred in the philosophy of the National Park Service concerning the identity and purpose of the national parks. While the development of park facilities remained a priority,[1] the preservation of desirable species and their habitats became a primary focus of park expansion efforts. In adding this new mission, the agency was influenced by the scientific directions of the day. Advances in the natural sciences (based on a belief in the existence of orderly and immutable laws of nature) and a fascination with biological (and social) engineering[2] led scientists like John Merriam (paleon-tologist, head of the Carnegie Institution in Washington, D.C., and advisor to both the Park Service and the California-based Redwood League) to advocate national parks as ideal places to improve society and to provide laboratories where natural processes could be preserved and studied.

The study of ecology, which focused on the interactions of entire communities or ecosystems, emerged as an alternative to the narrower focus of traditional biological science and translated into ecologically based resource management. However, differences soon arose about how evolution worked, leading to debates over whether natural selection was one-directional, from least to most developed form (ortho-genetic), or whether there was randomness in the process of natural selection. Though the latter view won out by the 1950s (Schrepfer 1983), during the earlier years belief in unidirectional change that led to a climax stage of perfection prompted much effort to ensure optimal environmental conditions for desirable species.

Ecological concepts also underpinned much of the social engi-neering of the period. Merriam and his colleagues believed that the march of civilization was destroying important natural phenomena that would advance human knowledge and lead to a betterment of society.[3] In the 1910s, this belief had underpinned efforts to promote natural parks as field laboratories for scientific research and as class-rooms for educating the public (Schrepfer 1983). A decade later, the Park Service was following through on these ideas by creating park interpretive programs and by pressing for expansion of park holdings.

The situation was tailor-made for Park Service officials such as Ste-phen Mather, Horace Albright, and Arno Cammerer,[4] whose expan-sionist philosophies did much to shape the early trajectory and image of the Park Service. Rather than simply preserve scenic vistas for the public to enjoy, the parks would shelter wildlife—especially popular species such as deer, antelope, and bighorn sheep—by incorporating entire habitats within the absolute spaces of park boundaries. Because some of the hoofed species, in particular, had large ranges, justification was at hand for very large additions to the parks.

A New Round in the Park Expansion Contest

At Grand Canyon, no sooner had park boundaries been revised than new contests arose. As in previous and subsequent contests, Park Service efforts to enlarge the Grand Canyon on biological grounds soon prompted the Forest Service to ally itself with local businesspeople and resource users.

These new contests over park expansion were occurring at the same time that the hardships of the post–World War I recession and the beginnings of the Great Depression were placing enormous stresses on the nation. Although documentary evidence contained in the archives of the park from this era includes no significant mention of the state of the economy, certainly the intensity of the contest over the spaces of the greater Grand Canyon and the successes of local interests in averting any major changes were at least in part due to the effects of the depression on both the local and the national economy. In any case, the lack of adequate staff to monitor parklands can be directly attributed to depression-driven reductions in congressional appropriations.[5]

Likewise, documentation of efforts to enlarge the park does not directly mention the great drought of the late 1920s and into the 1930s, though this natural event too was surely instrumental to local resistance. Ranchers and public land managers did recognize, however, the impacts of one of the most important administrative actions of the New Deal era: the passage of the 1934 Taylor Grazing Act.

The major innovation of the decade in natural resource policy, and an example of federal response to the crises of the 1930s, the Taylor Grazing Act created a new federal land management agency: the U.S. Grazing Service (later subsumed in the Bureau of Land Management). The agency's mission was to manage the vast acreages of federal lands that had not been absorbed by other agencies. Soon after its establishment, the Grazing Service issued a series of regulations, including a reduction in the number of livestock allowed to graze on its lands. These actions prompted livestock owners in the greater Grand Canyon area to fight even harder to prevent losses of land and resources to the Park Service.

At Grand Canyon National Park, in the meantime, administrators apparently failed to recognize these stresses, for serious efforts were afoot to significantly expand the park boundaries based on biological criteria. Vernon Bailey, the chief naturalist of the U.S. Biological Survey (which in 1940 was combined with the Bureau of Fisheries to form the U.S. Fish and Wildlife Service), became the catalyst for the effort when he advised acquiring more range for wildlife—especially the large North Kaibab deer herd (Bailey nd; Cammerer 1929). According to Bailey, Grand Canyon National Park, like many others, had been created without adequate attention being paid to the need to provide sufficient range for wildlife (Bailey 1929; Bailey nd; Kauffman 1954).

Bailey's comments prompted the Park Service to issue a report on possible boundary extensions. The report asserted that every national park was—and ought to be—a game preserve and that the boundaries ought to incorporate feeding and breeding grounds for all seasons of the year. The area encompassed should be large enough to sustain reasonable numbers of animals under the most natural conditions possible (Kauffman 1954). The report used Grand Canyon National Park as an example: a two- to ten-mile extension of the South Rim boundary was needed for the proper management of deer, antelopes, and bighorns. An additional five to fifteen miles were required for habitat protection on the North Rim. Anticipating criticism that boundary extensions on the South Rim would create economic hardship, the Park Service predicted that losses could be counterbalanced by the additional income the area would receive from tourism. This was no small matter, for altogether the park would be expanded by 222,720 acres (348 square miles) on the North Rim and 154,880 acres (272 square miles) on the South Rim (Kauffman 1954).

Not surprisingly, given the magnitude of park officials' designs, the proposal, issued in a draft report by the Park Service, generated immediate and strong resistance from both the chief of the Biological Survey and the head of the Forest Service, neither of whom believed that the Park Service was capable of managing wildlife effectively (Redington and Stuart 1930).[6]

While the debate continued at the federal level, state and local resistance to the Park Service's expansionist activities intensified. C. W. Person and James A. Diffin (respectively, secretary and president of the Arizona Game Protective Association, which advocated hunting and fishing) sounded the call to arms against the latest flurry of proposals:

> Again the sportsmen of the state must don their war bonnets! There's a battle to be fought. . . . In February 1927, the National Park Service succeeded in getting about 45,000 acres added to the Grand Canyon National Park. Now, a still more ambitious "grab" is contemplated. . . . There is no logical or sensible reason for thus extending the boundaries of the Grand Canyon National Park— unless it be to cater to the interests of invested capital at Grand Canyon and V.T. Park! We already have a complicated conservation problem on our hands up there, as regards the management of the

Kaibab deer. It would be most unfortunate to complicate it further by introducing a third agency with policies that differ from those of the Arizona Game and Fish Commission and the United States Forest Service. We all hope to see our own State Game Department, in the not far distant future, assume the entire management of the Kaibab deer. Let us do all in our power to keep those deer out of the hands of the National Park Service. (Person and Diffin 1930)

The association subsequently invited Park Superintendent Minor R. Tillotson to make a presentation on the issue. While remaining cautious about being involved in a dispute before the Park Service's strategy had even been finalized, Tillotson agreed, admitting to Park Service Director Albright that they should explain the situation before the opposition got any stronger (Tillotson 1930a). But when it came time to meet with the association on May 5, 1930, Tillotson committed an irremediable blunder: he told the assembled crowd that the idea for the boundary adjustments had originated with a member of the Biological Survey, not with the Park Service (Tillotson 1930b). The Biological Survey, outraged at the gaffe, dissociated itself from the Park Service's plans and vociferously denied having made the recommendation.[7] Any opportunity that may have existed for substantial additions to the park on biological grounds came crashing down.[8] Ultimately, on June 2, 1930, the Flagstaff Game Protective Association went on record formally opposing park expansion (Flagstaff Game Protective Association 1930).

The Park Service's activities came under further attack when Chief Forester Robert Stuart wrote to Senator Carl Hayden that the South Rim lands recommended for addition to the park in the 1929 biological survey were the same lands that had been involved in a timber sale to the Saginaw and Manistee Lumber Company shortly after the 1927 boundary change. The sale, Stuart complained, had been discussed with all interested parties and no one had raised any objection at that time. Besides, Stuart asked, how were the contract holders to be reimbursed (Stuart 1930)?

In the midst of the fray, Edmund Seymour, president of the American Bison Society and a widely recognized leader in the conservation movement, attempted to resolve the issue by participating in a field investigation on June 8, 9, and 10, 1930. To the immeasurable disadvantage of the park, the inquiry did not include any Park Service representation, though it did include park opponents T. E. McCullough, chairman of the Arizona Game and Fish Commission; R. Lee Bayless, Arizona state game warden; and Walter T. Mann, forest superintendent for the Kaibab National Forest (Seymour 1930).

Both McCullough and Seymour documented their conclusions. McCullough wrote to Senator Henry Ashurst three days after the field trip that "the Forest Service, in charge of this Federal Game Refuge, is working with the Arizona Game and Fish Commission in complete harmony, with the . . . idea . . . of reducing the deer herd as soon as . . . [possible]." Any park boundary extension, he warned, "would inject right into the very heart of the summer deer range, as well as the winter range, a department of the Government whose definite and fixed policy is one of strict conservation, with no hunting. How in the name of common sense could any improvement result in this serious problem by injecting the Park Service into the situation?" He even accused the Park Service of wishing to eliminate the Buggeln Cattle Company and the Babbitt CO Bar ranch operation, since the proposed boundary on the South Rim would include those cattle ranges, and he added, "I believe that if the truth were known, this proposed extension is backed by both the Union Pacific and the Fred Harvey [Company] of the Santa Fe [Railroad]."[9] He attacked Vernon Bailey as well, accusing Bailey of being a sentimentalist with regard to his love of outdoor life and wild game and also accusing Bailey of being used by the Park Service "to pull their chestnuts out of the fire." He concluded by pronouncing the Kaibab deer problem to be too great for the "injection of Park Service ideals" and advised Ashurst that "the sentiment in Arizona is overwhelmingly against this proposed Park boundary extension" (McCullough 1930).

It was Seymour's report, however, that sent hopes of expanding park boundaries into a tailspin. On August 18, 1930, Seymour reported to the Park Service that he had found strong opposition on the North Rim to the boundary extension proposal, because the Park Service restricted hunting and because local residents believed that the Forest Service had already worked out a good plan for managing the deer. "To separate part of this territory from the Forest Service," he observed, "would complicate the deer problem." He was, however, willing to agree with the Park Service in one area: "It would be better to have the Park Service have the VT Valley [VT Park]. . . . This is a beautiful valley and the deer summer here and are seen a great deal by tourists. . . . [The] herd of deer is much more valuable to the United States and to the State of Arizona than any grazing privilege that could be given to sheep or cattle men." But even here, Seymour hedged his support by noting that there would be no harm in granting a few cattle-grazing privileges for people living in the district (Seymour 1930).

Developments in Indian Country

Many Indians fought in World War I and came home with a strong desire to have greater control over their own destiny. The odds against them were great, however, for the General Allotment Act of 1887 was still in force. The tide changed in 1921 when former U.S. senator Albert Fall of New Mexico, a man known to be hostile to Indian rights, became the secretary of the interior under President Warren Harding. Fall immediately proceeded to issue a series of proposals detrimental to Indian interests, but his strategy backfired, for it mobilized a wide array of opponents ranging from the General Federation of Women's Clubs to Indian rights organizations. The ensuing battle brought to the fore a man who went on to become one of the most influential commissioners of Indian Affairs in U.S. history: John Collier. A social science teacher at San Francisco State College and a seasoned social reformer, Collier organized and headed the American Indian Defense Association and testified on behalf of Indian rights before Congress. In 1933 he assumed the position of commissioner of Indian Affairs.[10]

Collier's efforts culminated in the Indian Reorganization Act of 1934, a major piece of New Deal social legislation designed to improve the economic situation of the Indians. Although most Indians never saw much change in their economic status as a result of the act (due in part to the meagerness of congressional appropriations for realizing development plans), they did experience major changes in their political lives, for the act promoted self-rule by requiring the tribes to adopt a constitution and set up a formal governance structure. Once set up, the governing body could negotiate directly with federal, state, and local governments and to veto the sale, lease, or encumbrance of tribal property and assets (Deloria and Lytle 1984). The new tribal governments provided an identifiable entity with which governmental and private authorities could negotiate. But on many reservations, they also generated tensions between traditionalists, who held to the old ways of making decisions and regulating tribal life, and more pragmatic tribal factions, who worked to maximize their people's position within the structure of mainstream American life.

Geographically, among the most important features of the Indian

Reorganization Act was the repeal of the General Allotment Act provisions. No longer would Indians be pressured to divide their tribal lands among current members and to relinquish the remaining lands, for a small financial reimbursement, to the federal government. Unsold surplus lands that had been open for sale to non-Indians, with some exceptions,[11] were returned, in trust status, to the tribes. The act also empowered the secretary of the interior to create new Indian reservations on land that had been acquired under the provisions of the act (Deloria and Lytle 1984).

Collier's long history of activism (including his twelve years as commissioner—the longest on record for the Office of Indian Affairs) and his string of successes encouraged many Indians to renew their efforts to improve their lives. The Havasupais were among those who were inspired to fight strongly for the return of their lands.

Havasupai Persistence

The Havasupais' Indian Affairs representative, Patrick Hamley, made a case for the enlargement of their reservation to the commissioner of Indian Affairs, citing their obvious need for grazing land. He requested that the approximately 90,000 acres of Forest Service grazing land that the Havasupais were then leasing, at no cost, from the agency be turned over to the tribe. These were lands, he reminded the commissioner, that the tribe had always used for grazing and winter residence. Hamley also testified before the Senate on May 21, 1931, reiterating that the Havasupais needed more grazing land and that the Forest Service had no objection to such a transfer. In the end, as before, nothing changed for the tribe (Havasupai Tribe 1973), due in no small part to Park Service resistance.

Preservation by Proclamation

While opponents continued to thwart efforts to expand the park based on biological criteria, and the Havasupais lost another bid to enlarge their reservation, a new contest arose over territory lying west of the park. Arizona Governor George H. Dern first raised the idea of creating a recreation area after visiting the Toroweap Valley on the North Rim in 1927. The Park Service soon followed up on the suggestion but proposed adding the area to the park. Eivind T. Scoyen, superintendent of Zion National Park in Utah, visited the area in 1929 and waxed eloquent about its beauties. Roger W. Toll, superintendent of Yellowstone National Park, inspected the area on June 16, 1932, and also found it worth protecting (Kauffman 1954).

Park Superintendent Tillotson, ever practical about local public relations, expressed reservations about the size of the Toroweap addition because it would encompass patented lands (Kauffman 1954). The issue of private lands was apparently not an important one to Secretary of the Interior Conrad Wirth, however, for he approved the proposed addition, noting that it provided views of the inner gorge (views that were better than those obtainable from anywhere within the existing park boundaries) from points that could be reached by automobile. But rather than adding the area to the park, he proposed that it be declared a national monument—a designation that would be less restrictive than national park designation and would avert strong opposition from the water-power lobby.

The concern over dams was not an idle exercise, for the Bureau of Reclamation completed the construction of Boulder (the name was later changed to Hoover) Dam in 1936. That same year, Lake Mead National Recreation Area (then called Boulder Dam National Recreation Area) was created in the area. Between the western boundary of the park and the slackwater of Lake Mead, at the mouth of Bridge Canyon, the Bureau of Reclamation planned to build yet another dam.

A New Monument Emerges — And Is Challenged

On December 22, 1932, President Herbert Hoover, soon to be replaced by newly elected Franklin Delano Roosevelt, signed Proclamation No. 2022 establishing Grand Canyon National Monument (Kauffman 1954). The new monument encompassed 273,145 acres of canyonlands adjoining the west boundary of the park, including the Bridge Canyon Dam site. Most of the land for the monument lay north of the Colorado River, between the park and Lake Mead National Recreation Area, but the monument also included a tract of the lands on the South Rim that the Havasupai had been using for grazing. The tribe now had to deal with the Park Service as well as the Forest Service for survival.

Much of the North Rim had been used for grazing also, and the ranchers were quick to enlist Arizona Senator Carl Hayden in their efforts to eliminate or drastically reduce the size of the new monument. The Park Service had acquired the monument lands at the expense of the Forest Service and Grazing Service and their local constituencies, without any participation by local interests. Therefore, it is not surprising either that strong opposition erupted or that opponents found considerable sympathy in Congress. The only surprises, perhaps, are the length of time required to reduce the size of the monument and the relatively small amount of territory that the opponents won back.

The campaign to alter the boundaries of the monument soon became enmeshed in arguments about whether—and how—to adjust the boundaries of Grand Canyon National Park. Tillotson, dissatisfied with the monument designation in general, drafted a bill that would have added to the park approximately 149,760 acres and would have returned to grazing status the remaining 123,385 acres (Tillotson 1935). He had a good reason for wanting to eliminate so much land from the monument, for park staff had found "a number of cases of damage to Government property in the monument, evidently with malicious intent." It was impossible, he maintained, to give adequate protection to the monument lands with an annual allotment of only $200 (Tillotson 1936).

On March 19, 1937, the Department of the Interior submitted a new draft bill to adjust the boundaries of Grand Canyon National Park. Like Tillotson's draft, the bill would have abolished the national monument and added parts of it to the national park (National Park Service 1937). The rest would have been returned to previous jurisdictions, an acknowledgment of the importance of ranching to the economy of the Arizona Strip. Predictably, the portions to be incorporated into the park were those containing scenic attractions, an interesting cinder cone formation, prehistoric cliff dwellings, and wildlife habitat. Surprisingly, the bill also proposed including lands that were reserved under section 24 of the Federal Water Power Act: three power-site reserves and two water-power designations. The remaining land, more than 117,000 acres, would be returned to the public domain (National Park Service 1937). The pending bills to revise the boundaries of the park died with the adjournment of the 74th Congress, but Senator Hayden continued working with local ranchers to resolve the conflict.

Having met with livestock growers and other representatives of the Arizona Strip, Hayden reported to Arno Cammerer (who by then had become the director of the Park Service) that the ranchers on the Arizona Strip had suggested an alternative boundary. He advised Cammerer that he was sending to Cammerer, and to the ranchers of northern Arizona, a Senate committee print of H.R. 7264, a compromise proposal, which—although it would not be entirely satisfactory either to the livestock growers or to the Park Service—he hoped would end the controversy (Hayden 1937).

Soon thereafter, Representative John R. Murdock of Arizona, at the request of the Department of the Interior, introduced an alternative bill to revise park and monument boundaries. Whereas Hayden's bill would have eliminated 145,345 acres (53 percent) from the monument, Murdock's bill (which was based on Tillotson's recommendations) eliminated only 117,825 acres (43 percent) (Demaray 1937).

Tillotson made his own trip to the Arizona Strip to confer with residents, including influential ranchers Charles McCormick and Elmer Jackson. Apparently convinced that his recommendations, contained in Murdock's bill, were unrealistic, he reported to Hayden that, since the ranchers appeared willing to accept Hayden's bill, he was willing to compromise (Tillotson 1937).[12]

Nevertheless, the dispute continued to rage. E. B. Pratt, deputy highway supervisor and deputy Coconino County supervisor of Fredonia, Arizona, advised Hayden that the ranchers were against the loss of any more range suitable for grazing, because the Taylor Grazing Act was limiting range use on the lands to which they did have access. Due to the grazing restrictions, combined with the long drought then being experienced and an increase in population, the monument boundaries should include no more territory than that needed for the proposed game population, and the grazers "should be given every bit of the range they can make use of, and not [be] cut . . . off from improved waterholes and springs where their cattle have watered for the past forty or fifty years" (E. B. Pratt 1937). Hayden also received a letter from Elwin Pratt (cattle inspector, also of Fredonia), who stressed that "the public sentiment is to help the poor man to live, rather than transpose his range into an unused richman's [*sic*] unneeded play ground" (Elwin Pratt 1937). As a result of these letters, Hayden requested Tillotson to go to Fredonia to confer yet again with the two Pratts and with ranchers Charles McCormick, Elmer Jackson, Thomas Jensen, and Asa Judd (Hayden 1938a).[13]

In place of Tillotson, who was already on his way to Washington, Assistant Park Superintendent J. V. Lloyd held the requested meeting in Fredonia on January 12, 1938, and succeeded in working out a set of mutually acceptable boundaries (Lloyd 1938). Early in 1938 Hayden introduced a new bill, S. 3362, reflecting the compromise boundary; Murdock introduced a companion bill, H.R. 9314, in the House. Yet opposition continued. On March 4, 1938, the Flagstaff Chamber of Commerce went on record with a resolution that opposed "any withdrawal or exchanges or adjustments of boundaries of any National Park, Forest, Monument or Game Reserve or the creation of any new areas" that did not have the consent of the county board of supervisors, the city council of Flagstaff, and the affected individuals. The resolution argued, with good cause, that taxable wealth was being jeopardized by continual withdrawals and exchanges of federal lands. The resolution also observed that Coconino County, the second largest political subdivision in the United States, was 90 percent owned by the federal government, making it difficult to sustain the levels of economic activity that were needed to generate taxes to support local government, schools, and municipalities (Walkup and Huffer 1938).

Tillotson corresponded both with the Mohave County Board of Supervisors (Tillotson 1938a) and with J. D. Walkup of Flagstaff (Tillotson 1938b) to remind them that the entire area in question was within Mohave County, not Coconino County, and that even within Mohave County, the bill actually returned large parcels of land to the public domain, thereby adding to the potential taxable wealth. To Walkup, Tillotson also stressed that 55.4 percent of the monument would be returned to the public domain.

Unimpressed by Tillotson's argument, Walkup, in his capacity as chairman of the Coconino County Board of Supervisors, wrote to Hayden and Murdock to relay the board's opposition to any further additions to Grand Canyon National Park. Furthermore, he asserted, "We feel that if this extension boundary bill goes into effect, . . . an amendment should be made to it or a new bill be drawn that a portion of revenue derived from this natural wonder and natural resource . . . be returned to the State and counties in the same proportion as that now received from the natural resource within the boundaries of the National Forest" (Walkup 1938b; 1938a).

Hayden, having apparently become impatient with local intransigence, responded by lecturing Walkup about economic realities:

Frankness compels me to say that I do not see the force of your statement that the establishment of the Grand Canyon National Park has deprived the County of Coconino and the State of Arizona of one of its natural resources. The annual report of the Secretary of the Interior shows that during the last travel season 270,000 people visited the Grand Canyon National Park, and I cannot believe that these individuals went through the Park without leaving in Coconino County and Northern Arizona a considerable amount of money which has materially added to the wealth of our people. Were the Grand Canyon National Park privately owned and therefore subject to a real property tax on the part of Coconino County, I frankly doubt that area would have had as many visitors, and I am inclined to believe that the people of Coconino County would not have come near realizing, either in the form of taxes or revenues on tourists, the sums of money which have come to the County in the past. Real estate taxation is based upon tangible value, and I doubt if the County would be able to tax the Grand Canyon on the basis of its value as one of the seven wonders of the world. (Hayden 1938b)

Hayden suggested that it would be possible for him to add a section to the bill that would provide for money to be paid to Coconino County each year from park revenues, but he was sure that Congress would, in that case, demand that the county also bear the cost of administering the park area (the cost of which considerably exceeded revenues). Ever the politician, though, Hayden softened his remarks by expressing sympathy for the county's desire to increase assessed valuation and promising to do all he could to promote the county's interests (Hayden 1938b).

Shortly thereafter, in two letters to the director of the Park Service, Tillotson revealed his penchant for going out of his way to avoid controversy. It would be a good idea, he said, to return the areas of the monument south of the river to the public domain to appease Coconino County (but not, apparently, to relieve the difficulties of the Havasupai, who most depended on these lands). Besides, he argued, there was no geological or scientific reason to retain those lands (Tillotson 1938b; 1938a).

The Bureau of Reclamation injected new problems into the boundary revision project, proposing language that stipulated that nothing in the act would be deemed to prevent the construction (as needed to conserve the usefulness of Hoover Dam) of dams, reservoirs, and appurtenant works within the area added to the park.[14] The Park Service began to back down. Dam building remained objectionable, the Park Service admitted, but "in the event it is necessary to build a dam to protect Boulder Dam, nothing that we can do can prevent its authorization. We believe it would be much better to permit the invasion of a national monument with such a nonconforming use than to have to permit the invasion of a national park. . . . It may be desirable to give consideration to the eliminations proposed from the Grand Canyon National Monument" (Cammerer 1938).

On May 18, 1938, Hayden introduced a new bill, S. 4047, to reduce the size of the monument. In apparent response to the objections of the Bureau of Reclamation, this bill omitted mention of any addition of monument territory to the park (Kauffman 1954).

Hayden introduced yet another boundary-modification bill, S. 6, on January 4, 1939. It was this bill (after some modification) that, on August 7, 1939, finally passed both houses of Congress. The battle was not over, however, for President Roosevelt vetoed the bill on the grounds that insufficient consideration had been given to the matter. He called for a thorough investigation of the issue (Kauffman 1954).

In response to Roosevelt's call, a full-fledged investigation regarding boundary adjustments at Grand Canyon began on September 16, 1939 (Kauffman 1954). A report of the investigation, submitted to the Park Service on October 6, 1939, recommended several boundary adjustments: the southwestern boundary was to be extended westward to protect antelope; the lava flows in the Toroweap area were to be included, presumably for their unique geological value; and all the territory east of Toroweap Valley up to 36 degrees, 25 minutes north latitude, encompassing all of Tuckup Canyon and as much of Kanab Canyon as possible, was to be included to protect bighorn sheep (McDougall October 6, 1939, cited in Kauffman 1954, 24).

Park Service Director Cammerer had another idea. In a memorandum to H. C. Bryant[15] (the acting superintendent of the park at this time), he supported the inclusion of the Toroweap lava flows in the park but suggested that the remainder of the monument be transferred to Boulder Canyon (i.e., Lake Mead) National Recreation Area (Cammerer 1939).

All of the disputes, contests, proposals, and counterproposals came to an end at last when, in December 1939, the investigating team issued its final recommendations. Soon thereafter, Secretary of the Interior Harold Ickes recommended to President Roosevelt a proclamation reducing the size of the monument. The new boundaries would include the heads of side canyons and the principal volcanic formations located on the western boundary but would exclude the privately owned lands for which there was little hope of acquisition, as well as grazing land not deemed essential for monument purposes (Kauffman 1954).

Apparently satisfied that the matter had indeed been thoroughly investigated, President Roosevelt signed Proclamation No. 2393 on April

4, 1940, eliminating 71,854 acres from the monument (Kauffman 1954). The opponents of the park won the skirmish, though they did not win back all the lands they sought.

Looking Backward and Forward

In retrospect, the Park Service, in dropping its bid to incorporate the remaining monument lands into the park, opened the way to compromise and ultimately to the retention of much of the land within the monument, where less stringent rules would allow grazing and other activities such as hunting and dam building to be more easily dealt with. The change in strategy enabled the Park Service to retain influence over the definition and use of the relative spaces of the monument, in addition to the absolute spaces of the park. It also allowed the possibility of stretching the representational spaces of Grand Canyon across both park and monument lands. In this regard, one of the more important decisions was the one that made the superintendent of Grand Canyon National Park the manager of Grand Canyon National Monument as well. The arrangement also ensured that the development of facilities and roads would be done by the Park Service, as would the promulgation and enforcement of regulations and the interpretation of the area. All of these factors eventually enabled the incorporation of the monument into the park.

In the end, the spaces of the greater Grand Canyon were partitioned yet again, but—again—redefinition was only partial. Park advocates failed to incorporate as much wildlife habitat and scenic forest into the park as they wanted, and conflicts over the preservation of lands west of the existing park boundary proved resistant to legislative resolution.

As in the past, preservation was accomplished only through a presidential action that overrode congressional will. Not surprisingly, the boundaries of the national monument not only failed to extinguish opposition, but, as revealed in the next chapter, actually escalated it.

CHAPTER SIX

Frustrated Expansion Efforts and a New National Monument: 1940 to 1969

During the 1940s, the nation's attention was focused first on World War II, then on postwar recovery. The 1950s saw the election of war hero Dwight Eisenhower to the presidency, a turn away from the liberalism of the New Deal, and a determination to remove constraints on free enterprise. The 1950s also saw the beginnings of the civil rights movement in the South and, for many white, mainstream citizens, unprecedented wealth and leisure time. But by the 1962 election, liberal politics again held sway, and John F. Kennedy assumed office, riding the crest of popularity generated by his New Frontier agenda of democratic participation, world leadership, and social activism. Kennedy's assassination in 1963 brought Lyndon B. Johnson to power; the New Frontier mutated into the Great Society with its focus on civil rights legislation, the War on Poverty, and the Vietnam War. Social protests, war, and environmental activism came to dominate domestic politics.

Substantial changes occurred during this era in federal land management. An important reorganization of the Department of the Interior in 1946 consolidated the General Land Office and the Grazing Service into a new agency, the Bureau of Land Management. The consolidation made it the nation's largest land management agency. Also during these years, important legislation was passed to improve the management of public lands and resources. Congress enacted the Multiple Use–Sustained Yield Act in 1960, for example, because the Forest Service insisted on having its mission formalized before it would acquiesce to environmentalists' long-sought goal of setting aside wilderness areas. Indeed, the Multiple Use–Sustained Yield Act accorded federal recognition to the agency's resource management philosophy: pursuit of coordinated resource use without impairment of the productivity of the land (Robinson 1975, 56).

Once the Forest Service had attained its formal mission statement, the environmentalists succeeded in persuading Congress to pass the 1964 Wilderness Act. The act, however, created only 9 million acres of wilderness within the national forests, in contrast to the 60 million acres sought by more radical wilderness advocates (Nash 1982; Robinson 1975). Also enacted during this era were the Land and Water Conservation Act of 1964, the National Wild and Scenic Rivers Act of 1968, and the National Environmental Policy Act of 1969. These laws changed the way the federal land management agencies did business, gave recreation and preservation advocates a new and more effective voice in decision making on environmental issues, and set important precedents for the environmental legislation passed in the 1970s.

The War and the Park Service

World War II refocused the nation's efforts away from nonessential activities. The Park Service made way for war offices in the nation's capital by moving its operations to Chicago (Foresta 1984). Arno Cammerer relinquished his position as Park Service director to head up the Park Service's Region One office in Richmond, Virginia. Newton B. Drury was named the new director.

Drury had a long history of activism in wilderness preservation, especially with regard to the redwood groves of California. He had been a vocal critic of some of the Park Service's policies and brought with him a very different philosophy from that of the previous directors. He was a purist: a dyed-in-the-wool preservationist who deplored the promotion of the national parks as playgrounds (Schrepfer 1983). He advocated only minimal development of facilities within the parks and asserted that the Park Service's sole role should be that of caretaker (Olsen 1985). His position may have helped him avoid frustrations arising from wartime shortages of monies and manpower; it also prompted him to actively protect the parks from intense pressures to exploit their resources—such as the spruce forests of Olympic National Park—for the war effort.

After the war, economic growth and an increase in leisure time put tremendous pressures on the national parks. Park visitation, which had totaled 440,000 in 1941, dropped to a low of 65,000 in 1944 before rising precipitously to 500,000 in 1946 and to more than one million in 1956 (Hughes 1967). At the same time the Park Service lost much of the support it had received from business and professional elites (Foresta 1984). Within this changing context, the Park Service found that it needed to reexamine its priorities.

Drury resigned as Park Service director in 1951 and was briefly succeeded by the aging Arthur Demaray, longtime Park Service staff member and expert congressional liaison. Demaray soon retired, and in December 1951, Conrad Wirth, a landscape architect who had previously headed up the Civilian Conservation Corps program for the National Park Service, assumed the agency's directorship. He immediately set to work to decide what the agency's priorities should be, and he developed an ambitious plan: "Mission 66," a ten-year plan to upgrade national park facilities. With this program, the pendulum moved strongly away from pure preservation and back toward definition of the parks as playgrounds.

Indian Voices

Indians found new voices after World War II, as a younger generation educated in the ways of the nation's mainstream culture began to occupy positions of authority and to turn the knowledge they had accrued from association with the dominant society to the betterment of their own people. They began to hire their own lawyers, to participate more frequently in public meetings and congressional proceedings, and most important, to press for land or monies as restitution for past injustices.

The Indian Reorganization Act of 1934 had unleashed a torrent of Indian claims against the federal government. By 1946, the deluge of claims finally prompted Congress to establish a special Indian Claims Commission. The Indian Claims Commission was empowered to hear arguments regarding the extent of individual tribes' aboriginal claims but could grant only financial restitution—not the return of any land. The restriction was singularly unfortunate for the Indians, for it was land that most tribes wanted. Even determining the size of the territory to be recompensed was problematical: the commission required that the claimant tribe prove *exclusive* use of the territory (Rosenthal 1985). In many cases, as was true for the tribes of the greater Grand Canyon, considerable areas of land—principally those used for hunting and gathering—could not be proved to be the exclusive aboriginal domain of any one tribe. For these lands, the tribes were disqualified from receiving any compensation.

Also important to Indians throughout the United States was a new threat: the federal government instituted a termination policy that aimed to end all government support received by the tribes. The policy was an outgrowth of the belief that government supervision of the tribes had limited Indians' progress and assimilation into mainstream society. Termination advocates, who wanted to end all bureaucratic control over the Indians, captured key congressional committees by 1948, convinced the Bureau of Indian Affairs to adopt a formal termination policy in 1950, and captured the executive branch of the government with Dwight Eisenhower's election in 1952. In 1953, Congress began a serious (but largely unsuccessful) move to transfer jurisdiction of the tribes to the states (Deloria and Lytle 1984).

By the mid–1960s, inspired by student and civil rights protests, some Indians began to stage protests. The most militant of the protest groups, the urban-based American Indian Movement, arose in 1968. Also in 1968—the same year that Martin Luther King and Robert Kennedy were assassinated—Congress passed the American Civil Rights Act, which incorporated the First and Fourth through Eighth Amendments of the U.S. Constitution into a package of individual Indian rights that tribal governments were forbidden to abridge (Deloria and Lytle 1984).[1]

The Havasupai Struggle Continues

In 1940, Dean Sinyella, chairman of the Havasupai Tribal Council, requested that the tract of land lying between the park and the Hualapai Reservation (at that time part of Grand Canyon National Monument) be added to the tribe's reservation (Greenwood 1943; Pooler 1940). Nothing came of his request. In 1941, the Supreme Court (in *U.S. v. Santa Fe,* 341 U.S. 339, 345) ruled that released railroad lands were subject to the aboriginal Indians' prior rights of possession. Based on this decision, on May 28, 1942, the *Examiner's Report on Tribal Claims to Released Railroad Lands in Northwestern Arizona* affirmed the Havasupai Tribe's rights to the odd-numbered sections of land that had been granted to, then forfeited by, the Santa Fe Railroad. The decision met with political resistance, however, for Congress passed a bill that blocked the return of railroad lands to Indian tribes. According to Arizona Congressman John R. Murdock, the Indians did not need the lands, which could be put to better use for activities such as grazing (Havasupai Tribe 1973).

A. W. Simington, a field agent for the Office of Indian Affairs, dismissed the tribe's expansion ideas, saying they were unfeasible because thousands of acres of state-owned and privately owned lands were involved. He did offer an alternative, however: the additions that had been recommended in February 1943 by John O. Crow (superintendent of the local Indian Affairs Office). Crow's proposed boundaries would have expanded the reservation by 264,959 acres and would have included all of Grand Canyon National Monument south of the Colorado River, all of the South Kaibab National Forest lying west of a drift fence that had been built to control the movement of Havasupai livestock, and the portion of Grand Canyon National Park that lay south of the Colorado River and west of Royal Arch Creek (Simington 1943).

A meeting on the proposal took place on April 19, 1943. Crow stressed the Havasupai Tribe's need to have possession of the designated lands to develop water on them. As long as these lands were controlled by the National Park Service, he argued, water development could not be accomplished because Indian Affairs rules did not permit investments on non-Indian lands. After the meeting, Indian Affairs Commissioner John Collier sent a formal request on behalf of the Havasupai to Park Service Director Drury, stressing that the recent decision giving the odd-numbered sections of forfeited railroad lands to the tribe also provided justification for claiming the even-numbered sections in that area, since the tribe had never given up title to those lands either (Collier 1943). Later that month, in a conference held at Grand Canyon National Park, Crow announced that the Forest Service had "informally approved the transfer of National Forest lands west of the drift fence" (Bryant 1943a).[2] Unfortunately the meeting resulted in nothing more than an agreement to undertake yet another study of the issue.

The group that examined the issue included J. D. Ratcliff (park ecologist), V. D. Smith (Havasupai Reservation Indian Affairs Office), Park Superintendent Harold Bryant, and landscape architect Frederick Law Olmsted, Jr. The report acknowledged that the Havasupais badly needed sources of income that were consistent with their way of life; that increasing the size of the tribe's cattle herd was the best way to accomplish this; that bringing their grazing activities under a single administrative structure that had the tribe's welfare as its primary objective would facilitate management; that the amount of land requested was modest for the purposes expressed and no better lands were available elsewhere; and that acquisition of the lands would greatly improve tribal morale and enable the Havasupais to better control visitors. However, although the authors recognized that there had been no legal extinguishment of the tribe's rights to occupy and use the aboriginal lands that had been included within the national park, monument, and forest, they expressed concern about "eliminating from a great National Park approximately one-fifth of the entire area deliberately included within its boundaries by Congress" and transferring those lands to an agency that privileged commercial, industrial, and other economic objectives rather than protecting the natural environment. The proposal, they observed, would reduce the amount of river contained within the park by forty miles—a "radical and deplorable change in a supposedly permanent public policy." Furthermore, most of the area proposed for elimination had quite different scenery from the rest of the park—and thus, presumably, should be retained on the basis of this uniqueness. Finally, one of the two valuable research areas in the park would be lost if the Great Thumb area were transferred. In what had to have been the most offensive passage of the report from the Havasupai point of view, the report went on to oppose the transfer of the Havasu Canyon area on the grounds that the area was uniquely interesting and beautiful and would remain so "for centuries to come—perhaps long after the last of the Havasupais shall have passed away." In the meantime, the best way to preserve the area was to retain it within the park, while instituting restrictions that would protect the tribe from "any appreciable interference by park visitors or park activities."

The authors did concede that if the national forest lands the Havasupais had been exclusively using for grazing were to be added to the tribe's reservation, they could see no serious objection to transferring to the tribe *some* of the national monument lands on the South Rim. The authors stated flatly, however, that there were serious objections to excising from the monument the land all the way down to the river. The river area, they argued, presented "distinctive and notable scenic and physiographic qualities" that must be retained (Olmsted, Bryant, and Ratcliff 1943).

Further resistance to giving land to the Havasupais followed immediately, for no sooner had the ink dried than Park Service Director Drury asked whether these lands would not "serve as good a public purpose" by being included in the national monument as they would by being made part of the reservation (Drury 1943a). Park Superintendent Bryant concurred with Drury but, certain that resistance would rise to any new addition, warned that changes should first be approved by the Arizona congressional delegation (Bryant 1943b).

Drury quickly tabled the matter, recommending that, because of unrest over public land matters, boundary changes be deferred until later, perhaps to be synchronized with boundary changes expected to occur when the long-anticipated Bridge Canyon Dam was built within Grand Canyon. While leaving the door slightly ajar to changes in the boundaries of the national monument, Drury cautioned that the Park Service "would be opposed to the elimination of any land from Grand Canyon National Park" (Drury 1943b). In a final letter to Crow on the matter, H. M. Critchfield, director of lands for the Office of Indian Affairs, observed, "If this area is useless to the Indians, if no water can be developed at reasonable cost, then it seems to us that we should cease to work for the addition of the monument and park lands to the Havasupai Reservation" (Critchfield 1943).

The Havasupais achieved a small victory in 1944, however, when they acquired a 2,540-acre addition to their reservation. The addition, which included four sections in a dry canyon located thirty miles south of the main reservation, was intended to provide the tribe with control over a critical portion of the waters of Cataract (Havasu) Creek. In actuality, the addition did almost nothing to improve the tribe's self-sufficiency.

In 1955, Mission 66—the Park Service's plan for making substantial improvements to the infrastructure of the national parks by the year 1966—intruded into boundary issues between the park and the Havasupai. Park Superintendent John S. McLaughlin (who had replaced Bryant) noted that a portion of the Havasupai Reservation would make "an ideal development site" (McLaughlin 1955).

In this era when national policy was aimed at terminating the status of Indians as dependents of the federal government, McLaughlin revealed a scheme to take over the Havasupais' reservation entirely. He portrayed it as a plan that would "better satisfy the Indians, eliminate a grazing problem, and give us a development site and water supply in that section of the Park." He went on to note, "As we pointed out in MISSION 66, we could well afford to pay the Indians dearly for their lands, and it would still be a cheaper approach to development than installation of a water supply system to pump water up to the South Rim" (McLaughlin 1955).

Ben H. Thompson, chief of the Park Service's Cooperative Activities Division, liked McLaughlin's ideas. Resettlement might take years, he observed, but because the Department of the Interior was pressing for the resolution of boundary issues associated with Grand Canyon National Monument, the project would have to be initiated right away (Thompson 1955).

The idea came up against a brick wall in the 1960s, however. Arizona Congressman John J. Rhodes wrote to Secretary of the Interior Stewart Udall that the tribe needed more land, and in 1968, Arizona Congressman Sam Steiger introduced a bill (H.R. 19072) into the House Committee on Interior and Insular Affairs to transfer the Havasupais' permit lands to their reservation. Though these efforts failed, they signaled to the Park Service that strong support for the tribe existed.

In 1969, the Indian Claims Commission offered the Havasupais a settlement of $1,240,000 for 2,257,728 acres of their aboriginal non-reservation lands. The Havasupais tried to refuse the money but were told by their attorney that they could never recover their lands and should accept the settlement (Paya 1973; Sparks nd). The majority of the tribe agreed to accept the money, only to learn later that other tribes (including Taos Pueblo, which regained its sacred Blue Lake) had received a monetary settlement and had still succeeded in acquiring land as well. The Havasupais redoubled their efforts to acquire their plateau lands, an effort that occupied them—and many opponents—until 1975.

Renewed Efforts to Expand the Park

At Grand Canyon, failure in the 1930s to expand park boundaries on biological grounds did not discourage advocates from persevering, though there was a change in the arguments they marshaled to support their position: they began to stress the need to protect the geological integrity of the Grand Canyon complex. Ranchers on the North Rim, reinforced by powerful allies on the South Rim, continued to argue that substantial portions of the Park Service's lands—especially those in the national monument—contained valuable resources that should be made available for exploitation. As was true in other parts of the

West, resentment that so much of the land base was under various federal jurisdictions lent energy to efforts to protect and, if possible, expand rights to own the private lands and exploit the natural resources. Their primary strategy was the same as it had been for more than fifty years: defend and enlarge their privileged access to public lands and resources, while at the same time minimizing their own risks, costs, and obligations.

Meanwhile, ranchers also worked to change the rules governing the permits they held to graze livestock on Grand Canyon National Monument lands. Whereas the Park Service restricted grazing privileges to the lifetime of the permittee and did not allow transfer of the permits to others, the ranchers sought to have their permits made transferable to their heirs or to purchasers of their property. The crux of the argument was that the value of their ranches depended on the possession of the grazing permits. Withdrawal of any of the permits decreased the value of their holdings in inheritance or sale transactions. Thus, the ranchers asserted, they had a right (not a privilege, as would later be maintained by all federal land management agencies) to grazing permits on federal lands and the right to pass that right on to others.

In 1944, World War II and resistance by ranchers notwithstanding, Park Superintendent Bryant detailed several desired boundary revisions. First, because the southern boundary had been drawn too close to the canyon rim to preserve ecological values effectively, he recommended transferring from the Forest Service the portion of Long Mesa that separated the southwestern corner of the park from the national monument (this was the area that the Havasupais and the park administrators had both wanted to incorporate into their respective domains two years earlier). The Forest Service, Bryant said, had no particular use for the area since it was "only" being used for Havasupai horses (horses remain even today the primary mode of transportation into Havasu Canyon). He recommended several other additions and deletions of land on the North and South Rims but concluded by warning that residents of Arizona, which was a state's rights state, were dissatisfied that 72 percent of the land in the state was owned and controlled by the federal government. Local ranchers, chambers of commerce, politicians, and bureaucrats would protest every change of land status in which the government acquired private lands or in which mining or grazing access was restricted. Therefore, he advised, any boundary changes would have to be handled with great care (Bryant 1944).

Minor Tillotson, by now promoted to regional director of Region

Three, continued to voice the same opinions he had expressed as park superintendent at Grand Canyon. He believed that further deletions should be made from the monument and, citing the history and vehemence of local opposition, advised against making additions to the park (Tillotson 1945). Bryant strongly objected to Tillotson's ideas. Among other things, he said, the elimination of two tiers of land on the south side of the monument would benefit only the Arizona Livestock Company, which had, he noted, the largest range in Arizona.[3] In direct challenge to Tillotson's penchant for appeasement, Bryant went on to argue that recommendations for boundary changes "should be made on the basis of a far-reaching view of needs to improve federal holdings, not on the basis of ease of securing them. Compromise should come later, not with the proposal" (Bryant 1945).

The end of the war brought renewed efforts to reclaim the North Rim grazing lands. North Rim resident L. Elmer Jackson wrote to Senator Carl Hayden accusing the park of poor land management and of driving ranchers out of business by eliminating grazing on its lands. "We do not object to a reasonable area being used for Park purposes," he argued, "but we do object to such vast areas as the Grand Canyon National Park and Grand Canyon National Monument being allowed to go to waste while so many people need additional range and returning soldiers need range if they are to become good, contented citizens." Jackson went on to ask Hayden to introduce a bill immediately to return substantial portions of national park and monument lands to the Grazing Service, claiming that Senator Abe Murdock of Utah—among others—could be counted upon to support the initiative (Jackson 1945).

Tillotson thought Jackson's deletions from the national monument were too large but that some reduction in its size might blunt the criticism that was then being leveled at the park. However, Tillotson remained adamantly opposed to Jackson's recommendations for eliminations from the park. Superintendent Bryant was more generally critical of the proposal, terming Jackson's motives "selfish and personal" (Bryant 1946).

The Dam Controversy

By 1944, planning was proceeding for a dam at Bridge Canyon, and the Bureau of Reclamation was recommending that the western boundary of the park be changed to permit construction entirely outside park lands.[4] The boundary the agency proposed would have placed within its jurisdiction eleven miles of river channel and approximately a hundred feet of elevation for reservoir backwater (Bashore 1944). The proposed boundary was unsatisfactory to Park Superintendent Bryant, though he admitted that there would have to be some adjustment of the boundary to keep the reservoir that would be created by the dam out of the park (Bryant 1944). Tillotson, tending—as always—toward appeasement, recommended giving in entirely on the Bridge Canyon project in hopes of getting, in exchange, legislation that would provide stronger protection against future water projects within the national parks (Tillotson 1949).

In making their recommendations, Bryant and Tillotson reiterated a longstanding Park Service inclination to give up territory whenever the "integrity" of the national parks was threatened, rather than change the mission of the parks as defenders of unspoiled Nature. But Park Service voices were not unanimous, even on the Bridge Canyon Dam issue. Ben H. Thompson noted, "It would be difficult to hold that the inundation of so small a fraction of the park, at the edge of its boundary and at the bottom of the Inner Gorge, would be inconsistent with the primary purposes of the Park"—and besides, "protection of the Park from more fundamental hazards would be weakened by 'crying wolf' over this issue" (Thompson 1945).

The Sierra Club looked at the issue from the opposite position: Bridge Canyon Dam should not be authorized "until Grand Canyon Park as a part of the overall development of the Colorado is satisfactorily stabilized." Thus it was necessary to find a defensible western boundary line above which no reservoir would be permitted. Kanab Creek, the boundary point selected by the Bureau of Reclamation because it was located above the outlet of a proposed water tunnel, was unacceptable. The project would have diverted 90 percent of the water of the Colorado River from the upstream stretch of the canyon through forty miles of tunnel to a hydropower plant to be located on Kanab Creek (Nash 1982). As Sierra Club leader Bestor Robinson asked with more than a little Socratic irony, "Did Nature in her great wisdom terminate the superlative portion of the Grand Canyon at the exact spot selected by twentieth century engineers for a hydro-electric power house?" (Robinson 1950).

The contest became even more intense, because the 1950s saw impassioned efforts to preserve Dinosaur National Monument from being flooded by a Bureau of Reclamation dam. The outcome of the Echo

Park controversy was both a victory and a defeat for environmentalists. It was a victory because the 1956 Colorado River Storage Project Act declared that no dam or reservoir associated with the act could be built within any park or monument—and this included Dinosaur. It was a defeat because, in exchange, the beautiful Glen Canyon, lying between Dinosaur National Monument and Grand Canyon National Park, was flooded instead.

The controversy over dams entered a new phase when, in 1964, Arizona finally ended its dispute over the Colorado River Compact by settling for 2.8 million acre-feet of Colorado River waters plus the flows of the tributaries running within the boundaries of the state. Having cleared away the last obstacles to its water development plans, the Arizona congressional delegation, headed by the venerable Carl Hayden, convinced Congress to pass the Colorado River Basin Project Act in 1968. Delivery of water to central Arizona, a major feature of the project, was not to be powered by dams in the Grand Canyon, however.

The closing of the gates of Glen Canyon Dam in 1963 had galvanized environmentalists to fight even harder against the dams planned for the Grand Canyon. Spurred on by Sierra Club leader David Brower's vivid imagery (which compared building dams in the Grand Canyon to flooding the Sistine Chapel in order to get a closer look at the frescoes; see Nash 1982), a broad spectrum of the general public rose in opposition to Bridge Canyon Dam, which featured prominently in the central Arizona water reclamation project. The effort culminated in 1968, when Lyndon Johnson signed the Central Arizona Project bill into law. The act placed a moratorium on the construction of dams in the Grand Canyon between Glen Canyon and Hoover Dams. In the end, coal-fired power plants were built in the Four Corners area instead—eventually creating yet another problem: regional air pollution.

Park Expansion Efforts Persist

In the meantime, not willing to wait for a resolution of the Bridge Canyon Dam issue, Park Service Director Conrad Wirth urged that boundary changes go forward, given that no one knew when or if the dam project would be authorized. In a rebuttal to Tillotson's arguments, Wirth stressed that expected increases in park tourism would lead to much greater use of the contested areas. He reminded Tillotson that "the fact that a segment of the canyon is remote from development centers today may not be a fact in the future." Havasu Canyon and Kanab Canyon, he observed, would be the most practical western boundaries for the park. As for recurrent ideas that Marble Canyon should be incorporated into the park, Wirth gave his opinion that incorporation was probably impractical; however, "since Bestor Robinson [of the Sierra Club] has repeatedly recommended the addition of this area to the park, it is highly desirable that it be examined, photographed, and included in your report" (Wirth 1954).

That same year, park planner John E. Kell made a study of park and monument boundaries and recommended that approximately seventy-three square miles (46,720 acres) be added to the park—some on each side of the canyon. The recommendation for the addition south of the river—which involved acquiring the tip of Long Mesa—as usual ignored Havasupai claims to the area. Kell argued that adding the tract of land to the park would eliminate the problem of intervening lands that separated the park from the monument in that area. Kell also recommended that some twenty-four square miles (15,360 acres) of the monument, mainly sagebrush flats, on the south side of the river be deleted for grazing purposes and (ironically, given his willingness to appropriate lands that the Havasupai had long been using) that Marble Canyon not be added to the park because park encroachment on the Navajos' lands would probably generate opposition (Kell 1954).

Barry Goldwater Enters the Park Expansion Debate

In 1955 Arizona Senator Barry Goldwater entered the fray over the boundaries of Grand Canyon National Park. Elected to the seat that Carl Hayden had relinquished after fifty-seven years in office, Goldwater was intent upon making his own mark in Congress.

The Goldwater family had been in Arizona since territorial days, and Barry's uncle Morris had been a member of the state constitutional convention. Aside from serving on the Arizona Interstate Stream Commission and being a city councilman in Phoenix, Barry Goldwater was an accomplished photographer, a congressionally recognized authority on Indian affairs, and a frequent visitor to Grand Canyon. He was also a conservative Republican, representing a state that had just turned decidedly Republican (Shadegg 1986). Like his predecessor, Goldwater represented a state that resented federal control over 70 percent of its land and that still relied heavily on the exploitation of natural resources for its wealth. Goldwater became known on the national scene when he ran against Lyndon Johnson in the 1964 presidential race. He lost the election and returned to the Senate, where he resumed his role of defending Arizona interests—including those of the greater Grand Canyon.

As early as 1956, Goldwater requested that the Park Service provide a draft bill to expand Grand Canyon National Park. Director Wirth obliged, though he cautioned that the draft was being furnished without commitment on the department's position (Wirth 1956).

The Park Service went on to further develop its recommendations for new park boundaries and referred its recommendations to the Forest Service for comment (Wirth 1956). The boundary revisions included the transfer to the park of 11,130 acres of national forest lands on the South Rim, including 4,500 acres of good rangelands. Significantly, these lands were, at that time, part of the Havasupai grazing allotment. The transfers would have given the park control over Hualapai Canyon and the main trail to the Havasupai Reservation in Havasu Canyon.

Chief Forester Richard E. McArdle was willing to agree to these changes but wanted the park, in return, to give up lands on the North Rim in the areas of Crazy Jug Point, Fire Point, and Mount Trumbull.[5] He argued that these were areas where the Forest Service needed better fire control, where timber cutting would make important contributions to the local economy, where a seed orchard could be established, and where park-quality uniqueness was significantly lacking. Besides, the transfer would make the area available for recreational development and—shades of the disputes of the 1920s and 1930s—would allow for deer hunting as a means for controlling persistent overpopulation and consequent overgrazing problems (McArdle 1956).

On January 17, 1957, Senator Goldwater introduced S. 693, the bill drafted by the Park Service. The bill would have added three areas to the park and deleted two areas from the national monument. The first of the additions included Havasupai grazing lands on Long Mesa and in Little Coyote Canyon, Beaver Canyon, and Hualapai Canyon—these were all areas the tribe had sought to add to its reservation. The purpose of the addition, according to the bill, was to preserve the scenic and scientific values of the side canyons and to create a common boundary between the park and the monument. The second area to be added, approximately 42,265 acres, was on the North Rim and included the lower seven to eight miles of Kanab Canyon. The Park

Service valued this area for its scenery. The third addition was on the east and would have added 1,120 acres to provide a buffer between park lands and national forest lands along the park access road at Desert View.

The lands earmarked for deletion, though somewhat responsive to local demands, fell far short of McArdle's expectations. The first exclusion would have returned to the public domain some national monument plateau lands in the vicinity of SB and Tuckup Points on the North Rim. These lands were among the areas that had been most assiduously sought by local ranchers. The second deletion would have returned 4,080 acres on the South Rim to the public domain (Scoyen 1957).

These boundaries did not please the Bureau of Reclamation. The bureau argued that the Marble-Kanab tunnel project should not be foreclosed, as would occur if Kanab Canyon was added to the park. The Bureau recommended that S. 693 be amended to delete all language that changed the status of the Kanab Creek watershed and to eliminate the areas that would be inundated by Bridge Canyon Dam— that is, all lands below an elevation of 1,876 feet (Nielson 1957).

Park Service Director Wirth argued, in return, that the bureau had been directed by the secretary of the interior to abandon the Kanab Canyon project in 1949 and that, after abandonment, the Park Service had voiced no objection to a proposed Marble Canyon Dam. The Park Service, he said, considered Kanab Creek to be integral to Grand Canyon National Park and, in any event, the wording of the organic act for the park left open the possibility of development of power projects, an arrangement that would not be changed by the new legislation (Wirth 1957). In the end, nothing came of the bill.

Apparently frustrated by the lack of congressional action, on January 13, 1961, Secretary of the Interior Fred A. Seaton attempted to bypass Congress by submitting to President Eisenhower a draft proclamation to make additions to Grand Canyon National Monument (including 42,265 acres in the Kanab Creek area) and two deletions from the monument (Seaton 1961). Eisenhower never signed the proclamation, however.

John F. Kennedy succeeded Dwight Eisenhower as president shortly thereafter and moved quickly to name Stewart Udall of Arizona as his secretary of the interior. A strong supporter of parks and conservation, Udall went on to serve throughout Lyndon Johnson's administration as well, supervising a massive enlargement of the Park Service that included entire new categories of parks and recreation areas that, as part of the president's Great Society agenda, were designed to provide recreational opportunities within the reach of urban dwellers. During his tenure, Udall also made many changes in the Park Service, the first of which was forcing the resignation of Conrad Wirth (Foresta 1984), followed by the hiring of George B. Hartzog, Jr. Trained in law, and apparently closest to Mather in style, Hartzog served as the director of the Park Service from 1964 until 1972 (Everhart 1983).

The Havasupai Issue Resurfaces

The Havasupais' latest bid to acquire Park Service and Forest Service lands for their reservation prompted Secretary Udall to remind Congressman John Rhodes of Arizona that the park contained only the minimum area needed to preserve park values and the maintenance of as nearly natural vegetative conditions as possible along the rim. He assured Rhodes that the uses authorized in the park organic act continued to be recognized—including those accorded to the Havasupai. There were no plans to discontinue Indian grazing uses in the area, he maintained, although plans between the park and the tribe were underway to limit the numbers of livestock to the carrying capacity of the ranges (Udall 1966).

In 1967, at around the same time that the Park Service was attempting to set rules for Indian grazing on its lands, the Havasupai Tribal Council called for a return of lands from the Park Service and Forest Service, declaring that the lands were needed for tribal economic development and the expansion of its tourist and cattle industries, that Park Service policy made it impossible to improve the range in terms of water development and reseeding, that the lands were "desperately needed for our younger generation to make a living and to have room to build homes," and that it was an "immoral act for the Havasupai to be deprived of these lands in the first place." The resolution petitioned the secretary of the interior to introduce legislation that would add the desired lands to the Havasupai Reservation (Havasupai Tribe 1967). As in the past, this effort came to nought.

Marble Canyon National Monument Emerges

With the renewal of environmentalism, possibilities again arose for repartitioning the spaces of the greater Grand Canyon. On January 20,

1969, his last day in office, President Lyndon Johnson signed Proclamation No. 3389, creating Marble Canyon National Monument. It was a controversial action that reverberated throughout the greater Grand Canyon.

Much of the ensuing controversy revolved around concerns about the effect the proclamation would have on construction of the planned Marble Canyon Dam, which—along with Bridge Canyon Dam—had originally been expected to support the Central Arizona Project. Over strong protests by the power lobby, the proclamation put a new roadblock in the way of Marble Canyon Dam and protected the area from any power development schemes that did not have express congressional approval. It was an important victory for environmentalists and an interesting example of the politics of Johnson's last days in office. President-Elect Richard M. Nixon had just announced that he intended to name development-minded Walter Hickel (at the time governor of Alaska) as his secretary of the interior. The announcement gave Secretary Udall considerably greater leverage in persuading Johnson to preserve desirable natural areas like Marble Canyon.[6]

The Boundaries in Retrospect

By creating a new quasi-relative space, Marble Canyon National Monument, preservationists were able to prevent undesirable developments (such as dams), but at the same time other uses (such as grazing) could continue. As in the case of the other territorial partitions accomplished through presidential proclamation, the newly constructed space, and its functionally defined boundaries, immediately became a precondition—and thus an input—to subsequent efforts to redivide and redefine the spaces of the greater Grand Canyon.

In subsequent years, notwithstanding earlier evaluations of the area as not being of park quality, efforts to expand the park included the incorporation of Marble Canyon National Monument—as well as Grand Canyon National Monument—into the park. The battle was not yet over.

CHAPTER SEVEN

Park and Havasupai Reservation Expansion: 1970 to 1975

By the 1970s, opposition to the Vietnam War had defeated President Lyndon Johnson. His successor, Richard Nixon, was more interested in foreign policy than in domestic affairs but nevertheless presided over the greatest growth period in the history of the Park Service. Under the directorship of George Hartzog, the national park system acquired sixty-two new parks. At the same time, the National Environmental Policy Act of 1969 was changing the way decisions were made with respect to public lands and resources. The act required more openness, more citizen participation in decision making. Environmental groups such as the Sierra Club, Wilderness Society, and Audubon Society took advantage of every opportunity and forum to press home their agendas, especially with regard to preserving wilderness and turning the parks into representative samples of ecosystems. Building on their successes of the 1960s, when passage of the 1964 Wilderness Act effectively buried the tourism-development orientation of the Mission 66 program (Foresta 1984), the environmentalists got important new legislation enacted, including the Endangered Species Act of 1973.

The problem of what to do with the vast federal holdings in Alaska came to a head at this time, in part driven by oil companies interested in exploiting the petroleum resources in the state. The Alaska Native Claims Settlement Act of 1971, an unusual alliance of oil companies and Alaskan natives, extinguished all native claims to Alaska lands in return for a grant of a billion dollars and 44 million acres of federal land in the area (Everhart 1983, 128). The question was, what to do with the remaining lands? In 1973, Interior Secretary Rogers Morton submitted legislation to Congress that would have created 83.5 million acres of national parks, forests, refuges, and wild rivers, the boundaries of which excluded all known mineral and oil deposits. Due to the lack of strong support from Presidents Nixon and Ford, however, nothing was actually accomplished until 1980, just after President Jimmy Carter had been defeated in his reelection campaign. Recognizing that Ronald Reagan's landslide victory (including a new Republican majority in the Senate) would make the process even more difficult, Congress passed, and Carter signed, the Alaska Lands Bill in December 1980. The bill more than doubled the size of the national park and national wildlife systems and more than tripled the size of the national wilderness preservation system (Everhart 1983). For the Park Service, it meant new responsibilities but not nearly enough new funding.

Meanwhile, a new emphasis on planning within the federal government led in 1974 to enactment of the Forest Service's Forest and Rangeland Renewable Resources Planning Act (amended in the 1976 National Forest Management Act) and the Bureau of Land Management's 1976 Federal Land Policy and Management Act. These pieces of legislation clarified the agencies' missions and provided new opportunities for outside voices, such as those of environmentalists, to modify the resource management process.

The decade of the 1970s was also a time of activism for American Indians. Determined to force the government to recognize their treaty rights, militant Indians associated with the American Indian Movement arranged a march on Washington, D.C. during election week in 1972. The protest culminated in the occupation of the Bureau of Indian Affairs headquarters. The Nixon administration retaliated in early 1973 by confronting and overcoming members of the American Indian Movement and traditionalist Lakota Tribe members at Wounded Knee on the Pine Ridge Reservation in South Dakota. The episode proved to be a major setback to the Indians' quest for self-determination (Deloria and Lytle 1984).

At this same time Nixon coldly politicized parts of the federal bureaucracy that had heretofore remained outside Washington power circuits. The Park Service was among the agencies that felt the impact of the new politics that gave top jobs to political appointees rather than to career veterans and specialists (Foresta 1984). The process began when, in 1972, Secretary Morton, at Nixon's behest, fired Park Service Director George Hartzog.[1] Into Hartzog's place stepped Ronald Walker, a career politician who not only had no experience in managing a large organization, but had no experience in either environmental issues or park management. With this move, the White House gained significant new power over the Park Service. Yet, surprisingly, Walker turned out to be an enthusiastic—but inept—supporter of the parks, even as he became an increasing liability to the administration.

Shortly after Nixon resigned in 1974, hounded out of office because of the Watergate scandal, Morton called for Walker's resignation. In Walker's stead, Morton hired Gary Everhart, formerly superintendent of Grand Teton National Park and a popular figure within the environmental community. Yet even Everhart could not undo one important change that had actually begun when Stewart Udall forced Conrad Wirth's retirement: control of the agency had been transferred upward to the department level.[2]

At the same time, Congress, suspicious of the agency's penchant for empire building, began asserting more power over the national park system. Congress also began to treat the establishment of national parks in members' districts as "park barrel" political plums (Everhart 1983). The Park Service had little say about what parks were added to the system. Worse, Congress consistently declined to appropriate enough funds to properly administer the burgeoning system (Foresta 1984).

Despite all the turmoil within the Park Service, an intensive effort was put forward to expand Grand Canyon National Park so that park boundaries would encompass the entire ecosystem. As usual, opposition was fierce and the battle was protracted.

Renewed Efforts to Enlarge Grand Canyon National Park

At Grand Canyon National Park, the late 1960s and early 1970s saw park staff members developing a master plan that would address boundary changes as well as provide new guidelines for development and management. The drafts of this plan, and the positive and negative response to it, contributed to new efforts, beginning in 1971, to enact park expansion legislation.

Meanwhile, in Congress, Arizona Senator Barry Goldwater and New Jersey Senator Clifford Case introduced competing bills to enlarge Grand Canyon National Park. Goldwater's bills, which he introduced into virtually every Congress from 1957 until 1973, reflected his persistent attempts to find a compromise among factions of his constituency—including hydroelectric power interests, Indian groups, ranchers, miners, timber companies, and hunters as well as some park and wilderness preservation advocates. The bills introduced by Senator Case beginning in 1967, by contrast, called for a park whose size and configuration reflected the recommendations of various national environmental groups such as the Sierra Club and Friends of the Earth.[3]

The Buffer Zone Idea Emerges

By 1971, the park master plan featured an attempt to solve boundary problems through the creation of "zones of influence." The zone concept was important for its movement away from attempts to delineate and maintain control over areas of absolute space and toward efforts to establish a sharing of jurisdiction over relative space. The zone, in essence, would filter out undesirable uses and establish a gradient: a transition zone in the landscape between radically different land-use practices.

Even environmentalists initially favored the concept. Sierra Club representative John McComb defined the buffer concept as a "scenic easement or other method wherein the National Park Service could prevent undesirable developments, logging, juniper eradication projects, etc. in an area within about 1 mile of the rim" (McComb 1971). The easements were to function as buffer zones in areas where the Park Service had little likelihood of gaining outright control. Yet, though aimed at all incompatible uses, the provision for zones of influence was primarily intended to forestall potential development projects on sensitive portions of the Navajo and Hualapai Reservations. The only dispute revolved around how wide the zones should be. The 1971 draft management plan for the park called for scenic easements of only one-half mile on sensitive rimlands rather than the one mile recommended by McComb (Grand Canyon National Park 1971). A 1971 draft bill to expand the park, requested by Goldwater and Arizona Congressman Morris Udall (brother of Interior Secretary Stewart Udall and throughout his long career in Congress a steadfast supporter of environmental causes), also featured one-mile easements (Goldwater and Udall 1971).

The Forest Service demurred, preferring to formalize cooperation through a memorandum of understanding negotiated between the two agencies rather than having to deal with legislatively delineated buffer zones, which, presumably, would be less amenable to negotiation or modification (Suazo 1972). The agency's reservations were well founded, given the long history of Park Service efforts to wrest large amounts of lands from its control. Under the buffer zone concept, the Forest Service might have had to fundamentally change the way in which it managed the edges of its lands to accommodate the preservationist agenda of the Park Service. More important, the concept had the potential to establish a precedent of park dominance over the adjacent lands. Once the precedent was established, it could lead—as had happened in the past—to a full transfer of lands into Park Service hands. If there was one thing the Forest Service did *not* want, it was the loss of any more lands or natural resources to its arch rival.

New Park Boundaries

The apprehensions of the Forest Service were well founded at a larger scale as well, for the acquisition of major tracts of land—much of it from the Forest Service—was high on the list of priorities for Grand Canyon National Park. The 1971 draft of the park master plan called for the acquisition of Lower Kanab Canyon on the North Rim, as well as of Long Mesa and Cataract (Havasu) Canyon on the South Rim. Park administrators also wanted jurisdiction over the Colorado River bed, as well as over the lower Colorado River gorge downstream as far as Separation Rapids. In return, they proposed to transfer 49,250 acres of Grand Canyon National Monument to the Forest Service or Bureau of Land Management, as appropriate (Grand Canyon National Park 1971).

The best location for a boundary on the South Rim portion of Grand Canyon National Monument continued to be a source of concern to park officials, particularly with regard to management of the bighorn sheep in that area. Park research biologist N. G. Guse, having been directed to study the issue by Superintendent Robert R. Lovegren, recommended that the new park boundary be drawn to retain sufficient suitable habitat for the bighorn sheep and to protect "a vegetation community unlike any other present" within the park. This vegetation community was, ironically, sagebrush—hardly a rare species in the area! Yet Guse revealed that such details hardly mattered: "It may sound ridiculous to want to 'save' sagebrush, but it is within our philosophy to do so and should rank along with any other vegetation type we might want to preserve" (Guse 1972).

Guse's report fails to mention another crucial issue: these lands were among those long claimed by the Havasupai. Park administrators, however, were certainly cognizant of the issue, for they decided to fight transfer of the disputed monument-area lands to the Havasupai Tribe. What lands park administrators did not want, they were willing to see transferred to the Forest Service for Havasupai use—but not transferred to the tribe (Lovegren 1972a).

Park administrators, in an attempt to prove that they were not land grabbing, proposed deletions from the Slide Mountain, Tuckup Point, and Jensen Tank areas on the North Rim of Grand Canyon National Monument (Lovegren 1972b). Deletion of the North Rim lands was not to be so easy, however, for soon thereafter, anthropologist Richard A. Thompson described the areas as being rich in archeological potential (Thompson 1972). This argument was used in all subsequent efforts to retain the lands within an enlarged park.

At the same time, ranchers, still among the strongest opponents to park expansion, persisted in seeking to have the lands transferred to the Bureau of Land Management. They had been allowed to continue grazing the area ever since Grand Canyon National Monument had been established, and they wanted to retain their grazing rights—something they would not be allowed to do if the lands were incorporated into the park.

Park Expansion on Ecological Grounds

By the early 1970s, environmentalism had become a potent force in U.S. culture. Stewart Udall's book on environmental issues, *The Quiet Crisis* (1963), presaged the avalanche of writings that ensued. Writers such as Edward Abbey (e.g., 1977) and Colin Fletcher (1967) celebrated wild nature and extolled the virtues of the canyonlands of the Southwest. To these and many other authors, humans were not only fouling their own nests with air and water pollution, overcrowding, and other evils, they were destroying the last remaining vestiges of unspoiled America. Even the preservationists who had for so long fought to keep the Park Service out of the redwood stands of California had finally decided that the federal agency might be the best steward after all, since state management had proven to be so weak (Schrepfer 1983).

Sierra Club representative John McComb was among the many activists who sought to put into practice what authors Wallace Stegner, Donald Worster, Wendell Berry, and so many others wrote about, and he was consistently—and insistently—vocal in support of major enlargements of Grand Canyon National Park. He favored extension of the park boundaries from Lees Ferry all the way to Grand Wash Cliffs and northward to include all of Kanab Canyon. These boundaries, he said, would encompass the ecological Grand Canyon. More to the point, McComb's proposed extension was clearly a bid to bring the absolute space contained within park boundaries into alignment with the representational space that he and other environmentalists defined as the "Grand Canyon." The argument was reminiscent of those advanced in the 1930s, when park advocates tried to use laws of nature to justify what was, in essence, a very political redrawing of park boundaries.

While acknowledging that the neighboring Indian reservations impeded efforts to encompass the entire ecological Grand Canyon within the park, McComb repeatedly advocated finding a way to incorporate reservation lands into the park, including those bordering Marble Canyon, the Little Colorado River Gorge as far upstream as Blue Springs—both within the Navajo Reservation—and upper Havasu Canyon, on the Havasupai Reservation (McComb 1971).

Environmentalists also set their sights on the community of Tusayan, located just south of the main entrance to the park on the South Rim, asserting in no uncertain terms, "One of the most disturbing scenes . . . is the abortion called Tusayan—the miscellaneous and unplanned sprawl of motels, motorcycle rental places, stores, helicopter pads, etc., just south of the south Park boundary. . . . It . . . is hardly deserving of existence anywhere, and least of all at the entrance to the state's most important Park" (Eiseman 1972).

The Havasupai Struggle Continues

Representatives of the Havasupai had traveled to Washington eight times in sixty-five years in efforts to get their reservation enlarged, but as the 1970s opened, they still had not achieved their goal.[4] Grand Canyon National Park staff members met with the tribe on December 27, 1971, to discuss the potential for a land transfer. The park representatives drove a hard bargain, though, because they insisted that a detailed list of conditions be met before any transfer would be made. In return, park officials would be willing to hire tribal members, provide training, and help the tribe with tourism development and road construction (Grand Canyon National Park, nd).

The trade-off was quite uneven, for the list of restrictions included a repeal of provisions in the park organic act that allowed the Havasupai to use park lands, a demand of assurance from the tribe that outside interests would not be allowed to undertake any commercial exploitation of tribal lands, a requirement that there be public meetings and government agency concurrence regarding any developments other than grazing improvements on lands that were formerly part of the park, protection of bighorn sheep, and allowance of Park Service and visitor access. The tribal council eventually accepted the terms, but the Havasupais' outrage at the council's compromise soon forced the resignation of the tribal chairman.

The Havasupais remained embattled on another front as well, for the outcome of the Indian Claims Commission proceedings continued to provide a potent source of resistance to reservation expansion. Oscar Paya, chairman of the Havasupai Tribal Council, responded to the argument that the tribe had already received compensation from the Indian Claims Commission for lands it had lost by arguing that the tribe had tried to refuse the money and in any case had yet to receive a cent of that monetary settlement. He went on to declare, "We . . . still stand ready to forego settlement money at 50 cents an acre for whatever lands we can regain now by doing so" (Paya 1973).

Juel Rodack, head of Arizonans for a Quality Environment, immediately reacted, denying that the tribe had a right to the contested lands and intimating that the Havasupai would allow inappropriate development to occur:[5] "You must realize that opening the smallest portion of our preserved lands to commercial use creates the precedent through which the special interests will seek to destroy the entire structure of our national preserves. No such commercial use must be permitted. Not a single acre! The land that once was yours is held now in trust for you and your descendants and for that of all mankind. . . . Obviously adequate grazing must be made available for your horses, but beyond that, nothing" (Rodack 1973).

Rodack sent copies of his and Paya's letters to Goldwater, urging that the senator drop the proposal to enlarge the Havasupai Reservation "so that we may throw our complete support behind your bill." Apparently not wishing to appear completely insensitive to the tribe's plight, he recognized that the Havasupais should be "treated with compassion now that they have been given hope that they may obtain lands for economic development. Since it is completely intolerable that current park lands be so converted, we urge that you investigate the possibility of providing them with lands outside the park boundaries, possibly within the National Forest" (Rodack 1973).

The controversy prompted Goldwater to call for Morris Udall's support in getting reservation enlargement legislation passed during the 1973 congressional session:

> I am a realist, I know that we are not going to get what we are asking for, but I do think they are entitled to the hilltop and to some land where their power plant is and a little more grazing land than they are already using. When we consider that about three hundred Indians live on a little over five hundred acres, I don't think that is exactly fair in anybody's book, but, on the other hand, I know there is great opposition, particularly from the Sierra Club to granting them a great deal more land and I don't think this will come about. . . . I am asking this as a personal favor. This is the first time I have ever done so because I attach so much importance to it, not for what it might mean to my name or the co-sponsors, but what it will mean to our state of Arizona. I hope you will help me all you can on this. (Goldwater 1973)

It would be some time before he realized his aspirations.

Dams in the Canyon

As mentioned previously, in 1968, in response to voluminous public pressure, Congress had passed legislation that put a moratorium on the Federal Power Commission's right to sanction (or even study the possibility of) dams within the Grand Canyon. Yet, due to the refusal of water-power interests to give up the fight, the Hualapai Dam remained a stumbling block to congressional efforts to enlarge the park. On one hand, if the park was to encompass and represent "untouched nature," then either the boundaries had to be drawn far enough upstream to eliminate the dam and all slackwater associated with its reservoir, or construction of the dam had to be prohibited. On the other hand, if the rules were relaxed to allow human modifications of nature to exist within the park, then the boundaries could be extended farther downstream. The contest pitted hydroelectric power interests, the Bureau of Reclamation, the state of Arizona, the Hualapai Tribe,[6] and Mohave County against environmentalists and the Park Service.

The Park Enlargement Effort Proceeds

Concern over the inability to reach consensus on a bill to enlarge the park finally prompted Goldwater to hold two meetings at his Phoenix home. The first meeting, which took place on December 9, 1972, ended in disappointment when John McComb and Jeff Ingram, both active in the Sierra Club's Southwest Division and seasoned opponents of dams in the Grand Canyon, announced that Goldwater's bill should be unanimously opposed by conservation groups. The bill, they complained, enlarged the park by only 2 percent; furthermore, the idea of granting land to the Havasupai Tribe, while possibly justifiable, was unacceptable (Bracey 1973). The second meeting at Goldwater's house took place on January 29, 1973 (National Park Service 1973a), and included a broader range of people: representatives of the Arizona congressional delegation, environmentalists, Indians, and representatives from state agencies and the Park Service. Although, again, no consensus on new park boundaries was achieved, Goldwater indicated that new legislation would be introduced within a month.

Still anxious to modify park boundaries, administrators issued a new version of the park master plan (Grand Canyon National Park 1973). The western boundary would be extended westward, all the way to the Grand Wash Cliffs. The eastern boundary was to begin at Navajo Bridge (just downstream from Lees Ferry). Again casting covetous eyes on Navajo lands, the master plan indicated that this boundary would incorporate the east rim of Marble Canyon—provided the Navajo Nation concurred (a highly unlikely prospect). In addition, park administrators wanted a scenic easement established that would preclude undesirable developments on reservation lands visible from the Colorado River. Easements, for that matter, would also be desirable on South Rim lands managed by the Forest Service.

Park administrators, having finally recognized that they could not ignore—or dispossess—the Havasupai Tribe, also included in the master plan an acknowledgment that tourism was the tribe's "most promising economic asset" (Grand Canyon National Park 1973, 13) and noted that a study would be made regarding the possible transfer of lands to the tribe. The plan suggested that an enlarged reservation might include about 20,000 acres of land on Tenderfoot Plateau (then within Grand Canyon National Monument) and about 43,000 acres in the Manakacha/Topocoba area. In exchange for this land transfer, however, park administrators again insisted that provisions allowing the tribe to use other park lands be deleted from the 1919 organic act.

Indian efforts began to bear fruit in another area of concern as well, for the new draft plan explicitly recognized traditional Indian religious uses and assured that these uses would be honored. The plan even went so far as to commit the park to regional planning and cooperation with Indian tribes and with other agencies.

With these new commitments, park officials at long last acknowledged that the park existed within a larger regional context, that they would have to cooperate more fully with others in the area, and that maybe they would even have to make some concessions in the absolute space of the park to accommodate the representational spaces of its neighbors. Such reciprocity would certainly have made resource management more context-specific. But it also made management more complex: many years passed before regional cooperation began to be realized in practice.

The two bills that finally led to enlargement of the park, S. 1296 and H. R. 5900, were introduced on March 20, 1973, by Barry Goldwater and Morris Udall, respectively. Reflecting the revised park master plan, the bills proposed boundary revisions that would have created a single national park extending from Lees Ferry to the Grand Wash Cliffs and would have included tributary side canyons and surrounding plateaus. The bills included zones of influence and provided for enlargement of the Havasupai Reservation—a significant advance for tribal interests over the environmentalists' agenda.

Perpetuating the contest between supporters of the Goldwater compromise approach and the environmentalists, Senator Case introduced on June 19, 1973, a rival bill that, like his previous ones, came close to encompassing all of the lands wanted by the Sierra Club. It was this bill that environmental groups, such as the Sierra Club, again favored (Freemuth 1975).

The very next day, on June 20, 1973, the Senate Subcommittee on Parks and Recreation held a hearing on Goldwater's bill. Goldwater's testimony focused on inclusion of buffer zones (the provision required the secretary of the interior's approval for any development within one mile of the river); deletion of the Tuckup Point, Slide Mountain, and Jensen Tank areas; and enlargement of the Havasupai Reservation (U.S. Senate 1973a).

The Park Service favored conducting a study before any enlargements of the Havasupai Reservation were made and recommended that the boundaries omit the slackwater area of Lake Mead from the park.

Going against the master plan draft drawn up by administrators of Grand Canyon National Park, perhaps in recognition of strong political opposition to the concept, the Park Service also recommended that the zone of influence provision be deleted from the bill, noting that the existing land management agencies already possessed the authority needed for proper land management in those areas (U.S. Senate 1973a, 43–46).[7]

The Forest Service not only objected to the idea of buffer zones, but also opposed the enlargement of the Havasupai Reservation, noting that approximately 100,000 acres of the lands would come from National Forest lands that were being used at that time by both Indians and non-Indians. Like the Park Service, the Forest Service supported doing a detailed study before any lands were transferred (U.S. Senate 1973a, 54–57).

Predictably, John McComb opposed S. 1296 because it endangered the integrity of the national park system and Grand Canyon National Park itself, and worse, it actually decreased the amount of land in the national park system by 47,000 acres. He again argued that park lands should not be transferred to the Havasupai, but he displayed more than a little hypocrisy when he announced that he was willing to negotiate boundaries on the North Rim lands, where the continued power of local resource users—especially timber interests and hunters—militated against large additions to the park. On the North Rim the Sierra Club was advocating the addition only of those areas that were particularly important for their scenery, biology, or geology: DeMotte (formerly VT) Park, the North Canyon–Cockscombs area, all of Kanab Canyon and adjacent plateau lands, Toroweap Valley (now called Tuweep Valley), the southern end of the Uinkaret Plateau, Whitmore Wash, Parashant Canyon, Andrus Canyon, and a portion of the Shivwits Plateau. South Rim additions should include the Tusayan area and upper Havasu Canyon.

McComb, reversing the earlier environmentalist position, came out flatly against the zones of influence. McComb infuriated Goldwater—who believed he was addressing a key environmentalist demand—when he testified that the Sierra Club opposed the buffer zone provision because the arrangement was dependent, for its implementation, on the will of the secretary of the interior (Freemuth 1975). Goldwater was so angry, in fact, that he canceled his membership in the Sierra Club (Freemuth 1975).

The Hualapai Tribe advocated the exclusion of North Rim lands that had previously been marked for construction of Hualapai Dam.[8] The tribe also objected to a feature on the map accompanying the bill that showed the reservation boundary as being on the south bank of the river. Even though there was text on the map establishing the south bank as the boundary "with the concurrence of the Hualapai Nation," the Hualapais reiterated their longstanding claim that the reservation extended to the middle of the river and asserted that such language on the map was unnecessary because they had no intent of ever giving up any of their land.[9] Finally, the Hualapais objected to the buffer zone provision, arguing that the provision placed unacceptable restraints on their freedom to develop their reservation lands near the river and that it constituted a taking of their lands without compensation (U.S. Senate 1973a).

The Navajo Nation, in contrast to earlier intimations that it was open to the idea of a buffer area in the Marble Canyon area, came out flatly against the idea, arguing that it infringed upon the tribe's rights to pursue its own development and land-use plans. The greatest risk the Navajos faced, however, may well have been that the zone of influence could have nullified their claim that the reservation boundary extended to the middle of the Colorado River through Marble Canyon. This claim was essential to its plans to establish its own tourism facilities, a river-running enterprise through Marble Canyon, as well as trail access to the river's edge.

The Navajos also voiced concerns that lands they used for grazing in the vicinity of Desert View and Cape Solitude would be included in the park. Finally, the members of the Cameron and Bodaway chapters of the tribe, whose lands lay closest to the park boundary, and who thus would be most affected by boundary changes, were concerned that the zone of influence provision would involve negotiations with the tribal government in Window Rock (on the eastern side of the reservation), rather than directly with themselves (U.S. Senate 1973a).

Havasupai Tribal Councilman Augustine Hanna, while willing to allow some side-canyon areas that they had been using to be designated as wilderness, admonished the committee, "Not many of you would stand the humiliation we stand every day. We live in a Park Service zoo. We have to open our house to somebody else's guests. Remember, we used to own the whole place" (U.S. Senate 1973a, 72). Hanna went on to object that conservation groups' warnings that the tribe wanted the land for large development plans was "just crazy. We don't have any way to do that and we don't even want to. . . . Some big business operation would change us into white people, and we like our way if life. . . . We think it is better than yours" (U.S. Senate 1973a, 73).[10]

The Havasupais reinforced their testimony in a written statement where they specified that they wanted added to their reservation all their park and Forest Service grazing allotments and other permit areas, the 160-acre Supai Camp within Grand Canyon Village (as a permanent, though spatially separate, segment of their reservation), the lands forfeited by the Santa Fe Railroad in the 1941 Supreme Court ruling, and Havasu Campground (a campground in Havasu Canyon that was built on a tribal burial ground). They also wanted usage rights in the Indian Gardens area within Grand Canyon National Park, which had been part of their original territory (U.S. Senate 1973a; Wray 1990).

S. 1296, as reported to the full Senate on September 21, 1973, re- tracted the proposed park boundary from Lees Ferry to Navajo Bridge and retained Tuckup Point, Slide Mountain, and Jensen Tank within the park, though with a provision that a study be done regarding pos- sible subsequent deletion of these areas from the park (U.S. Senate 1973b, 2). Whereas the Goldwater version would have designated large areas of the park as wilderness areas (thus closing those areas to all but "primitive" uses), the committee version deleted the provision. The committee's amendments also left the door ajar for construction of a dam at Bridge Canyon.

The greatest amount of space in the report was dedicated to a dis- cussion of the committee's position on the proposed enlargement of the Havasupai Reservation. The committee directed the secretaries of the interior and agriculture, within one year of enactment, to conduct a comprehensive study and make detailed recommendations to Congress and the president for expansion. Cognizant of the danger that pro- longed study might result in no action, the committee report stressed that positive recommendations had to be made and that the study had to be conducted in close cooperation with the Havasupai Tribal Coun- cil. The committee even suggested the study of a specific alternative: the possibility of the tribe's acquiring private land, rather than Park Service or Forest Service lands. At that time, the Boquillas Ranch (also known as the Three-Vee Ranch) was for sale. In the 1940s the tribe had identified this ranch as a desirable addition to their reservation. Environmentalists had also been promoting this ranch as a solution to the problem.[11]

The Senate approved the amended bill on September 24, 1973, and referred it to the House Committee on Interior and Insular Affairs the next day (Freemuth 1975). A subsequent House hearing on the bill (Hulett 1973) revealed support for immediate enlargement of the Havasupai Reservation from Arizona Congressman Sam Steiger and from members of the tribe. Environmentalists continued to oppose the idea, and the Forest Service reiterated its call for a study of the issue (U.S. Senate 1973b). In a new wrinkle, John McComb transformed the "zone of influence" idea into an outright call for incorporation into the park of a strip of land about one mile wide along the western boundary of Marble Canyon, along the upper portions of four tributary side canyons to Marble Canyon, as well as in several plateau locations downstream (McComb 1973).

Hualapai leader Sterling Mahone, Arizona Power Authority Chairman Marshall Humphrey, and Mohave County again worked to keep the Hualapai Dam project alive (Humphrey 1973; Ketchner 1974; Mahone 1973), while members of the timber industry and the Forest Service reiterated their opposition to the zone of influence (Conkin 1973; Housley 1973; Kulosa 1973; Young 1973).

The Navajo Nation supported the Goldwater bill, as passed by the Senate, although in a written statement Tribal Chairman Peter MacDonald noted that the Navajos had set aside land in the contested area of Marble Canyon for a Navajo Tribal Park. This area, he maintained, was already protected from development, though the Navajos intended to continue using some of it for grazing and related activities (MacDonald, nd).

As congressional proceedings continued, a highly significant breakthrough occurred for the Havasupais' cause. Members of the Sierra Club from the Prescott, Phoenix, and Tucson chapters met with the Havasupais and came away supporting enlargement of the tribe's reservation, provided they received assurances that the tribe would manage the area carefully. This placed McComb and Ingram, who continued to oppose the land transfer, in an ambiguous position: Sierra Club policy was to allow local chapters to take the lead in such activities, but the national office continued to oppose the transfer. Thus, they found themselves representing only the members of the national environmental coalition that covered their expenses (*Canyon Shadows* 1974; *Qua-'Toqti* 1974b). Yet, even at the national level, internal dissention arose: the club's National Native American Issues Committee came out in favor of an enlargement that included park lands, again provided reasonable environmental restraints were included (Sierra Club 1974).

At about this time, it became apparent that Congressman Udall had decided to oppose inclusion of the reservation enlargement provision in the bill. The chagrin felt by the tribal leadership is clearly apparent in a telegram dispatched by Oscar Paya to Udall: "You are making a terrible mistake in your stand on returning land to our people. This land holds our entire life and entire history. We beg you to talk with us here and see what is at stake before presenting H.R.5900 to the Interior Committee" (Paya 1974). Udall, in his response, chose to echo politically driven objections: it would be difficult to get congressional approval for a land transfer to the tribe because the Indian Claims Commission had already awarded the tribe a monetary settlement for the lost lands and because concerns persisted that an unacceptable precedent would be set by the transfer. Furthermore, national conservation groups and others were firmly opposed to the measure and made up a considerable block of opposition. According to Udall, "I concluded that we could not win on this point" (Udall 1974a). Not coincidentally, at this time Udall was considering running for president (Byler 1974).

In an about-face a month later, Udall decided to support an enlargement of the Havasupai Reservation after all. Perhaps cognizant of his need for a larger political base for his presidential campaign, he explained his position change in terms of a lack of other acceptable alternatives; it looked as if immediate transfer in trust was preferable to waiting for another study to be completed because the tribe would not have much opportunity for legislation to increase their reservation in the next Congress, "and this they desperately need." However, Udall's statements clarified that such a transfer would have to include a study, land-use planning, and strong environmental and scenic protection (Udall 1974b).

As the debate wore on, the Havasupais achieved a major boost when the CBS television show *60 Minutes* covered their struggle (*Canyon Shadows* 1974). They also gained important support from President Richard Nixon (Nixon 1974) and Senators Edward Kennedy and Hubert Humphrey (*Qua'Toqti* 1974b, 1974a). However, the Havasupais still faced an uphill battle, for an editorial critical of their efforts appeared in the *New York Times* (1974). The editorial prompted many readers to write to Congress to object to the taking of park lands for the proposed reservation enlargement, though most writers supported some other means of enlarging the tribe's land base (*Conservation Report* 1974a).

At a House Interior Committee session held on July 31, 1974, seven amendments to S. 1296 were debated. Most of the discussion centered on Udall's proposal to transfer lands to the Havasupai Tribe and at the same time to retain within the park a considerable tract of land to be defined as "Havasupai Use Lands." These were lands that the Havasupais would be allowed to use for restricted traditional purposes. Over objections that the move would set an undesirable precedent, the committee reversed a vote that had been taken by its Parks and Recreation Subcommittee and approved the immediate transfer of land to the Havasupais (*Conservation Report* 1974b).[12]

On September 25, 1974, the House Interior and Insular Affairs Committee reported S. 1296 to the full House. Reflecting the greater strength of environmental interests in the House, the amended bill called for a larger amount of land to be added to the park than had the Senate version. On the east, the boundary was extended upstream to the mouth of the Paria River rather than just to Navajo Bridge. The committee also added the Parashant Allotment and upper Kanab Creek areas to the park, though with a provision that they—like Slide Mountain, Jensen Tank, and Tuckup Point—be studied to determine whether they should remain in the park or be returned to the public domain. The amended bill called for a study of possible wilderness designations within the enlarged park. It also provided for immediate enlargement of the Havasupais' reservation and stipulated that certain lands below the rim, which the tribe had long used for traditional purposes, were to be designated Havasupai Use Lands, though retained within park boundaries and under park jurisdiction. Tribal members were to be allowed to use these lands for religious and other "traditional" purposes.

This version of S. 1296 passed the House on October 11, 1974, after lengthy debate. All amendments to the House version of the bill were approved by voice vote, except the expansion of the Havasupai Reservation. When the voice vote on this amendment appeared to be "no," Arizona Congressman John J. Rhodes asked for a recorded vote. In a tension-filled vote count, the final tally was 180 in favor and 147 opposed, with 107 members not voting (Hirst 1976; U.S. Congress 1974).

At this point, a Senate-House conference was required to reconcile the differences between the two bills. This conference provided yet another opportunity for opponents of the bill's provisions to attempt to influence the legislation.

The mining industry, for example, finally awoke to the possibility that its interests might be negatively affected. A geologist at Phelps Dodge Corporation's Western Nuclear Division telephoned Congressman Udall's aide, Dale Pontius, to express concern about the boundary negotiations for the park. The geologist admitted that there had been no mining industry testimony previously, but it was "another problem now." Hack Canyon, a western finger of Kanab Canyon, had been proposed for inclusion in the park. Extensive uranium development would soon be required to meet the demands of proposed nuclear power plants, and this area and Parashant Canyon constituted two good prospects for development (Pontius 1974). The president of the company, Robert W. Adams, was careful to emphasize the low impact of the proposed operations and assured Udall that the Hack Canyon claims would not be seen from within existing park boundaries (Adams 1974). This sentiment dovetailed with hunting interests, who were also concerned about the large areas of Kanab Canyon that were being proposed for inclusion in the park (Herman 1974).

Ranchers on the Arizona Strip continued their efforts to keep North Rim grazing lands out of the enlarged park, asserting that they needed the land to maintain the profitability of their operations. Their power was certainly out of proportion to their numbers, for by 1974, there were only empty ranch buildings on the Arizona Strip except for small settlements at Cane Beds, Colorado City, Kaibab, and Moccasin. The entire population of the Strip amounted to only some 1,000 people. A few others ran livestock on the Strip but lived in southern Utah (Malach 1975).

At the same time, although many influential groups supported the Havasupais' cause and supportive articles and editorials had appeared in many newspapers, the tribe became increasingly worried that its quest would again fail. Only a few weeks would elapse between Congress's return from its election recess and final adjournment, and opponents were expected to seek delays. If the bill was not enacted before adjournment, the Havasupais would have to start all over again when the new Congress convened (*Indian Affairs* 1974). To make matters worse, news of the Havasupais' victory in the House was slow to reach the reservation, for "throughout the crucial two-week period between the time that the House Rules Committee acted until the full House voted on S. 1296, all telephone contact was knocked out—ingeniously sabotaged—jeopardizing not only the Tribe's chances in Congress, but also endangering the health and safety of the people" (*Indian Affairs* 1974; see also Byler and Byler 1991). Within this climate of hostility, the Havasupais and their attorney, Joe Sparks, mounted an intensive lobbying campaign to get the bill enacted before adjournment (Hirst 1976).

The Senate and the House met on December 12 and 13, 1973, to resolve the differences between the two versions of the bill (Freemuth 1975). The same three points that had been disputed in earlier congressional hearings caused difficulties at the conference. The first related to areas the park and its advocates wanted included within the new boundaries: the Parashant-Andrus-Whitmore Canyon area, Kanab Canyon, and the Shivwits Plateau. The ranchers provisionally won this battle when the conference members recommended that these areas not be incorporated into the park in S. 1296 but that a study be done by the secretary of the interior regarding possible future inclusion. The results of the study, together with recommendations, were to be transmitted to Congress. The second point concerned the three long-disputed areas that had been part of Grand Canyon National Monument but that ranching interests wanted transferred to the Bureau of Land Management: Jensen Tank, Slide Mountain, and Tuckup Point. The Park Service and environmentalists provisionally won this contest: the conference members directed that the lands be included in the park. However, the conferees also insisted that a study be done on whether these lands should be deleted.

The third disputed provision was the enlargement of the Havasupai Reservation. The Senate bill had postponed the issue pending further study, and the House bill had enlarged the reservation immediately. The Havasupais won this battle. However, the tribe's control would be less than absolute because the conference specified stringent controls over the types of use the Havasupais could make of the area and required that the tribe develop, issue for public comment, and abide by a management plan covering intended uses of the new lands (U.S. House of Representatives 1974b).

The amended version of S. 1296 drew immediate opposition. The Park Service recommended to the secretary of the interior that the bill as amended be vetoed, citing several reasons. First, the transfer of lands to the Havasupai Reservation set a dangerous precedent for claims by other tribes on other park lands. Park Service Director Dickinson warned that "both the Navajo and the Hualapai Indian Tribes have also expressed interest in lands at Grand Canyon National Park; the Hualapai Tribe has also expressed a similar interest in lands at Lake Mead National Recreation Area; and other interests have been noted by the Blackfeet Indians at Glacier National Park" (Dickinson 1974). Surely the success of Taos Pueblo in acquiring Blue Lake from the Forest Service gave added urgency to the Park Service's argument (Gordon-McCutcheon 1991). Second, the transfer of the lands to the Havasupai might have a negative effect on the resident bighorn sheep population, not in the least because the tribe might allow them to be hunted. The third reason was that not enough study had been done on the economic or cultural benefits that would accrue from the transfer.[13] The fourth reason for opposing the bill was that the boundaries detailed in the bill included a slackwater portion of the Colorado River (Dickinson 1974). The Park Service did not consider this humanly altered landscape to be an appropriate addition to the park.

In the end, the Senate and the House passed the compromise version of S. 1296—objections by the Park Service and others notwithstanding—and President Gerald Ford signed the bill into law as P.L. 93-620 on January 3, 1975. The expanded park stretched from the mouth of the Paria River to the Grand Wash Cliffs and included tributary side canyons but fell far short of including the North and South Rim lands pursued by the environmental lobby. The act created a park of some 1.2 million acres but stipulated that lands could be taken from valid Indian reservation territories only with the approval of the tribe's governing body. The proviso was largely aimed at the Navajo lands along Marble Canyon that had been included within the new boundaries of the park. Grazing rights on Grand Canyon National Monument lands were grandfathered for the lifetime of the person holding the lease; other grazing privileges would be allowed to continue for only ten more years.

On their newly added reservation lands, the Havasupais were to be allowed to hunt, gather wild plants, and engage in grazing, agricultural, and burial activities, as well as to pursue community support projects such as schools and local businesses. However, the act imposed unprecedentedly strict environmental controls over the tribe's use of its new lands, for, in addition to requiring development and approval of a detailed land management plan, the act specifically prohibited the Havasupais from engaging in commercial timber or mineral extraction operations. The act also required the tribe to allow visitors en route to adjacent park lands to cross the reservation. In total, the Havasupai Tribe received trust title to 185,000 acres of land. The Havasupais also received restricted usage rights on another 95,000 acres designated as "Havasupai Use Lands." These lands (lying between the expanded reservation boundary and the Colorado River) were within the boundaries of the park, but the park was required to allow the Havasupais access for "traditional" uses.

P.L. 93-620 addressed increasing problems associated with aircraft overflights by authorizing the Department of the Interior to work with the Federal Aviation Authority, Environmental Protection Agency, or other responsible agencies to regulate threats generated by the activity to public health or safety, or to the natural environment. On a broader regional level, the act encouraged the park to enter into cooperative agreements with other federal, state, and local departments and agencies and with interested Indian tribes to "provide for the protection and interpretation of the Grand Canyon in its entirety." It retained the hydropower provisions of the 1968 Colorado River Basin Project Act—which required congressional approval for any reclamation projects in the canyon. At the same time it amended the original 1919 park organic act to allow reclamation projects on lands that had been part of Lake Mead National Recreation area immediately before the enactment of P.L. 93-620.

Persistence and Change in the Newly Configured Park

P.L. 93-620 represented a hard bargain for national environmental interests in their battle with local resource users. The environmentalists succeeded in winning eastern and western park boundaries that closely accorded with their recommendations; however, they failed to achieve important goals, notably, acquiring significant tracts of land on the North Rim and preventing expansion of the Havasupai Reservation. Ultimately, the new boundaries encompassed lands that had already been controlled by the park, either as national park or national monument lands or that had been part of Lake Mead National Recreation Area (also managed by the Park Service).

Hunters managed to protect their access to game animals. River runners using motorized craft won a battle too: the bill included none of the wilderness designations that would have precluded motorized travel on the Colorado River. Though the issue had seemingly been settled in 1966, the Bureau of Reclamation, the Hualapai Tribe, power industry officials, and politicians from the interested states lost what they had seen as another opportunity to get Hualapai (Bridge Canyon) Dam built. The power lobby had collided with public sentiment that had become disenchanted not only with large government projects, but with a Congress that had become parsimonious with regard to funding such projects. Too, the efforts of the environmentalists to evoke images of the damage that would be done by flooding the Grand Canyon, and opposition from influential members of Congress, weakened the power lobby's voice. That no permanent injunction against dam building in the canyon was included in the act, however, gave proof that the lobby was far from dead.

The park sustained some losses as well: P.L. 93-620 transferred considerable portions of its South Rim lands to the Havasupai Tribe, even in the face of strenuous objections from the Park Service and its constituents. The loss to the park was less than total for two reasons, however. First, the Havasupais had already been using the transferred lands for many years, and second, the secretary of the interior was empowered to approve or disapprove tribal use plans for those lands. Such approval was not apt to occur if the plans or activities were detrimental to park values.

The invisibility of the Bureau of Indian Affairs in the negotiations over park enlargement was quite remarkable: its absence allowed the Indians to be directly heard, and seen, to an extent that had seldom occurred in the past. This activism, reflective of the larger movement for self-determination among American Indians, allowed the Navajo, Havasupai, and Hualapai Tribes to present their issues through the lenses of their own cultural experiences and viewpoints.

The Havasupais, who had the largest stake in the proceedings, were most successful in this regard, having broadened the problem from one simply of how to enlarge the park to one of how to apportion contested land equitably. By broadening the problem, they forced the contestants to consider a wider array of possible solutions not only to their problems, but to the larger issue of how and under what conditions partitioning of the spaces of Grand Canyon should be done: no longer could the contest proceed in the absence of consideration of issues of human equity.

The Navajos and Hualapais were able to maintain the status quo for their reservation lands, though no resolution was achieved with regard to their particular boundary disputes. The defeat of the zone of influence provision was probably their greatest gain.

While the Paiutes and Hopis did not participate in the negotiations over park enlargement, they at least gained recognition within the master plan for Grand Canyon National Park, for, after many years, park administrators formally recognized that they had legitimate interests in the area and that efforts should be made to build cooperative relationships. These peoples later became more active in pursuing their agendas with the land management agencies and other entities of the greater Grand Canyon.

The curious fight over buffer zones was an important aspect of the contest over how to define and divide the spaces of the greater Grand Canyon. The justification given for creating zones of influence was that park values—especially those associated with scenic views—could be protected only if the lands adjacent to the boundaries were maintained according to similar values. While ostensibly to be done in agreement with the adjacent land holder, in practice, the restrictions were very one-sided, because the zones lay outside the park boundary, rather than straddling it. It is interesting, however, that the Havasupai Use Area emerged as the only mandated form of buffer zone. Although never called an easement, buffer, or zone of influence per se, the area extended Havasupai interests into park lands. Though the park can severely restrict use of the area, it cannot completely prohibit Havasupai access.

No zone of influence was ever proposed to prevent damage generated by park policies or conditions to lands or resources outside park boundaries—for example, to deal with the problem of pest damage to Forest Service trees (due to the Park Service's philosophy of letting Nature take its course). Opposition to the concept, arising as it did from its advocates as well as from its opponents, suggests a general unwillingness to tolerate ambiguity in the geographies of power and jurisdiction. Yet the problem remains an important one, for neither ecological processes nor human perceptions end at arbitrarily drawn boundary lines.

Some insight into how the problem might be handled has been provided by Joseph Sax. In his discussion of how to deal with problems arising from private holdings within—or adjacent to—park lands (1976), he notes that, ideally, park boundaries should be modified to accord with established principles of ecological management. However, in some cases it might only be necessary for the federal government to regulate specific activities that have created a nuisance. Where such external activities threaten park values, a park could threaten to initiate nuisance litigation or, if appropriate statutory authority existed, to initiate condemnation proceedings. Sax cautioned, however, that parks' jurisdictional powers should be limited to a clearly defined distance: perhaps two to three miles beyond the boundaries. This is double or triple the one-mile buffers originally advocated by John McComb and Barry Goldwater. While provocative, however, Sax's ideas have not been adopted as Park Service policy, for the political geography of natural resource management still favors boundaries over zones.

On to the Next Contest

As with all previous redefinitions of the spaces of the greater Grand Canyon, the new boundaries became artifacts of the previous political battles, and inputs to subsequent contests. As revealed in the next chapter, some of these contests have been resolved; others have not.

Subsequent and Ongoing Boundary Issues: 1976 to 1995

With the election of Ronald Reagan in 1980 came the Sagebrush Rebellion and the highly controversial policies of Interior Secretary James Watt. The Sagebrush Rebellion, a call for the return of federal lands to the states, fell flat, but policies aimed at intensified resource management—and against preservation efforts—dominated the official discourse. Though a less contentious secretary soon replaced Watt at the Department of the Interior, the policies of exploitation remained a strong factor in public land management throughout not only Reagan's two terms, but George Bush's one term as well. It was against this backdrop that environmentalists and recreationists struggled to defend their achievements—and possibly add to them.

For the Park Service, the major innovation of the period was a movement toward acquisition of less-than-fee easements and creation of greenline parks.[1] Funds for full purchase of park lands had all but dried up, but these less-expensive alternatives provided a more politically expedient way for the agency to extend its influence over valued lands and resources. By 1981, more than 25,000 acres of lands were covered by easements and development rights (Foresta 1984).

For the Indians, the last years of the 1970s produced an important new piece of legislation: the 1978 American Indian Religious Freedom Act. Based on the First Amendment of the U.S. Constitution, the act was Congress's response to charges that federal agencies were, even if inadvertently, impairing the religious freedom of Indian peoples (U.S. Department of Agriculture 1988). Under the act, agencies such as the Park Service and the Forest Service were obliged to evaluate their policies and procedures in light of how they affected the religious rights and cultural identities of Indians. Where negative effects were found, the agencies were expected to take appropriate action.

Like many other regions of the country, the Grand Canyon and its environs hold many religious sites important to area peoples. Thus, the act posed major issues for how the Forest Service, Park Service, and Bureau of Land Management handled tribal claims to privileged access to Grand Canyon lands on religious and cultural grounds.

In 1976, however, issues of Indian religious freedom remained in the future. The main concern at Grand Canyon was making decisions about the lands designated for study in P.L. 93-620, for although the boundary revisions of the 1975 park enlargement act may have expanded the park, the act also set in motion another series of efforts to bring the representational spaces of the park into better alignment with the new absolute spaces. The lands Congress designated for study were the same ones that had generated the most intensive controversy during the preceding years because they contained timber, grazing, and mining resources of value to the national, regional, and local economies and at the same time exhibited characteristics and contained resources that preservationists, archeologists, and others wished to protect under the more stringent Park Service rules. Two studies emerged from the requirements of the legislation: the Park Suitability Study and the Adjacent Lands Study.

The Park Suitability Study

P.L. 93-620 instructed the secretary of the interior to report, within one year of enactment of the legislation, on whether the long-contested North Rim areas of Jensen Tank, Slide Mountain, and Tuckup Point should be retained within or deleted from the national park. Proponents of deletion, objecting to having only the Park Service involved in the study, succeeded in having the Bureau of Land Management and Forest Service included in the project (Byrnes 1975; Steiger 1975). Thus, the study team came to include—in addition to members of the park staff and specialists from the Park Service's Denver Service Center—representatives from the Bureau of Land Management and the Forest Service, as well as an array of consultants specializing in archeology, ecology, economics, forestry, geology, wildlife management, recreation, and grazing.

The study team defined its task to be the determination of the national significance of the contested lands and the examination of the

economic issues associated with existing and potential grazing, recreation, timber harvesting, hunting, and mining activities, as well as
aesthetic, recreational, and scientific values. Whereas the study team's
goals might have seemed guaranteed to achieve deletion of the lands,
the deletion proponents' strategy of packing the team with their supporters failed: the Park Service's recommendation to Congress was that
the lands be retained within park boundaries (Grand Canyon National
Park 1976b; U.S. Department of the Interior 1976a). Clearly, in the
changing politics of the time, not the least of which was a substantial
growth in support for environmentalist activism, the voices of local
users—especially ranchers—had been considerably weakened.

Yet the disarray of the Park Service (which had five different directors between 1972 and 1981) and its ongoing budget woes put it in a
weak position to acquire adjacent lands that Congress had excluded
from the park but had designated for study for possible future incorporation. Park advocates had fought hard to acquire these lands, but
political realities again defeated their efforts.

The Adjacent Lands Study

Upper Kanab Canyon, portions of the Shivwits Plateau, and Whitmore, Andrus, and Parashant Canyons had long been targets of park
expansionism[2] but had always been strongly defended by resource users. Such was the case in the struggle to enact P.L. 93-620. These were
the lands that the new legislation had excluded from the park but had
designated for future study. Unlike the provisions for study of the Jensen Tank, Slide Mountain, and Tuckup Point areas, however, P. L. 93-
620 did not specify any time limit for reporting recommendations
to Congress. Evidently, Congress had seen much greater urgency in
exploiting the possibility of returning Jensen Tank, Slide Mountain,
and Tuckup Point to multiple use than in adding even more lands to
the park.

The lack of a congressionally imposed deadline did not deter the
Park Service from pursuing the issue, nor did the observation from the
acting superintendent of Lake Mead National Recreation Area, Gary
E. Bunney, that local ranchers had installed chain gates on private
property outside Park Service boundaries, effectively preventing road
access to the Shivwits and Sanup Plateaus. Their purpose, Bunney
warned, was to discourage any further study, "the results of which they

feel will eliminate additional lands from grazing" (Bunney 1976). Preliminary work on the study began in 1976.

In 1977, the Park Service, Bureau of Land Management, and Forest Service held public workshops in Tucson, Flagstaff, and Phoenix, Arizona, and in St. George, Utah, to obtain local input on the potential transfer. As it turned out, concern about sport hunting—not grazing, mining, or logging—dominated all of the meetings except the one in St. George, where grazing was paramount (Grand Canyon National Park 1978). In response, the three agencies broadened the scope of their study to include resource values and land management needs and to decide which agency was most appropriate to address those values and needs (Grand Canyon National Park 1978; O'Brien 1981).

The review draft of the study, issued in March 1981, reported that there had been considerable public opposition to any changes that would eliminate grazing, sport hunting, or mineral development but that there had been "almost total agreement that the uses must be of a non-consumptive nature" (Grand Canyon National Park 1981a, 43). In the face of these findings, and in recognition of the multiple-use value of the lands, the document conceded that the Forest Service and the Bureau of Land Management had the capability and the legislative authority to protect the contested areas and that none of the areas should be added to the park (Grand Canyon National Park 1981b; 1981a). Thus, as in the previous study, the boundaries created by P.L. 93-620 proved resistant to change.

Contests over Navajo Lands and Boundaries

The Navajo Nation and Grand Canyon National Park share a common boundary between Lees Ferry and the confluence of the Colorado and Little Colorado Rivers. Ever since the enactment of the 1975 legislation and the completion of the mandated studies, this boundary area— and the Little Colorado River Gorge—have remained contested territories.

As mentioned previously, the Navajos had established their own parks in the 1960s in the Marble Canyon area as a defense against expansion of the national park into their lands. The Navajos, however, have never developed the lands as "parks," in the generally understood sense of establishing boundaries and administering the areas separately from surrounding lands. Moreover, the tribal parks lacked—and continue to lack—effective administrative control. Even today, there is only one tribal ranger for the whole district, and his responsibilities do not include giving precedence to tribal parkland protection (Yazhe 1992). A lack of adequate funding from tribal headquarters in Window Rock, where—understandably—social welfare projects such as housing and health care have received higher priority, has made matters worse. So has the long-standing Navajo-Hopi land dispute: the contested lands are located within what has become known as the "Bennett Freeze Zone," an area where legal restraints have prevented either tribe from undertaking any activities aimed at changing the status quo, unless those changes received the express approval of the other tribe (Yazhe 1992). Given the history of the disagreement between the two tribes, reaching such an agreement was—and remains—highly unlikely to occur.

Recognizing the Navajos' constraints on adequately protecting these lands, park administrators have persisted in trying to gain control. A 1983 memorandum circulated among staff members of Grand Canyon National Park suggested incorporating into the park not only the Navajo lands within the Marble Canyon area, but also the entire Little Colorado River Gorge, beginning at Blue Springs on the upstream end and continuing downstream to the confluence of the Little Colorado River and the Colorado River. The memorandum gave two reasons for wanting to acquire this area. First, the area was the only known significant nursery for a rare fish species, the humpback chub; second, Blue Springs was valuable because it was the primary year-round water source for the Little Colorado River (itself identified as a biologically significant stream). The hitch, though, was that the park was unlikely to gain control of the area unless it fully compensated the Navajos (Saux 1983). Given Reagan-era purse tightening, the chances of obtaining monies for such compensation probably would have been nil.

Even park staff members differed on the issue. A handwritten note attached to Curt Saux's memorandum not only challenged the desirability of including Blue Springs in the park, but observed that the water was heavily saturated with chemicals and was unpotable and unsuitable for livestock or irrigation use. In general, the unidentified author stated, "I do not see where having the gorge within the park would in reality provide any more protection for the area than it presently gets from benign neglect by the tribe."

Word apparently leaked out, for Park Service Director William Mott found himself assuring Arizona Senator John McCain that the proposal was still informal. Defending the Park Service's failure to contact the Navajos about the proposal, the director explained that since no formal land exchange proposal existed that was acceptable to the Park Service, Navajo tribal comment had not been requested. Clearly the Park Service was concerned, however, for Mott went on to advise McCain, "We believe this is a sensitive issue and one that needs to be addressed" (Mott 1985).

Mott also revealed that the Park Service did not consider the "zone of influence" concept to be dead: he resurrected it in the guise of the easement acquisition strategy that the Park Service had successfully begun using elsewhere, noting that the draft land protection plan for the park called for protection of the viewshed and restrictions on nonconforming uses in Marble Canyon. Such protection, Mott advised McCain, would be accomplished through the purchase of a conservation easement. Nothing has ever come of the idea, however, perhaps due to consistent budget shortages and ongoing tribal resistance.

Also in Marble Canyon, from River Mile 0 to River Mile 61 (river miles are measured downstream from Lees Ferry), a question has continued to exist regarding exactly where the boundary between the reservation and the park is located. Gayle E. Manges (1969), field solicitor for the Department of the Interior, concluded that the reservation boundary began one-quarter mile east of the river and, therefore, that the eastern boundary of the park (the eastern cliffs of Marble Canyon) overlapped the Navajo Reservation boundary. The area of overlap comprised 24,288 acres of reservation lands lying between the river and the Marble Canyon cliffs. These were the lands that Congress had designated in P. L. 93-620 for addition to the park, provided the Navajo Nation agreed. The Grand Canyon Land Protection Plan (Grand Canyon National Park 1989a) later identified this parcel as the largest tract of "privately owned land" remaining within the park. Unoccupied, undeveloped, and unused (except for hiking and camping by "trespassers"), the area extends fifty-seven miles along the Colorado and Little Colorado Rivers.

The position of the park on this parcel of land has been that the views of the area are integral to Colorado River raft trips, which—not coincidentally—are the primary visitor use of the area. Any land uses that would detract from the natural appearance of these lands would be considered incompatible, although limited grazing and other traditional uses could be allowed (Grand Canyon National Park 1989a).

Again, to ensure that the viewsheds in the area were not degraded, park administrators saw their only feasible alternative to be the acquisition of a scenic easement (Grand Canyon National Park 1989a). The Navajo Nation responded by pointing to the legal documents that enlarged the reservation into the contested area, arguing that these documents supported its position that the boundary was, in fact, at the edge (or, alternatively, in the middle) of the river.

Even without recourse to legal documents, the Navajos' long use of the area, and their resistance to losing control over any of their lands, has worked against successful implementation of an easement (or zone of influence) arrangement. Cooperation is made even more difficult by local Navajos' persistent resistance to decisions made at tribal headquarters in Window Rock and by the profound cultural differences remaining between the local residents (a significant number of whom to this day do not speak English) and the representatives of the agency.

A set of briefing statements prepared at the park in 1989 revealed that serious issues persisted between the park and the Navajos (Grand Canyon National Park 1989b). The main concern was "unregulated use and disregard for park regulations" in areas contiguous to the Navajo Reservation, lying in the Marble Canyon area between River Mile 0 and River Mile 36.[3] These areas, park officials complained, were "exposed to use by the local population, resulting in damage to the area's vegetation and aesthetic values." Yet their few proposals to remedy the situation were to maintain a dialogue with the local tribal governments, provide accurate information, increase park presence in the affected areas, and "educate" users. On the one hand, the solutions indicate that park administrators had begun to recognize that they could neither ignore nor bully their Indian neighbors. On the other hand, these briefing statements gave little—if any—real weight to accommodating nonconforming tribal activities: "incompatible" uses (mining, visitor accommodations, etc.) would be discouraged; by contrast, pastoral uses and "appropriate" tourism development (not defined in the statements) would be acceptable. In essence, the park was bent on changing portions of the tribe's absolute space into a shared relative space. Less benignly, by restricting Navajo options for developing the area, this arrangement would have allowed a significant expansion of the representational space of the park, at the expense of the tribe. It would also have empowered park staff members to undertake surveillance of Navajo activity in the area to ensure that only acceptable behaviors and resources uses occurred.

Recently, a park staff member, Frank Buono, again challenged the

Navajo claim, based on the same sources of justification used earlier by Manges. Interestingly, Buono's research also revealed that some tracts of land exist between the authorized park boundary and the reservation boundary. These tracts are located in areas where a quarter-mile withdrawal of land was made some years ago for hydroelectric power development but was never exploited. In these areas, the park boundary is actually located closer to the river than is the reservation boundary. Title to lands that lie within the quarter-mile withdrawal but outside the authorized park boundary (defined as the rim of Marble Canyon), Buono suggested, were unreserved lands that probably came under the jurisdiction of the Bureau of Land Management (Buono 1992; 1990).

Plans to build a new bridge to replace Navajo Bridge near Lees Ferry brought the issue to a head. Construction of the bridge could not proceed until it was determined which land management entity was authorized to issue the required permit, because the eastern abutment was to be located on the undefined land (Grand Canyon National Park 1990). In a letter to the superintendent of Glen Canyon National Recreation Area, the Phoenix Office of the Bureau of Land Management defined land ownership in the same way that Buono had: the western boundary of the Navajo Reservation lay a quarter-mile east of the Colorado River; the eastern boundary of Grand Canyon National Park was the East Rim of the Grand Canyon. However, "There may be a strip of land lying between the two boundaries that is not under either jurisdiction. This strip of land would be . . . designated for exclusive use and occupancy by the Navajo Indians until . . . required for power purposes or other uses under the authority of the United States. . . . [I]f they are required for other uses under the authority of the United States, they would be considered as unreserved public lands under the administration of the Bureau of Land Management" (McClure 1991). With the issuance of this opinion, the Navajos' position regarding the location of the boundary was considerably weakened. Yet the tribe continues to believe that if the issue were litigated, its position would prevail.[4]

Ongoing Issues Concerning the Havasupai Tribe

The enactment of P.L. 93-620 did not settle all boundary issues between the park and the Havasupai Tribe, although it did set the stage for better relations than those that had existed previously, especially during the 1950s and 1960s (Hough 1991; Wray 1990). The most persistent remaining boundary issue concerns the Havasupai Use Lands. As mentioned earlier, though not so designated, these lands constitute the only formalized buffer zone in the region—and ironically, constitute an extension of tribal influence into national park lands rather than an extension of park influence into adjacent lands.

The first effort by park administrators to exercise authority over the Havasupai Use Lands involved a study to determine whether the grazing of tribal horses was degrading the environment. The Havasupais had been grazing their horses on these lands since the late 1800s, but a 1982 study determined that the Havasupai Use Lands had a zero carrying capacity for domestic livestock, due to the shallow, easily eroded soils and lack of available forage (Grand Canyon National Park 1989b; Marks 1984). The park used this study to ban tribal horses from the lands, and in a 1982 memorandum of understanding, the tribe agreed to remove the animals.

Today, grazing has been eliminated on these lands, except for trespass events (Crumbo 1992); however, the struggle over the spaces of the Havasupai Use Lands continues. The Havasupais, while continuing to use the lands for "traditional" purposes, claim that much of this area is rightfully theirs, invoking rules, based on history and tradition, that equate long-term occupancy and use with more general rights to the lands and their resources. Park administrators, relying on ownership and control over absolute space as defined within the enabling legislation, contend that the Havasupais, by receiving the reservation lands transferred to them under P.L. 93-620, lost their claim to other lands in the area. To date, except for being unable to halt continued Havasupai use of Supai Camp near park headquarters on the South Rim, the position of the park has prevailed and undoubtedly will continue to prevail unless Congress again steps in.

Another ongoing boundary issue with which the Havasupais must cope is the requirement in the enlargement act that the tribe allow visitors to cross the reservation to reach the park lands beyond (Hough 1991). Here the issue involves lack of control over the absolute spaces of the reservation with regard to rights of passage. The Havasupais have sought to assert themselves by charging access fees, but the lack of park cooperation in collecting fees at remote access points has impeded the tribe's effort.

Finally, the Havasupais continue to be constrained in the options available to them for using the lands and resources granted them in

P.L. 93-620. Any marked changes in land use must be accompanied by a revision to the land-use plan mandated by the act. The tribe is required to issue the revisions for public comment and must obtain written approval from the secretary of the interior. Due to these requirements, the Havasupais have less latitude to act autonomously than do other tribes having reservation lands in the area and must manage their reservation as a quasi-relative space, rather than as an absolute space.

Recently, park representatives—especially through the efforts of staff anthropologist Jan Balsom—have established a more amicable relationship with the tribe, a development that should go some distance toward facilitating the settlement of issues between the park and the Havasupais. The experiences that evolve from these interactions may prove immensely useful to the park in dealing with other boundary issues, such as those involving the Hualapai Tribe.

Continuing Issues Involving the Hualapai Tribe

In 1976, the field solicitor for the Department of the Interior issued an opinion that—based on the January 4, 1883, executive order that established the Hualapai Reservation—the northern boundary was the Colorado River high-water mark that existed at the time Arizona joined the union, that is, 1912 (U.S. Department of the Interior 1976b). The issue is an important one, because the 1912 high-water mark would have been higher than is currently the case: Glen Canyon Dam controls Colorado River flows today and has effectively eliminated natural flood events. Thus, the stretch of land between the river and the historical high-water mark may actually belong to the park. If the park controls this stretch of land, then the Hualapais have no claim to the river for revenue-generating enterprises. This is a crucial point of conflict, because the tribe not only runs its own river rafting operation, but also receives significant income from charging per-person, garbage, and vehicle fees to people who either enter or exit the river at Diamond Creek. Amicable relations between the tribe and the park are critical, for to operate its revenue-producing enterprise, the tribe depends on the park and on river operators to notify the appropriate tribal authorities of dates of entry and exit.

Matters are further complicated by the fact that the 1883 proclamation stated vaguely that the northern boundary of the reservation ran "along the river" but gave no explanation of what that phrase meant.

To the Hualapais' disadvantage, another historical document that proposed to establish a reservation for the tribe—and that was supposedly approved by the majority of tribal members—stated clearly that no significant resources, including water, existed on the requested lands (Frizzell 1976). This document lends itself easily to an interpretation that the Hualapais agreed to reservation boundaries that specifically *did not* extend to the river.

Relations between the Hualapai Tribe and the park remained unfriendly in the late 1970s and early 1980s, primarily because of the dispute over the location of the reservation boundary and over tribal activities along the river. According to one tribal member, park administrators were very restrictive and "almost dictated to us what they would like to see happen" (Walema 1991). Park efforts to require the tribe to obtain a permit to engage in river running, for example, were interpreted by the tribe as a dislike of competition from Indians.

The arrival of a new park superintendent in the early 1980s led to improved relations between the park and the Hualapais, and joint efforts were initiated to clean up and patrol the river and the canyon within the tribe's sector. These activities have subsequently provided further opportunities for amicable and productive interaction between park staff and tribal members.

It is open to question, however, what changes might occur if the park ever asserts its claim to lands up to the historic high-water mark. If, as park administrators claim, it owns the land from the river up to that particular high-water mark, the Hualapais' river running operation would come under control by the park. For its part, the tribe has gone so far as to claim that because it owns at least half the river, it is entitled to a portion of the revenues from the nontribal river running concessions, as well as to run its own trips (U.S. Department of the Interior 1976b).

Other boundary issues also exist with regard to the Hualapai–Grand Canyon National Park boundary. The park superintendent's 1989 briefing statements identified as problematical the portion of the boundary stretching from River Mile 187 to River Mile 266. A helicopter flight operation near River Mile 187, made 2,000 flights a year in the course of moving river trip participants to and from the river beaches in that area. Additionally, a paved airport with a mile-long runway, a tramway, heliports, access roads, and a river-based powerboat marina had all been built near River Mile 266. Significant portions of this activity were occurring on lands below the historic high-water mark of the river.[5] Apparently not wishing to attract bad publicity, though park administrators took strong exception to the tribe's activities, the briefing statements alluded to merely trying to re- solve the problem through communications and education (Grand Canyon National Park 1989b).

The relations between the Hualapais and the park remain complex because, although the Hualapais have engaged in practices that may be seen as resistance to park control—such as building the airstrip within view of the river—they have also worked, in recent years, to build cordial relations with park staff members. For their part, park administrators have assisted the tribe by offering training for its river running operation rather than trying to keep the Hualapais off the river. In view of the tribe's potential revenue loss due to the killing of plans for the Hualapai Dam, encouraging tourist enterprises may have been park administrators' best strategy with regard to the tribe.

One park staff member has even suggested working out an ex- change, whereby the park would acquire a scenic easement along the tribe's portion of the river, in exchange for which the tribe would re- ceive land on the Lake Mead marina (Crumbo 1992). A new spin on the issue arose recently with regard to interpretation of a Supreme Court decision that indicates that the bed of a river belongs to the state, provided that the river was "navigable" at the time of statehood. In *Montana v. the United States* the court held that in cases where a treaty creating an Indian reservation was negotiated before the terri- tory became a state, and where the treaty is silent on the issue of own- ership of navigable streams, the assumption is that Congress des- ignated the state as owner of the streambed as of the date that state entered the nation. The big question, of course, is whether the Colo- rado River was in fact "navigable" at that time, a debatable point if the highly dangerous river running of early explorers such as Joseph Christmas Ives and John Wesley Powell is discounted. If a "navigable" ruling holds for the disputed lands of the Hualapai Reservation, then the state, rather than the park, might actually control the lands up to the historic high-water mark. To add to the complexity of the issue, more recently it has been suggested in a draft report prepared for the National Park Service that the federal government has the option to control activities associated with a federal purpose, even where there may be a conflict with state law (National Park Service 1991). The issue remains unresolved.

External Threats

No sooner had the park enlargement bill been passed than pressure began to intensify along park boundaries as a result of a boom in uranium exploration and mining brought on by the energy crises of the 1970s. During the exploration period, which extended from the late 1970s to the early 1980s, between 3,500 and 4,000 claims were filed on the Arizona Strip and considerable mining activity was undertaken, especially on the lands that had been designated in P.L. 93-620 for possible addition to the park. Opposition to inclusion of these areas in the park arose, in fact, immediately after the enactment of the park enlargement act when Exxon proposed exploration in the Parashant and Whitmore Canyon areas, just outside the park boundary (McComb 1975). In 1982, Energy Fuels Nuclear, a division of Phelps Dodge Corporation, proposed mining operations in the northern portion of Kanab Canyon, thus putting pressure on yet another of the sensitive boundary areas of the park. By 1985, Superintendent Richard Marks observed that three mines were operating close to the park, raising concerns about the introduction of radioactive wastes into park waters and the negative effects of the new mining roads: increased visitor use, possible increases in hunting pressures, and archeological vandalism (Marks 1985a; Ray 1992).

After the Chernobyl incident in 1986, the price of uranium dropped considerably; by 1988, uranium activity involved not much more than exploratory drilling, and a drop in uranium prices had forced the closing of one working mine and a cutback on the development of new mines (Ray 1992; Grand Canyon National Park 1988). Unfortunately for the park, however, one of the remaining operational sites lies 1.5 miles from the park boundary. Equally unfortunate for the ecological integrity of the greater Grand Canyon, the Havasupais recently lost an emotionally charged suit to prevent uranium mining in the headwater area of Havasu Creek. Obviously, the uranium mining problem remains quite alive.

The ability of park officials to influence the nature and scope of renewed mining activity near park boundaries in the future will depend on the extent to which they can devise strategies that convince politicians, bureaucrats, and the general public that this type of activity is detrimental to critical park resources—and that the park has a right to participate in land-use decisions in the relative spaces that adjoin park boundaries. Given that park enlargements have typically been justified in terms of protecting geological formations and scenic attractions rather than biological or water resources, the extent to which park officials will be able to influence relative spaces beyond the boundaries of the park remains uncertain at best.

The community of Tusayan poses a different set of problems. Whereas during the 1970s environmentalists had wanted to eliminate the settlement of Tusayan, which is located just outside the main South Rim entrance to the park, the Forest Service recently began to negotiate a series of trades with owners of land scattered throughout the South Kaibab National Forest. The aim of the Forest Service is to consolidate privately held land within the immediate Tusayan area and to eliminate inholdings in other areas of the forest that the agency wants to keep undeveloped (Gibbons 1992; Lindquist 1989; Lund 1992). Tom DePaolo of Scottsdale, Arizona, a developer specializing in factory outlet malls, together with Park West Development Corporation, has been instrumental in moving the project forward. Park West Development has a controlling interest in the private lands to be developed. Not coincidentally, it has undertaken similar development projects outside Yosemite and Yellowstone National Parks.

The project involves a trade of some 650 acres of land adjacent to Tusayan and 40 acres at Ten-X Ranch headquarters for approximately 1,210 acres of privately owned land comprising seven inholdings within South Kaibab National Forest (Lund 1994). Once the acquisitions are completed, the consortium of developers will be able to proceed with the project, called "Canyon Forest Village." As of early 1995, plans included the construction of almost 5,000 hotel rooms, 500,000 square feet of retail space, and 2,600 residential units, as well as spaces for community services and educational, transportation, and parking facilities (Lopez 1994).

In conjunction with the plan, federal officials have approved the construction of a new spur running off the Grand Canyon Railroad line and two new depots, both to be located just north of Canyon Forest Village. The Forest Service argues that if eight trains a day were to run between Williams and Grand Canyon Village, the number of cars entering the park could be reduced by 200,000 a year—and yet more than 700,000 tourists could be accommodated (Hawkins 1994).

In an effort to acquire support from the park, the Forest Service has defended the development as a way to utilize spaces outside park boundaries to address some pressing park needs—especially additional staff housing: park administrators have estimated a shortage of more than 700 dwellings for the 1,500 residents of the park. The Forest Service sees the provision of more visitor accommodations to also be a benefit to the park (Lund 1992).[6] The 1995 draft of the new general management plan for the park cautiously supports the development, provided that the park is not adversely affected. At the same time the Park Service is proceeding with its own plans to manage tourist crowding by establishing a reservation system for cars and expanding its existing public transportation system (Grand Canyon National Park 1995).

Most of the opposition to the project has come from interests in Tusayan and Williams who do not want any commercial competition (Gibbons 1992) and from environmentalists who are resisting further development in the area. Concerns have mainly focused on how many more visitors the development will attract and what the negative effects of water development will be on the ecosystem of the Grand Canyon region (Lund 1992).

The Grand Canyon Trust, a nonprofit environmental advocacy group headquartered in Flagstaff, estimates that the project would consume two million gallons of water a day. Considering that, for some time, Tusayan has trucked in most of its water from Flagstaff, the water issue is a major one. The development proposal calls for sinking wells into a large, deep-lying aquifer that was discovered during mineral explorations on the southern portion of the Colorado Plateau. Proponents see the water as the foundation of the Tusayan project. Critics assert that no one knows how much water exists in the aquifer or what the effects of intensive pumping would be on springs in the Grand Canyon area—especially Blue Springs on the Little Colorado River and Havasu Spring within the Havasupai Reservation—or on water availability for the existing settlements of the region (Hawkins 1994).

Environmentalists and park officials are also concerned that if all of the privately held parcels within South Kaibab National Forest are not traded, the possibility would continue to exist for undesirable development. Furthermore, the project might encourage additional development activity along Highway 64, which connects the main gate of the park with Williams (Hawkins 1994; Lopez 1994). Given the unsightliness of much of the development currently existing along this stretch of road, the concern is a valid one.

At the federal level, Interior Secretary Bruce Babbitt has voiced the opinion that gateway communities, such as the Tusayan plan, were

needed by all the national parks (Babbitt 1994). Unfortunately, because Babbitt was the legal counsel for Canyon Forest Village before
assuming the post of interior secretary, his neutrality on the issue has
been questioned,[7] further complicating prospects for consensus among
the contending parties.

With the growth of the commercial aircraft sight-seeing business,
the notion of drawing boundaries to divide up noncompatible uses has
moved into airspace. Among the disputes that arose during the events
leading up to the enactment of P.L. 93–620 was park officials' concern
about intrusive aircraft overflights. A problem that had come to the
fore with the development and diffusion of commercial and private
aircraft after World War II, the issue intensified dramatically in the
1960s and 1970s as low-level flights over the canyon increased in number. Few areas of backcountry were free of the roar of the aircraft, and
crashes occurred with enough frequency to stimulate efforts to assert
control over entry to, and behavior within, the airspaces of the Grand
Canyon.

The problem persists to this day. Despite earnest efforts to ban or
severely limit these overflights to specified corridors delineated on
maps, opponents have only partially succeeded, for aircraft noise continues to disrupt the wilderness experience of canyon hikers. P.L. 93-
620 mentions the problem but fails to give the Park Service authority
to set specific rules, requiring only that the Federal Aviation Agency
work with the Park Service in dealing with the problems. The upshot
has been that park officials have not been able to establish rules for
overflights independently, but have had to rely on cooperation with an
agency that has aviation companies as one of its primary constituencies. Though today aircraft must operate within designated corridors
and not fly below the canyon rims, the issue remains hotly contested.

Especially since the 1980s, degradation of air quality over parks has
become a significant problem. At Grand Canyon, pollution originating
from nearby coal-fired power plants—built to provide the power that
was originally to come from the dams to be built within the Grand
Canyon—prompted park officials to assert control over the entire airspace of the park (Fradkin 1981; Freemuth 1991). After a tortuous
series of negotiations pitting the park and its environmentalist and recreationist supporters against power interests, the federal government
mandated stricter controls over emissions from power plants. Yet the
battle is not yet won. Class I air quality in the region may prove as
ephemeral as the air currents themselves, because pollutants reach the

canyon from places as far away as the Los Angeles metropolitan area and mining districts in Sonora, Mexico—sources that are not easily controlled.

The operation of Glen Canyon Dam constitutes yet another significant problem for the park. It originates, like the activities causing air pollution, outside the jurisdictional boundaries of the park, yet threatens valued park resources. In this case, because of the drastic fluctuations in the timing and volumes of water being released from Lake Powell to satisfy peaks in electricity demands, the continued existence of important beaches and riparian areas along the Colorado River— not to mention the survival of indigenous species—is seriously threatened (Carothers and Brown 1991).

Park representatives have been actively participating in an interagency project to find ways to resolve the problem and have been involved in ongoing, intensive negotiations at the local, regional, and national levels (Bureau of Reclamation 1992; Carothers and Brown 1991; U.S. Department of the Interior 1989). Even so, achieving concurrence between preservationists and hydropower supporters on acceptable water release volumes and timings has proven frustratingly difficult.

Yet even this intensely fought issue has had positive effects, for it has activated a wide array of interests, including the Navajo, Paiute, Havasupai, and Hualapai tribes. As part of the interagency study, for example, anthropologists escorted members of the Kaibab Paiute band on a raft trip down the Colorado River to catalog and assess religious, archeological, and cultural sites threatened by the water management regime (Stoffle et al. 1993). This trip may prove invaluable in opening new avenues for productive interactions between the federal agencies and the tribes. It may also have established an important precedent for giving the local Indians a stronger voice, based on religious and cultural interests, in the development of resource management policies and practices throughout the greater Grand Canyon region.

Trespass Issues

Human trespass poses a thorny problem for the park. Because the park lacks both the staff and the resources to prevent all forms of trespass, administrators must choose which specific types of trespass they want most to prevent. Although people frequently cross park boundaries without paying the requisite fees, park officials in recent years have focused on specific forms of behavior once people are inside the park. One such form of behavior they have been particularly active in suppressing has been the unauthorized selling of jewelry by Native Americans, especially by Navajos who cross the boundary from reservation lands on the east side of the park. The driving force behind the effort is that the sellers' activities infringe on the preferential rights of concessionaires allowed to sell within the park. The problem is not minor: in 1988, for example, park employees made eleven arrests, issued fourteen violation notices, and seized $14,000 worth of merchandise (Grand Canyon National Park 1988).

In another trespass incident, in 1983, a heavy crop of pinyon nuts attracted a large number of local Indians to the park. The park implicitly—but not explicitly—allows such activity but expects certain standards of behavior in return. On this occasion, park officials found that the Indians had created considerable resource damage from off-road vehicle travel, tree cutting, illegal fires and camping, and littering (Grand Canyon National Park 1984). Park administrators continue to allow Indians to harvest pinyon nuts but at the same time carefully keep the arrangement informal in case they need to take stronger enforcement action.

Improper access to hiking trails within the Grand Canyon is another way the park defines "trespass." Hikers must not only have the proper permits, but must go only where their permit specifies, must demonstrate the kind of hiking experience that is required to survive a canyon trip, and must prove that they have proper equipment and adequate water. The requirements are not unreasonable: rescues are expensive and dangerous. Finally, the issue of raft trips down the Colorado River is yet another instance of park administrators' determination to restrict the numbers of people in the canyon at any one time. Permits to run commercial river trips are far fewer than the number of operators wishing to offer raft trips. The situation is even worse for private rafters who must often wait ten years to obtain permission to run the Colorado.

Wilderness Designations

As of 1990, the Colorado Plateau features 1,422,000 acres of designated wilderness and 10,300,000 acres classified as potential wilderness. Together, the two categories account for 19.7 percent of the federal lands and 10.9 percent of the total lands on the Colorado Plateau (Grand Canyon Trust 1990). Yet environmentalists want more.

Designation of wilderness areas within Grand Canyon National Park has been integral to efforts to define the park in terms of ecological preservation. Congress deleted the wilderness study provisions from P.L. 93-620, then reversed itself in an amendment passed six months later (P.L. 94-31) that mandated the completion of a wilderness study within two years. By 1976, the park had developed a plan that designated 82 percent of the enlarged park as wilderness and 10 percent as potential wilderness (Grand Canyon National Park 1976b). Park administrators completed the accompanying environmental impact statement in August 1980 and forwarded it to the Washington office of the National Park Service soon thereafter. Sadly, the proposal received a cold reception in the nation's capital. The hitch to the plans was that park administrators wanted to designate the Colorado River as part of the wilderness, and under the wilderness designation, to eliminate motorized rafting entirely. Utah Senator Orrin Hatch defeated the plan when, in 1981, he attached a rider to an appropriations bill for the Interior Department that specified, "None of the funds appropriated in this Act shall be used for the implementation of any management plan for the Colorado River within the Grand Canyon National Park which reduces the number of user days or passenger launches for commercial motorized watercraft excursions for the preferred use period," which runs from May 1 to September 30 of each year (quoted in Crumbo 1994). According to Kim Crumbo, a resource management specialist at Grand Canyon National Park, Hatch's rider, ostensibly arising out of a concern that motorized craft afforded more safety (an unsubstantiated concern), was "a successful backdoor attempt to circumvent a legitimate public involvement process for the economic benefit of a special interest group, the river concessioners" (Crumbo 1994). It certainly had the effect desired by river concessioners: it killed the Park Service plan to ban motorized craft on the river (see also Everhart 1983). Even in 1989, when the Park Service revised the 1981 Colorado River Management Plan, it was careful to omit any reference to wilderness status for the river corridor.

Although formal wilderness designation has not yet been forthcoming, park administrators, in accordance with the Park Service's management policies, have managed the vast majority of the lands in the park as de facto wilderness. Nevertheless, even the existing administrative practices (such as allowing increases in the levels of annual use of the Colorado River and construction of permanent research facilities) have had negative impacts on natural resources and visitor experiences within the park (Carothers and Brown 1991), prompting renewed efforts to have the designation legislatively formalized.

The current wilderness recommendation calls for the immediate designation of 1,109,257 acres of the park as wilderness—including the Havasupai Use Lands—and 29,820 acres (within the Colorado River corridor) as potential wilderness, pending the resolution of boundary issues and a decision on whether to ban or limit motorized watercraft on the Colorado River (Grand Canyon National Park 1993a). It remains to be seen whether this plan finds acceptance in Congress and with the general public.

Whereas the park damaged its own wilderness case in the early 1980s when park administrators insisted on banning motorized watercraft, administrators of the national forest have succeeded in attaining wilderness status for portions of the lands that have been most hotly contested over the years: Kanab Canyon and the Saddle Mountain portion of Houserock Valley, both on the North Rim (U.S. Forest Service 1987). Although not nearly as large as environmentalists wanted, the wilderness boundaries encompass important riparian communities and other natural features. The Forest Service's success in achieving legislative designation of these wildernesses is due in part to its willingness to maintain a higher degree of flexibility than the Park Service in redefining its mandate to manage public lands and resources for multiple uses, and in resolving conflicts in expectations between factions of its diverse constituency—including recreationists and wilderness preservationists. Yet the management of much of the wilderness lands administered by the Forest Service and the Bureau of Land Management continues to be sharply criticized by environmentalists and wilderness advocates, who want more preservation and less exploitation, and from resource users, who are now as apt to invoke states' rights to eliminate the federal presence altogether as they are to join with the Bureau of Land Management and the Forest Service in resisting their opponents' demands.

The Forest Service Versus the Park Service

Even in an era of interagency cooperation, boundary issues remain alive between the Forest Service and the Park Service. For the Forest Service, many of the current boundary problems are associated with overflow from the park, in terms of both visitor movements and biological management. In effect, the policies of the Park Service generate a zone of influence into adjacent lands, and in the eyes of the Forest Service, not all of the effects are beneficial. For example, insect infestations originating in park forests continue to damage timber on the Forest Service side of the boundary, and visitor overflow onto Forest Service lands poses threats to both lands and resources (Lund 1992). Although frequently an unintended consequence of the Park Service's management policies and actions, these negative effects on the surrounding national forest lands can be significant, in terms of damage to timber resources. Fire management remains an issue as well. The Park Service's policies regarding when and where to fight fires (rather than allowing them to burn themselves out) often puts the two agencies at odds with each other (Pyne 1989).

For the park, specific concern centers on timber cutting authorized by the Forest Service on and near the park boundary, particularly with regard to the impact on endangered, threatened, and sensitive species such as the Kaibab squirrel, goshawk, and spotted owl. Because these species freely cross park boundaries, they cannot be protected within the absolute spaces of the park. The problems demand cooperative solutions that involve interactions with neighboring land managers as well as with special interests such as hunters and ranchers. Though park officials, recognizing the necessity of open interaction and cooperation to address these issues, have stepped up their interactions with researchers from the Forest Service, conservation groups, and the Arizona Game and Fish Department (Ray 1992), the problem of how best to manage highly mobile species remains unresolved.

Ever watchful of activities outside park boundaries, park administrators keep a close eye on the Forest Service's attitudes and activities with regard to the potential development of recreational opportunities not only within the Tusayan District of South Kaibab National Forest, but also in the areas around Hull Cabin, Grandview, and Desert View (all on the South Rim) and in North Kaibab National Forest. Because little timber harvesting is occurring in the national forest at the present time, the Forest Service has increased its emphasis on recreation. But where the Forest Service sees its plans to develop trails and facilities complementary to park activities (Gibbons 1992), park officials see ever greater threats to park resources associated with increased visitation in previously unpressured boundary areas.

Plans for recreation development on the North Rim warrant special notice, because the area has remained remarkably undeveloped in the face of the exponential growth in tourism. As part of its recreation plan for the North Rim, the Forest Service wants to construct new facilities at DeMotte Park and Jacob Lake. On the positive side, the new developments would accommodate more of the visitors who today arrive only to find that the few available accommodations are already filled; they would also provide needed employment for North Rim residents, including members of the Kaibab Paiute band.[8] On the negative side, park administrators are concerned about the level and kinds of development the Forest Service plans to implement and about what kinds of land-use controls the agency intends to enforce—both of which would have considerable impact on the park (Chandler 1992).

Renewed Efforts to Expand the Park

One of the more recent efforts to address the boundary issues within the National Park System is detailed in a report issued by the National Parks and Conservation Association (February 1988).[9] Expansion of Grand Canyon National Park was one of the top priorities.

The background of the report is interesting because, apparently, the National Parks and Conservation Association requested Flagstaff attorney Robert Lippman (in his capacity as the Colorado Plateau representative for Friends of the River) to draft the proposal for Grand Canyon. In his draft (1987) Lippman observed that, because the park was surrounded by jurisdictions that were managed under multiple-use or Indian trust objectives, the park was experiencing negative impacts from external activities sanctioned by these agencies. According to Lippman's draft, and certainly in accord with the long line of expansionist recommendations regarding the lands of the greater Grand Canyon, the way to eliminate these threats was to incorporate the threatened lands into the park.

To prevent incompatible uses on adjacent lands managed by the Forest Service and Bureau of Land Management, Lippman recommended various boundary changes on the North Rim, affecting Toroweap Valley and—yet again—Parashant and Andrus Canyons and Whitmore Wash. For the South Rim, he recommended an adjustment to the fifty-seven-mile boundary between the park and the Navajo Reservation in the Marble Canyon area,[10] including a one-mile buffer between the canyon rim and tribal lands. Lippman also wanted to include fourteen miles of the Little Colorado River Gorge—including Blue Springs—citing problems associated with unrestricted access and helicopter landings.

With amazing disregard for Navajo land rights, Lippman advised that this boundary should extend one mile from the rim of the Little Colorado River along the entire extent of the addition. Nor was he much more sensitive to Havasupai independence: noting that grazing activity had affected the Havasupai Use Lands and that the tribe had denied visitor access to inner-canyon areas of the park via reservation lands, he advocated a boundary adjustment or concurrent management of that area. As for the boundary in the vicinity of the Hualapai Reservation (108 miles long), Lippman noted that mineral, industrial, and recreation and tourist development might occur in this area, as well as in tributary canyons and on the rim. He recommended that the boundary be placed on the canyon rim, with a one-mile buffer between the rim and tribal lands. Zones restricting mining and commercial use should also be designated, he asserted. Yet, though he raised the buffer zone idea once again, Lippman provided no better insight than had been given in the past regarding how such conjunctive management could be achieved politically.

Park administrators seemed to have a generally favorable attitude toward Lippman's recommendations, though staff members found some of his proposals unnecessary. Apparently, park officials were chary of having staff reactions set down in writing, however, for a note attached to the park's copy of the document advised that comments on the draft should be made by telephone, rather than in writing (Hodapp 1987).

The final report of the National Parks and Conservation Association reflected some of Lippman's recommendations but drew also on suggestions from Brien Culhane of the Wilderness Society (Ray 1992). The report once again put on the expansion agenda many of the same lands, mostly on the North Rim, that had been fought over in the 1960s and 1970s. It recommended addition to the park of approximately 15,000 acres in the Snap Point area, 14,600 acres of the Mount Logan wilderness area (an officially designated wilderness area managed by the Bureau of Land Management), the half of Mount Emma not then inside the park, approximately 150 acres in the Tuckup Point area, 90,000 acres of Shivwits Plateau land (managed by Lake Mead National Recreation Area), some 77,100 acres of upper Kanab Canyon, 36,000 acres of cliffs in the Little Colorado and Marble Canyon gorges, and Blue Springs. For Marble Canyon and Blue Springs, the final report—unlike the Lippman draft—formally acknowledged that, although P.L. 93-620 had authorized the extension of the park boundary to the eastern rim of Marble Canyon, the extension was subject to the concurrence of the Navajo Nation, an event unlikely to occur. The report was silent on Lippman's proposals for Hualapai and Havasupai lands.

In response to the National Parks and Conservation Association report park administrators took a more restrictive view of possible additions: areas that might qualify for inclusion in the park were portions of Kanab, Parashant, and Whitmore Canyons and the Shivwits Plateau (Grand Canyon National Park 1988). To date, nothing has occurred with regard to any of the recommendations. However, given past history, it is not unlikely that, if political receptiveness to park expansion again increases, these recommendations will constitute an important source of input. Another major source of input, of course, would be the boundaries set in the 1975 enlargement act, because these boundaries were not only the outcomes of power relationships among the various interests, but constituted the baseline from which new contests over the partitioning of the spaces of Grand Canyon would have to begin.

Implications for Grand Canyon as a "Place"

The various efforts that have been made in recent years to change the boundaries of the park and to cope with the activities and events occurring in the Grand Canyon area testify to the ongoing interest in protecting and enhancing those qualities that make the greater Grand Canyon a highly valued mosaic of places: scenic beauty, wildlife, recreation opportunities, resource exploitation opportunities, wilderness, climate, way of life. The deeply rooted values associated with ranching, logging, and mining lifestyles have continued to influence the management of the multiple-use lands on both the North and South Rims and have made efforts to repartition those spaces stubbornly difficult to achieve. Similarly, deep-seated tribal values associated both with reservation lands and with certain lands and resources that are within the domains of the federal land management agencies have contributed to a generalized resistance to further changes.

Recognition of Grand Canyon as a national—and international—treasure, a unique and priceless manifestation of Nature, and a mecca for recreation and tourism have made the park (and the larger context within which it exists) a permanent and highly visible entity.[11] Yet, ironically, while the park is passionately defended on the one hand, it is decried on the other as being overrun with visitors, plagued by environmental degradation, and inadequately protected more generally.

Though not entirely successful from any one interest's point of view, all the efforts to define and defend Grand Canyon as a place (or related set of places) have produced an increased interest in, and commitment to, cooperation among the various groups and agencies. As emphasized by the 1988 recommendations for boundary revision by the National Parks and Conservation Association, interest in repartitioning the greater Grand Canyon remains active. But, unlike the early history of the area, there is now a greater sense of pragmatism and a stronger interest in including a wide array of voices. Planning, problem-solving, and decision-making activities are all now open to wider input and participation, ensuring that future negotiations over the spaces of the greater Grand Canyon will take place in a very different political context.

CHAPTER NINE

Toward a (Re)definition of Grand Canyon

In recent years, a reform agenda for the federal government's lands and resources has picked up momentum. According to Interior Secretary Bruce Babbitt, this agenda "must start by recognizing that multiple-use planning has, for the most part, been a failure. . . . [It] skirts the central reality that in the new urbanizing West, there is no longer enough space to accommodate every competing use on every section of the public domain. Commodity production . . . is increasingly infringing on the broader public values of open space, wildlife, wilderness, and recreation" (Babbitt 1991, 167). He recommends moving away from the concept of multiple use, where all uses are supposedly balanced, to an approach based on the idea of "dominant public use," in which precedence is given to recreation, wildlife, and watershed uses. It remains to be seen whether the changes that would be required under the new concept can be readily implemented within existing political power arrangements. In the meantime, less radical changes associated with improved communications and a greater commitment to regional cooperation may smooth the way. With the increasing pressures on federal lands, and on all parks, these strategies have significant potential for improving the management and protection of park resources.

The Park Service's position on the matter appeared in a 1973 memorandum to regional directors: the parks needed to be less insular, and park managers needed to engage in regional planning to protect park integrity and to widen the base of support for park programs and plans. The new perspective had significant implications, especially with regard to how these regions would be defined in terms of size and boundaries. Planning regions, the Park Service suggested, need not have static boundaries and might vary in size from encircling the immediate neighborhood of the park to encompassing large, multistate areas. The criterion for determining the size and configuration of a region should be reasonable cohesiveness based on pertinent economic, physiographic, social, and visitor-use factors (National Park Service 1973b).

At the time, the Park Service recognized that this type of planning would not be a one-time effort but would require ongoing interactions between the park and other entities. Truer words may never have been printed, for administrators of parks such as Saguaro National Park, adjacent to and increasingly surrounded by the city of Tucson, Arizona, have found that regional interaction is absolutely essential to the survival of the parks. Yet even here, as at Grand Canyon National Park and elsewhere, the idea of "dynamic boundaries" remains largely untested, and external threats continue to pose severe challenges to resource management.

Progress in Cooperatively Managing the Greater Grand Canyon

With regard to broader regional cooperation, the expressed intentions of the land management agencies operating in the area have not yet been fully realized. For example, although park administrators have been evaluating the possibilities of interactive management through regional planning and cooperation, and although they maintain good relations with political entities such as the Bureau of Land Management and Forest Service (Reed 1992)—as well as with state and local governmental units—the park was, as of 1992, party to only one formal cooperative plan: an annual operating plan for joint fire protection involving the park, the Arizona Strip District of the Bureau of Land Management, Kaibab National Forest, and the Arizona State Land Department (National Park Service 1991). However, the 1995 draft of the general management plan stresses regional cooperation strongly and cites the participation of the park in regional development, provision of tourism information outside the park, and transportation planning as examples of productive outreach efforts (Grand Canyon National Park 1995).

At a more informal level, communications among the local offices of the Park Service, the Bureau of Land Management, and the Forest Service remain quite active as well. Further, all three agencies have more fully incorporated public participation into their planning processes, and public review of their planning and environmental impact documents is now routine. Even ranchers, historically resistant to changes in land management but seeing their profession increasingly embattled, have become convinced of the need to interact with all of the land management agencies in integrated planning and management activities (Metzger 1992).

Unfortunately, this cooperation is in danger of being subverted by the Wise Use movement. The movement does not seek to build upon existing natural resource management structures and practices so much as it aims to eliminate government presence from public lands management entirely. Even many of the less radical resource users have increasingly come to see the federal government in particular as a huge impediment to effective cooperation (Lund 1992; Metzger 1992). For all of these people, the ultimate goal has become assertion of local autonomy over resource management.

The Grand Canyon Trust, an environmental organization based in Flagstaff, arose in 1985 to promote conservation and sustainable use of the 130 million acres of the Colorado Plateau. Inspired by the land trust trend that seeks to empower localities to manage their own resources, the trust, in just ten years, has become an important voice in environmental issues on the plateau (Ruch 1992). True to its name, the trust has become a leading player in issues associated with the greater Grand Canyon and, in contrast to traditional environmental activism, has advocated a community-based approach that takes into account local and regional economic, cultural, and physical contexts. Since its inception, the trust has attempted to reinforce this broad-based approach through maintaining diversity within its board of directors. Members of the board have included, among others, James Trees (founder and honorary chairman), James Getches, James E. Babbitt (of the Flagstaff Babbitt family), Bruce Babbitt (also a member of the Flagstaff Babbitts; he relinquished his position upon becoming secretary of the interior), Vernon Masayesva (a Hopi leader), N. Scott Momaday (Kiowa author and artist), Terrence L. Bracey (former staff assistant to Congressman Morris Udall), and Stewart Udall.

The trust's approach, by placing the Grand Canyon solidly within the context of the larger Colorado Plateau region, is a worthy effort, but it will undoubtedly create new contests, for many advocates of multiple use see it as operating within the mainstream environmentalist discourse. Thus, inevitably, it becomes a target of opposition for the increasingly powerful states' rights, wise use, and property rights constituencies. Furthermore, the deep-seated differences that have long persisted among ranchers, municipalities, miners, environmentalists, and recreationists about natural resource management suggest that even the trust's successes may well be fragmentary.

There are geographical issues as well. In drawing boundaries on maps that define their area of concern, the trust runs the risk of creating yet another absolute space within which consensus becomes all but impossible to achieve: the very multiplicity of jurisdictional units within the Colorado Plateau poses a considerable challenge. The trust might well take a cue from the 1973 Park Service perspective on regions and move toward a more context-specific designation of regional boundaries, based on the geographical extent of specific issues (or sets of issues) and designed on the basis of identified relative and representational spaces. These regions might or might not coincide with—or overlap—each other. As in the case of air quality, they might even extend beyond the limits of the Colorado Plateau. Regardless, operating within a definition of social space that sees it as fluid and contextual would ensure that only relevant resources and voices were encompassed within the debate.

Interaction with the Local Tribes

Today, even though resource management policy at Grand Canyon strives to include a greater array of voices, from the Indians' point of view major issues remain. The Indians have a strong interest in developing (or expanding) tourism enterprises on their reservation lands and desire to receive park cooperation and assistance in setting them up. Furthermore, they want more than just an invitation to participate in planning processes and to pursue more open communications. At the very least, they want communications to be ongoing and institutionalized, rather than sporadic and informal (Balsom 1991).

The Havasupai, Hualapai, Paiute, Hopi, and Navajo (and Zuni) also want unrestricted entry to the park for religious and traditional activities, as well as park management policies and practices that accord more fully with their definition of the Grand Canyon as a profoundly sacred place: a place where one must make proper spiritual preparations before entering. Further, the five local tribes all fault the park for failing to incorporate Indian history, culture, and experience into visitor interpretation materials and displays. They find particularly troublesome the separation of culture from nature—an approach diametrically opposed to their own worldview, which interprets humans and Nature as being one and indivisible. The difference in worldviews is critical, for by focusing on separation instead of unity, the Indians believe that park administrators fail to take proper care of the Grand Canyon.

Yet changing interactions between the tribes and the park will not be easy. The discontinuity between the two ways of knowing, and of operating in the world, is deep. Because tribal members are still reluctant to communicate in writing, for example, effective discourse often requires lengthy personal visits and a building up of trust based on personal relations. Given the Park Service's long-standing policy of frequent supervisor and staff rotation, such personal relations are virtually impossible to maintain. The Indians have acknowledged that there are problems on their side as well. Changes in their tribal officers occur on a regular basis, and their policies are not always formally documented. Because the dominant society bases so much of its official activity on written documents and established procedures, these practices make cross-cultural interactions with the Indians even more problematical. Clearly, from both points of view, there is considerable need both for in-depth examination of precisely where the barriers to communication and cooperation lie and for concrete strategies to bridge those obstacles.

The task is made even more difficult because specific forms of knowledge and ways of structuring that knowledge vary considerably from one Indian group to another. To understand Hopi relationships with other land management entities in the area, for example, one must understand their perceptions of geographical space. First, the Hopis lay claim to specific places based on the spiritual values invested in those sites. Intervening sites having no special significance they do not claim. Second, the Hopi, like many Indian tribes, have no word in their language for boundary in the English sense. Rather, they have a word, *qalnani,* which, though technically equivalent to the English word *boundary,* is much more subtle in its interpretation. The concept entails joint stewardship (i.e., acceptance of responsibility) for protecting a valued place, with neither entity denying the affinity of the other for that place (Jenkins 1992). In this sense, the Hopi concept accords more closely to a form of relative (and representational) space, in which space is defined based on particular factors or values, rather than to any concept of absolute space where boundaries take on an exclusionary function. The concept of *qalnani* arises, for example, with regard to the very important Hopi religious sites within the park. Here, ongoing cooperation between the Hopis and park officials, in a spirit of "joint stewardship," has facilitated tribal members' access to and preservation of religious sites within the park.

These arrangements are only a beginning, however, for the Hopis have a more extensive agenda for increasing their influence over park affairs. Recently, the tribe and the park have been cooperating on a plan to improve cultural interpretation of the Grand Canyon—one that would at last fully acknowledge the Hopis' long-standing association with the area. For the longer term, the Hopis envision full partnership with the park, wherein they could be involved in the administration, implementation, and enforcement of policy, especially with regard to their sacred sites. They also look for the park to develop written (rather than the existing, very informal) policies detailing tribal rights.[1] Finally, in a clear assertion of tribal sovereignty, the Hopis anticipate developing direct communications with Park Service regional offices, as well as with the head office in Washington, D.C. (Jenkins 1992).

Pressures for major changes in park management come from other sources as well. In the past few years, the Zunis have been in contact with the park to assert their tribal religious interests (Balsom 1991). Likewise, the San Juan Paiutes have expressed an active interest in activities associated with the park and with the larger Colorado Plateau region (James 1992). The Kaibab and Shivwits Paiutes have also become active in regional affairs, especially with regard to identifying and protecting religious and cultural sites, entering the park to gather plants and fish and so on, and (for the Kaibab Paiutes) developing their own tourism enterprises.

Though issues between the park and the Navajo Nation remain unresolved, a relatively equal balance of power currently exists between the two entities with regard to the Marble Canyon area, ironically due to both parties' lack of adequate funding to patrol it. Lack of a strong desire to resolve the issue—stimulated by park administrators' recent "agree to disagree policy" (Chandler 1992)—also plays a role. Unfortunately, the lack of a strong surveillance presence facilitates degradation and general overuse of the area and its resources.

Resolution of the problem has proven stubbornly difficult to achieve. At a 1990 meeting between park and tribal representatives, when the Navajos expressed disappointment that the park was not managing the area well, park representatives countered that without jurisdictional authority, and without resolution of where the boundary was actually located, they could not manage the area effectively. While both sides agreed that a memorandum of understanding was needed that would allow management of the area as if it were part of the national park, the only action taken to date has been the manufacture of heavy-duty signs to warn hikers they are entering the park. The signs, placed in the two areas of heaviest use—Jackass Canyon and Saltwater Draw—are intended to afford the park the tangible territorial claim it requires to legally enforce its rules and issue citations (Law 1992). Yet, without adequate staffing, placement of the signs remains an essentially empty gesture.

The recently initiated proposal to designate the stretch of the Colorado within the Grand Canyon as a wild and scenic river, and to designate scenic easements along its shoreline, may open up new opportunities to work cooperatively with the Navajo Nation in the Marble Canyon area (Crumbo 1992). Contrarily, it may engender a new boundary dispute because tribal members who live there are more interested in developing tourist enterprises, issuing permits, providing guide services, and constructing a new campground than they are in preserving adjacent lands in the "natural" state desired for the park.

From a geographical point of view, framing the Marble Canyon issues as boundary issues is important because, like the Hopis, the Navajos have no word for "boundary" in the English sense of the word; rather, the Navajo emphasis is on interrelationships to which boundaries create undesirable barriers. Canyon de Chelly National Monument, for example, has no boundary in the view of the local residents; residents live in and use the canyon much as they always have.

Navajo Superintendent Herbert Yazhe (1992) points to the success his staff has had in instituting cooperative management between the monument and its neighbors. The newly instituted approach focuses on open interactions and a sense of local ownership, rather than enforcement of boundaries. Although not all use problems have been solved, the arrangement (similar to those used in biosphere reserves and in national parks in developing countries) poses an interesting alternative to current Park Service philosophies. While still far from the management practices at Canyon de Chelly, the newly drafted general management plan for Grand Canyon National Park prominently features cooperation with other interests among its management goals (Grand Canyon National Park 1995). Though how this cooperation will be realized in practice remains to be seen, it is an important step away from the bunker mentality that inspired national park policies for many decades.

A Broader Look at the Issues

To date, continued control by the executive branch of federal agency appointments, especially within the Park Service, and chronically inadequate congressional budget appropriations have impeded effective management of lands and resources by the Park Service, as well as the Bureau of Land Management and the Forest Service. And although many environmentalists remain committed to resource protection, intensified political and fiscal conservatism at all levels of government continue to make implementing new initiatives extremely difficult. Even day-to-day operations suffer. On the North Rim of the Grand Canyon, for example, the park has only enough staff to patrol as far as Kanab Canyon, leaving many square miles to the west unprotected and vulnerable to incursions of all kinds. In a situation like this, the impracticability of expanding the absolute spaces of the park becomes painfully apparent, and the question of how park officials could manage more land, when they cannot even fully protect what the park already has, becomes unanswerable.

Another stumbling block to park enlargement is the economy of the greater Grand Canyon region. Housing costs are high and per capita and median incomes are low, due in part to the prevalence of lower-paying service-sector jobs and the limited job opportunities available for local Hispanics and Indians. Tourism has spurred considerable job growth: 57,000 new jobs were added in 1993 alone, mostly in the service, retail, and state and local government sectors. However, whereas employment has increased by 145 percent in Coconino County, residents' per-job earnings actually decreased between 1970 and 1991. The 1991 unemployment rate in the county was high, at 8 percent (the overall rate in the state was 6 percent), rising to 10 percent in the winter. The statistic for Indians has been higher still: in 1993 the on-reservation unemployment rate was 22 percent, while the off-reservation rate was only 6 percent (Grand Canyon National Park 1995). The situation is made worse by the lack of a large land base (only 14 percent of the county is privately owned) and by a scarcity of good-quality water, both of which hinder the kind of development that would improve living conditions for local residents. Under these conditions, there is little likelihood of making significant additions to the park. Nor would such action be advisable unless new ways of generating adequate income were devised. In the meantime, local residents continue to defend their absolute, relative, and representational spaces vociferously.

The Ranchers' View

Ranchers, timber operators, and miners, acting as individual interests, remain strong voices in the definition and use of the lands and resources of the greater Grand Canyon, as do hunters and other recreationists. On the surface, this interest should make regional cooperation eminently attainable. Yet these groups' objections to the agendas and perspectives of environmental organizations (not least on the grounds that environmentalists consistently ignore local needs and lifeways) remain a large stumbling block. Criticisms of environmentalists' bigotry toward American Indians (Byler and Byler 1991) and of environmentalists' "excessive emotionalism"—presumably as opposed to rational scientific approaches!—(Metzger 1992) also impede cooperation. Even Bruce Babbitt has admitted that older members of his family who are still involved in ranching in the Flagstaff area continue to have expectations that the public lands they use might eventually be deeded over to them (Babbitt 1994).[2]

Yet, beneath it all, there is a wistfulness about the bygone days of ranching. Today, ranchers such as Billy Cordasco (grandson of John Babbitt and manager of the CO Bar and Cataract Ranches) and Jack Metzger follow Allan Savory's grazing philosophy, which involves the belief that intensive grazing on pastures and movement between fields as resources are consumed enhance the health and sustainability of rangeland resources. They complain about the damage elk herds are causing, especially to the fences needed to restrain livestock movements. Jack Metzger, who grew up at the Grand Canyon and worked for the Babbitt ranching operations before acquiring his own Flying M Ranch, deplores the vandalism that has accompanied recreational use of grazing lands and structures, and he looks back nostalgically to the days when ranchers were respected for their knowledge not only of livestock raising, but of Nature (Cordasco 1992; Metzger 1992). In many ways, they have a point: the lands would not be as attractive for other uses as they are today if ranchers had truly been rapacious land managers. And it is an understatement that not all recreationists are respecters of Nature. Nevertheless, persistent evidence of overgrazing, soil erosion, and disruption of native plant and animal communities is very real. In the end, agreement on what the landscape should look like and how its natural and human systems should function is critical if these problems are ever to be resolved.

The Potential for Regional Cooperation

Perhaps the strongest motivation for bringing local groups together in the cause of regional cooperation is concern about quality-of-life issues. To the extent that these concerns are in tune with larger concerns regarding management of natural resources, there exists a potentially broad base of support for managing the resources of the greater Grand Canyon in terms of relative spaces rather than in terms of the absolute spaces outlined by the many boundaries of the area. To the extent that advocates of park expansion and wilderness expansion ignore these opportunities, the gap between themselves and their rivals widens.

But boundary issues are far from the top of the list of priorities for the park. With more than four million visitors per year to manage, park administrators' priorities have, of necessity, been focused on how to protect park resources while accommodating the hordes of tourists (Travers 1992). Yet park officials continue to worry about real and potential noncompatible uses of adjacent lands (Grand Canyon National Park 1992)—these concerns, at heart, are boundary issues.

Will the use of cartographic boundaries as a resource management tool disappear? Not in the near future. But the boundaries may become more flexible, depending on the extent to which the various entities represented within the greater Grand Canyon region are able to develop truly cooperative management policies and practices. New rules and procedures will have to be established—ones that are based on the needs of the larger region, not on any one interest's agenda. Crucial to any new management regime will be recognition by park administrators that buffer zones and contextual issues extend *into the park,* as well as into lands extending outward from park boundaries. Bruce Babbitt's concept of "dominant use" might provide a useful starting point for such broad, cooperative management.

What constitutes that larger region must also be resolved: will it be the Colorado Plateau, as delineated by the Grand Canyon Trust, or will it be some other spatial configuration? The Colorado Plateau may be too large for effective cooperation to occur. What criteria will participants use to define that region? And what situations will cause the location, size, and configuration to be altered? How can we develop institutions to cope effectively with fluid geographical configurations? How will the power to define problems and to propose and adopt solutions to those problems be allocated? Who will be recognized as legitimate players? And, finally, who will lead the charge?

Though boundaries as political institutions are unlikely to disappear, boundary issues might finally be rendered obsolete if the idea of an ongoing, open forum were created that could reach consensus (or compromise) on outstanding issues while at the same time recognizing and respecting important social, economic, and cultural differences. For this to occur, the forum (whether facilitated by the Grand Canyon Trust or some other organization) would have to frame negotiation as an ongoing, never-ending process, rather than as a short-term effort to bring a narrowly defined problem to a "final solution." And there would have to be a much greater sense of urgency among the general populace than exists today with regard to the management of the natural resources of the greater Grand Canyon.

CHAPTER TEN

Looking Backward—and Forward

Looking back over the history and geography of the spaces and boundaries of the greater Grand Canyon, we see a progression from conquest to contest to incipient cooperation. In the years leading up to the creation of the first forest reserve, game preserve, and national monument, the native peoples were subdued, deprived of vast amounts of their lands, and restricted by concepts and practices—such as boundaries and private property—to a new form of space: reservations. In the meantime, settlers divided and subdivided the lands they had expropriated from the Indians, creating more spaces and boundaries, each defined according to its value and use. Some were absolute spaces, such as private property (and Indian reservations), and some were relative spaces, such as public grazing lands and forests.

As natural resource exploitation turned into environmental depredation, and as the United States changed more and more from an agrarian to an urban, industrial society, new efforts emerged to refine—and redefine—the spaces of the greater Grand Canyon. A new representational space of resource conservation, nature preservation, and tourism emerged and soon generated protracted contests with ranchers, loggers, miners, and other resource users over how much—if any—space should be dedicated to these ends. Out of the contests emerged new spaces: Grand Canyon National Forest and Grand Canyon Game Preserve, and the first (1908) Grand Canyon National Monument. All were relative spaces within which certain activities (such as the establishment of residences) were prohibited and others—associated with the exploitation of natural resources—were to be managed for long-term sustainability. The degree of protection afforded dictated the extent to which the areas gravitated toward becoming absolute spaces: Grand Canyon National Monument, with its stronger restrictions against uses that would degrade the scenery of the area, therefore, came closest to becoming an absolute space.

As events, conditions, and expectations changed at the national level, so too did the definitions and uses of the spaces of the greater Grand Canyon. With the creation of the U.S. Forest Service and the National Park Service came greater federal government intrusion into local affairs, including the management of natural resources. At the same time, the formal admission of Arizona to the Union established a framework within which regional demands could come to the fore. The combination of changes at the national and state levels found expression in the conversion of Grand Canyon National Monument into Grand Canyon National Park. The park boundaries, defining as they did a space within which all activities and resource usages would be governed, encompassed an absolute space of preservation and tourism. Yet the new boundaries were unstable, for they did not encompass the representational spaces of nature preservation envisioned by park advocates. The result was a new round of contests to bring the absolute and representational spaces of the park into alignment.

Park advocates won some additions to the absolute spaces of the park in 1927, but the power of the resource users and the Forest Service denied park supporters the representational spaces they so ardently sought. Efforts to justify major expansions in terms of wildlife management fell flat; ultimately, arguments based on efficiency of administration won only very limited additions to the park. Likewise, in the 1930s, substantial park expansions were advocated based on new knowledge arising from the sciences of biology and ecology, and on a desire to control entire habitats of valued game species. Again, the Park Service was unable to overcome criticisms of its game management policies (no hunting of game animals, but extermination of predators). The Park Service acquired a new Grand Canyon National Monument instead, justified on the basis of the uniqueness of its views of the Grand Canyon and of its volcanic formations. As was the case with the original national monument, the new addition constituted a quasi-relative space in which dams could be built and grazing continued. Also like the original monument, it was a presidential end-run around a Congress that consistently refused to "lock up" more lands from full resource exploitation. Subsequent efforts on the part of resource users to abolish the new monument failed (though they did win some deletions), heralding the beginning of an era in which urban-based recreationists and preservationists gained a stronger voice in how the public lands and resources of the nation would be defined, partitioned, and used.

The creation of Marble Canyon National Monument in 1969, as well as the 1956 and 1968 legislative victories that put huge roadblocks in the path of hydropower projects in the Grand Canyon, testified to the growing strength of the environmental lobby and brought to the fore once again issues of who was to be empowered to govern the uses of what lands, for what purposes.

The 1975 park enlargement act, P.L. 93-620, created a new absolute space, but that space essentially comprised only those quasi-relative spaces (Grand Canyon National Monument, Marble Canyon National Monument, and portions of Lake Mead National Recreation Area) over which the Park Service already had power. Again, preservationists lost their battle to extend the park into the resource-rich rimlands north and south of the canyon. Even the act's provision for a study of the most desired adjacent North Rim lands failed to achieve their incorporation into the park. As revealed by the National Parks and Conservation Association's recommendations for boundary revisions at Grand Canyon, and by park administrators' concerns about external threats, the absolute spaces of the park still do not encompass the representational spaces prized by preservationists. That the Park Service has made a significant transition to pursuing cooperative management of sensitive lands rather than pressing for further boundary modifications has done nothing to blunt the preservationists' agenda. Frequent appeals for donations mailed by the National Parks and Conservation Association continue to stress the need for major boundary adjustments, including adjustments at Grand Canyon as outlined in its 1988 report.

It would be erroneous, however, to read the history of the spaces of the greater Grand Canyon merely as a narrative of changes to park boundaries. The boundaries of the national forests at Grand Canyon follow the limits of the forestlands of the area quite closely, revealing the extent to which those boundaries enclose a relative space based on forests as units of natural resource production. They also testify to the early power and influence of Gifford Pinchot in retaining these valuable resources within the public domain, even in the face of strong local protest, and to the long-standing power of the agency he founded, the U.S. Forest Service, to not only repel repeated Park Service attempts to expropriate major portions of its lands, but to incorporate the values of the Park Service's preservationist and recreationist constituencies into its definition of its own mission. The malleability of the Forest Service's relative spaces—based on philosophies of multiple use and sustained yield for forestry, mining, grazing, recreation, and wilderness—has proven to be a powerful weapon in the agency's efforts not only to retain control of its lands, but also to maintain its legitimacy within the increasingly contentious world of natural resource management.

The Bureau of Land Management provides an even more striking example of an agency whose power is over relative space, for its holdings are often intermingled with state and private lands, creating a checkerboard pattern of boundaries. The pattern, as revealed in the material landscape of the greater Grand Canyon, is one of relative spaces devoted primarily to grazing, but also to hunting, recreation, and wilderness preservation. The question arises, however, can these lands ever be constructed as representational spaces? (The same question might be posed for Forest Service lands as well.) In fact, local resource users have over the years become more cognizant of their need to articulate their rootedness in the land, and they have become more adept in getting their perspective across to the public. And they have been notably successful in attracting support for their cause. The Wise Use movement is only the latest—and one of the more radical—of the groups. Others, such as logging communities and livestock growers' associations, also work to defend the resource user's way of life and to define the representational spaces they value.

The experiences of the Indians of the greater Grand Canyon constitute a narrative of loss, of efforts to learn new rules and to operate within an entirely foreign mode of knowledge. Despite the many impediments they faced, the absolute spaces of their reservation lands proved to be one of their most potent weapons in their fight for cultural (and sometimes physical) survival. The Navajos were by far the most successful in reacquiring major portions of their ancestral lands, eventually extending their reservation westward as far as the Grand Canyon. Indeed, of all the tribes, the Navajos have come closest to aligning their absolute spaces with their representational spaces, though they have never achieved control over some of their most sacred sites, including the San Francisco Peaks and the Grand Canyon itself.

The Havasupais, having lost almost all of their ancestral lands, fought with amazing persistence and intensity for more than seventy years to reacquire significant portions of their representational spaces. Their greatest adversaries were the Park Service and its preservationist supporters, but in the end, public sentiment favored the Havasupais' human needs—albeit within tight land and resource restrictions—over the Park Service's quest to protect Nature. Here, the contest over competing definitions of representational space ended in a compromise— one that traded complete control over absolute space (by either the park or the tribe) for a quasi-relative space over which the tribe could pursue low-impact development and use, but over which the park could exercise veto power with regard to nonconforming uses.

The Havasupais won another small victory over the park as well, for (just as they received use rights within the park in the 1919 act) the park enlargement act gave them limited use within an area designated as the Havasupai Use Lands. Although these lands, lying between the reservation and the Colorado River, were defined as belonging to the park, P.L. 93-620 required that tribal members be allowed to enter the area for traditional purposes such as hunting, gathering, and live- stock grazing. The Havasupai Use Lands constitute not merely the only "buffer" area included in the park enlargement legislation, but also a relative space defined in terms of traditional resource uses. They also form part of the tribe's representational spaces, which continue to ex- tend far beyond the reservation boundaries to include the entire Grand Canyon abyss as well as rimlands to the east and south.

The Hualapais, Hopis, and Kaibab Paiutes share experiences similar to those of the Navajos and Havasupais with regard to the loss of lands, acquisition of reservations, and continued lack of congruence between their absolute and representational spaces. All of these peoples (the Zunis and San Juan and Shivwits Paiutes as well) have strong cultural and spiritual linkages to the Grand Canyon itself; none (with the possible exception of the Hualapai Tribe) even comes close to having a reservation whose absolute space encompasses its ancestral lands. The San Juan Paiutes do not even have a territorial anchor— a reservation—on which to ground their cultural identity. Theirs is merely a relative space of residence and subsistence within the encom- passing Navajo Reservation.

For all of the voices of the greater Grand Canyon, the best promise the future seems to hold is the development of closer cooperation and more frequent and open communication. Such interaction implies a much greater movement toward coexisting within relative spaces of resource management and cultural affinity. Whether these efforts can produce better congruences with each group's representational spaces remains to be seen.

The story of the division of the greater Grand Canyon into different kinds of spaces is interesting in its own right, as well as for its echoes of other, often very similar, stories that permeate the history of U.S. public land management. Yet I believe the lessons of this story may be extended even further. By pondering on the dynamism inherent in society's construction of geographical spaces and how that dynamism is both embedded in and influences economic, political, and social institutions and processes occurring at various scales of social and spatial resolution, perhaps we will be able to improve our understanding of the relations between humans and their geographies. We remain at odds regarding which of our lands should be used—and how they should be used—and which should be preserved. The issues are local but at the same time national and international.

Perhaps at last we are beginning to realize the true extent of our physical, political, economic, and social interconnectedness. As revealed in recent international events—including the tragic war in the former Yugoslavia, the movement toward a European Community, and free trade between Canada, the United States, and Mexico—learning new ways to cooperate and live together is vitally important. We have only to consider the dismantling of the Berlin Wall to comprehend the dynamism existing within even rigidly defended spaces and boundaries. Likewise, we need look no farther than Palestine to appreciate the difficulties of choosing between constructing absolute and relative spaces in an area where representational spaces are completely overlapping and yet fiercely differentiated between Israelis and Palestinians.

The story of the partitioning of the greater Grand Canyon suggests that policies governing how differences come to be manifested in geographical space would profit immensely from deep inquiries into how these spaces and their boundaries are reaffirmed—or challenged—in everyday practices. Likewise, seeking out the muted voices of those who have been excluded from meaningful participation in the processes associated with the definition and partitioning of space could reveal hitherto unappreciated sources of resistance—resistance which would be likely to persist as long as the needs, values, and aspirations of marginalized groups continue to be unmet.

Even among dominant groups whose voices are regularly heard, challenges to existing spatial arrangements may emerge. Attention to factors such as how differences are defined, what objectives are being pursued, what strategies are being used to pursue those objectives, what rules and structures facilitate or constrain the process, and what rationales are presented for configuring geographical space in particular ways can open up new vistas on both the processes and the outcomes of these contests.

At the same time, full recognition of the dynamism inherent in socially defined space, and serious consideration of the limitations of print media (including maps) for representing that dynamism, are essential. Similarly, contexts are important in how such contests play out. The functions that the spaces and their boundaries are meant to serve are also important, both as outcomes of these contests and as inputs to subsequent contests. Only by capturing the process of spatial definition, partitioning, and delineation in all of its richness, dynamism, and diversity can we begin to understand the complexity of our very human relationships with the spaces we occupy, the resources we use, and the places we value.

NOTES

Introduction

1. The inspiration for this framework was derived from Michel Foucault (1982).

Chapter 1

1. "Usufruct" refers to a right or privilege to use a designated parcel of land, or the resources of that land, without interference from others. Unlike private property, however, usufruct is lost if the user fails to exploit the land or resource for some specified period of time. The usufruct, in such a case, reverts to the controlling entity (e.g., the tribe) and may be reallocated to someone else.

2. During formal proceedings of the Indian Claims Commission, the overlapping activities of the Hopis and Navajos prompted the commissioners to refuse to recognize the peaks as part of either the Navajos' or the Hopis' traditional domain, because neither could prove exclusive use. However, both tribes have persistently fought to maintain a voice in how the area is used. The tribes strongly object, for example, to the ski resort on Mount Humphreys (Rosenthal 1985).

3. The route selected for this road, running from Fort Smith, Arkansas, to California (Putt 1991), was generally the same one chosen some years later for the Santa Fe Railroad tracks (Hughes 1967).

4. The treaty process was not formally ended until 1871, though the last treaty was signed in 1868.

5. Two thousand Navajos, one-fourth of all those interned at Bosque Redondo, died there.

6. The Navajo Reservation was enlarged in 1878, 1880, 1884, 1900, 1901, 1905, 1907, 1933, and 1934, absorbing the San Juan Paiute lands (and thus for many years the Paiutes' identity as a separate tribal entity) and eventually encircling the Hopi Reservation. None of the other tribes in the area has been as successful in expanding its land base.

7. In subsequent years, the Navajos encroached more and more on Hopi lands. In 1958, a federal court declared that 1.5 million acres of the Hopi Reservation be set aside for exclusive use by the Hopis and ordered that the rest of the 1882 reservation lands be shared equally between the Hopis and the Navajos. The U.S. Supreme court upheld the decision in 1962, but conflict over this Joint Use Area continued. In 1974, Congress authorized the division of the Joint Use Area between the Hopis and the Navajos (which involved the drawing of a new boundary line between the two reservations and the relocation of people onto lands within their respective tribal domains), but even this

modification of the arrangement failed to resolve the dispute. Although relocation of Hopi and Navajo residents of the disputed area (known as the "Bennett Freeze Zone") was to have been completed by 1986, resistance continues, and the issue remains hotly contested by both sides.

8. This reservation was terminated in 1954 pursuant to U.S. House of Representatives Concurrent Resolution No. 108 (passed in 1953), which terminated U.S. trust responsibility for Indians. The Shivwits were among the Southern Paiute bands that were subsequently reinstated by the U.S. government, but as of 1986 they did not possess a territorial base (Kelly and Fowler 1986).

9. Ironically, in view of later events, the Mormons themselves facilitated the establishment of this reservation. The church, around 1900, obtained rights to one-third of the flow of Moccasin Spring for the tribe.

Chapter 2

1. Three other Babbitt brothers also arrived in Flagstaff, two of whom, George and Charles, stayed for the rest of their lives and contributed to the formation of the northern Arizona Babbitt dynasty. In addition to ranching, the Babbitt family was also involved in businesses ranging from Babbitt's general store to Indian trading posts, a lumber company, and even, for a while, a funeral parlor (Smith 1989).

2. Powell eventually took over from Clarence Dutton as the head of the U.S. Geological Survey, and he undertook the first major effort to produce a full set of topographic maps of the West. A student of Indians, he classified Indian languages and immersed himself in Indian folklore, activities that eventually led to his becoming head of ethnography at the Smithsonian Institution.

3. The Santa Fe Railroad profited particularly well from exchanges of Grand Canyon Forest Reserve lands: the company traded 50,000 acres of commercial timber for 260,000 acres of scrip redeemable for nontimbered federal lands and 115,000 acres of scrip redeemable for timbered lands located elsewhere (Putt 1991, 42–43).

4. It is interesting to note that this proclamation applied to deer and other animals recognized as "game animals" but did not apply to predators (Hughes 1978).

5. A copy of the map accompanying the proclamation is archived on microfiche in the L1417 files at Grand Canyon National Park.

6. Today, ecologists see the absence of such predators as a signal that the ecosystem is badly out of balance (Worster 1979, 261).

Chapter 3

1. The Geological Society of America had suggested naming it Powell National Park in honor of explorer John Wesley Powell.

2. Such sentiments for including in national parks only the "worthless" land have been common throughout the history of the national parks movement (Runte 1979).

3. Earlier drafts had not recognized the Havasupais' continued occupance of and need for the plateau lands above their reservation in Havasu Canyon.

4. A similar dilemma occurred on the Piman Ak Chin Reservation in central Arizona, where reservation boundaries influenced a series of bureaucratic decisions that eventually led to the construction of what turned out to be an irrational irrigation project (McGuire 1988).

5. For an early description of life among the Havasupai, see *People of the Blue Water: My Adventures among the Walapai and Havasupai Indians* by Flora Gregg Iliff (1954).

6. It was in 1919 also that Horace Albright first tried to resign from the Park Service. Mather persuaded him to become superintendent of Yellowstone National Park instead (Albright 1985).

Chapter 4

1. In addition, the state of Arizona holds 9,637,000 acres (13.26 percent of the total land area of the state); only 11,658,000 (16.04 percent) of the state is within the private domain (Walker and Bufkin 1986).

2. Only some 160 taxpaying individuals/families were actually living on the Arizona Strip as of 1936 (Malach 1975).

3. Although efforts continued for some years to add this area to the park, it has remained part of the Navajo Reservation.

4. Another area used by the Navajos, however, was recommended by Eakin for inclusion in the park, on the grounds that it would be good antelope habitat.

5. By the late 1960s, this area was being identified as one where a buffer zone was needed to protect park values.

Chapter 5

1. The Park Service's stress on tourism development and visitor accommodation prompted the Save the Redwood League to oppose creation of a Redwood National Park, during this era, within prime stands of the huge trees. In the league's estimation, the policies of the Park Service were ruining the landscapes it was supposed to be protecting (Schrepfer 1983).

2. The field of eugenics had become quite popular in the 1920s. The belief among its supporters was that through intervening in natural selection and evolutionary processes, the genetic makeup of species (including humans) could be improved. This, in turn, would contribute to the steady progress toward human and natural perfection. For some, the preservation and propagation, within parks and wildernesses, of those species that would contribute to human perfection were a means to this end. The Park Service, however, never incorporated eugenics into its programs or officially recognized it as a science (Schrepfer 1983).

3. Merriam also saw preservation of nature as a religious mission; at the parks visitors would be forced to think about creation (Schrepfer 1983).

4. Albright took over from Mather in 1929 and served as director until

1933. Cammerer assumed the directorship upon Albright's departure in 1933 and served until 1940.

5. With the advent of the Civilian Conservation Corps, improvements in trails and other facilities were accomplished—and accomplished so well that they have lasted for decades with little or no repair work having to be done.

6. Significantly, the Biological Survey did not want any publicity on Bailey's report and requested that the Park Service not give the report out (Albright 1930).

7. Though Bailey worked for the Biological Survey, the agency had never adopted his recommendations.

8. The wildlife management issue was particularly sensitive because the park prohibited the hunting of game animals but at the same time carried on a campaign to eliminate predators. In fact, until 1927, government hunters were paid to shoot predators within the park, and Grand Canyon National Park rangers continued, until 1931, to exterminate predators (Hughes 1978). The change of heart toward predators can be traced to the growth of the relatively new science of ecology, which stressed the importance of interactions in maintaining biological stability. The national parks provided ideal places to preserve predators, not only for the sake of the ecosystems, but also so that the public could, in safety, have opportunities to view them (Worster 1979). This decision was as unpopular with ranchers as the prohibition of hunting was with hunters.

9. McCullough's scattergun approach probably intensified resistance to the plans, but, although the railroads may have been sympathetic to park expansion for their own profit motives, the flurry of letters and memoranda that flew back and forth during this time show no evidence of railroad involvement.

10. Interior Secretary Fall, implicated in the Teapot Dome scandal, resigned in 1923 (Deloria and Lytle 1984).

11. The exception was an important one, for lands such as those that had been designated for reclamation projects were excluded from the provision, as were mineral lands claimed by the Tohono O'odham tribe of Arizona—a provision insisted upon by the mining industry and its spokesman, Senator Henry Ashurst of Arizona (Deloria and Lytle 1984).

12. Representative Murdock, discovering that his bill would have negative legal effects on power-site withdrawals in the canyon, decided to request that his bill be passed over without prejudice. A self-professed believer in national parks and monuments, he nevertheless believed that the natural resources of such areas should be exploited for utilitarian purposes (Moskey 1937).

13. Jackson, Jensen, and McCormick were the main spokespersons for Fredonia residents and were the leaders in the area on grazing issues. Jackson and Jensen were quite prosperous (Lloyd 1938).

14. Dam operators argued that siltation problems would shorten the useful lifespan of the dam unless another dam was built upstream to relieve the problem.

15. Harold C. Bryant, associated with the University of California, Berkeley, was a strong and prominent advocate of environmental education and for many years worked hard to develop and implement interpretive programs at

the national parks. He took over from Tillotson in 1939, serving as acting superintendent of the park from 1939 to 1940, then served as official superintendent of the park from 1941 to 1954. He had his greatest influence on the Park Service, however, in his position as the head of the Park Service's Branch of Education and Research, a position he held from 1928 to 1939 (Olsen 1985; Schrepfer 1983).

Chapter 6

1. Most people saw the act as a major step toward increased self-government, though whether it was successful remains debatable (Deloria and Lytle 1984).

2. Interestingly, when the tribe was asked whether any other lands besides those in the national park would be as satisfactory, they agreed that the Three-Vee Ranch would, but that the ranch was not for sale. This same ranch (also known as the Boquillas Ranch) was proposed as an addition to the reservation during the bitter contest over park enlargement in the early 1970s.

3. Presumably the lands controlled by the Arizona Livestock Company were part of those purchased by the Navajos as the Boquillas Ranch.

4. Environmental historian Donald Worster (1985) chronicles the history of the Colorado River's transformation from a free-flowing stream to a water reclamation project. The result of all the investments of money and technology, he argues, was a florescence of the West as a hydraulic society, beginning with the construction of Boulder Dam in 1935. For a fascinating account of the personalities involved, see John McPhee's *Encounters with the Archdruid* (1971).

5. McArdle assured Wirth that scenic strips of trees would be left along Point Sublime Road. Presumably, such a sleight-of-eye would not diminish the tourist's experience!

6. On this last day, Johnson added approximately 300,000 acres of federal lands to the national park system (Cahn 1969).

Chapter 7

1. Morton's predecessor at the Interior Department, Walter Hickel, had tried to oust Hartzog at the same time he fired all other bureau chiefs in the department, but he backed off when he realized that Hartzog enjoyed high respect in Congress and that Nixon's Interior Department programs would face rough weather if Hartzog was fired. Subsequently, a trivial incident involving the acquisition of land for Biscayne National Monument in Florida earned Hartzog Nixon's enmity and gave Morton the excuse he needed to fire Hartzog (Everhart 1983).

2. Stewart Udall believed that the National Park Service had become too professionalized and too narrowly focused. No longer did the agency respond to broad public needs; rather, it operated to protect its own narrowly defined self-interest. To alleviate the problem, Udall asserted more control over the department, setting a precedent that continues today (Foresta 1984).

3. Although companion bills to the Goldwater and Case bills were introduced in the House during the same congressional sessions as the Senate bills, it was the Goldwater and Case bills that stimulated the most action and controversy.

4. For an excellent analysis of the Havasupai dilemma and the extent to which the expansion they finally achieved was adequate to meet their needs, see Martin 1985.

5. Rodack cited an Arizona Office of Economic Planning and Development document that aimed to improve tribal welfare by undertaking intensive tourism development, including the construction of a tramway into the Grand Canyon. The tribe had long since disowned the plan.

6. The tribe expected to receive $1 million per year from power sales and job opportunities for tribal members, a considerable boon given the tribe's otherwise intractably poor economic status.

7. By this time, considerable opposition to the zone of influence concept had grown to include not only the National Forest Service, but also the town of Williams, Arizona, and various timber interests. Although opposition to the buffer zone idea had become widespread, it was not unanimous: the Arizona section of the National Wildlife Federation and the Arizona Cattle Growers' Association indicated their support for the concept—as long as hunting and grazing were allowed to continue (U.S. Senate 1973a).

8. Arizona Governor Williams also wanted the dam site excluded, arguing that recreational developments associated with the Hualapai dam and reservoir would offer spectacular recreation. Ultimately, however, Williams changed his stance and announced his support for S. 1296 (U.S. Senate 1973a).

9. This type of issue had arisen earlier when Lake Mead National Recreation Area was created: some Hualapai lands had been designated for inclusion there as well, provided the tribe concurred.

10. The argument pressed by environmentalists, and also used by the Park Service, for opposing the transfer of these lands to the tribe was that the tribe would allow inappropriate development to occur. The source of the worry over such development was the same study to which Juel Rodack had alluded (see note 5, above). Eventually, Congressman Morris Udall criticized the inaccurate references to these plans as "unfair and unworthy," and Congressman Sam Steiger labeled the environmentalists "green bigots" (*Akwesasne Notes,* early spring, 1975, 36).

11. The Havasupais decided to fight for the public lands they had been using rather than pursue the Boquillas Ranch lands, which were at some distance from the heart of their reservation in Havasu Canyon. Ultimately, in a scandal-ridden series of transactions, the Navajo Nation acquired the 500,000-acre ranch, in 1988, for more than $33 million. To date, plans for Navajo-owned tourism enterprises (including a theme park), a tribal cattle company, and distribution of lands to land-needy tribal members have not been realized. Rather, profits are generated by leasing the lands to a private company (Donovan 1995).

12. Apparently, environmental groups were proposing as an alternative that the tribe be given management of park concessions or of tourist facilities

just south of the park, presumably in the Tusayan area (*Environmental Action* 1974).

13. This was probably the only sound reason for objecting to the transfer. The addition held little prospect for significant economic improvement for the tribe, given the low quality of the lands and the restrictions on development options (Martin 1985).

Chapter 8

1. "Less-than-fee easements" involve the acquisition of development rights in areas near park boundaries, instead of the outright purchase of an entire property. The ownership boundaries do not change, but ownership by the Park Service of easement rights enables the agency to prevent specified forms of development or use within the easement zone. "Greenline parks" are specially designated regions that consist of a mix of public and private land ownership. The arrangement entails comprehensive planning aimed at ensuring preservation of the region's lands and resources. No formal category of greenline parks has ever been established within the Park Service, but the idea was quite influential in the way congressional legislation for new parks was written in the late 1970s. Cuyahoga Valley and Santa Monica Mountains National Recreation Areas are examples of "greenline park" units (Foresta 1984).

2. These lands had previously been within Lake Mead National Recreation Area, a less restrictive designation that permitted grazing.

3. These problems had arisen earlier as well. Park Superintendent Marks gave the Arizona Game and Fish Department permission in 1985 to expand the agency's law enforcement activities between Lees Ferry and Jackass Canyon because of increased use by fishermen (Marks 1985b).

4. The Navajo Tribe faced an earlier boundary problem when, in 1982, the Arizona legislature passed legislation to slice Apache and Navajo Counties in half, so as to separate Indian voters—of whom the Navajos were the largest in number—from non-Indian voters. The new boundary would have cut from east to west, severing the main Indian populations from the non-Indians. The reason for the move was that non-Indians were unhappy with Navajo majority votes that raised taxes for people living outside reservation boundaries (reservation Indians and their activities cannot be taxed) but directed the funds to reservation projects. Governor Bruce Babbitt vetoed the legislation on the grounds that it was a racially motivated solution to an essentially economic conflict (Phelps 1991).

5. The park claimed the "historical high-water mark area" as its southern boundary. The historical high-water mark is defined by the park as the highest level to which water reached before the dams were built.

6. The park could stand to gain from the project because, due to a lack of housing within park boundaries, jobs at the park have gone unfilled.

7. DePaolo claims ties were severed when it became apparent that Babbitt was in line for a position in President Bill Clinton's administration (Hawkins 1994).

8. Employment in the area is especially problematical because the Forest

Service has had to reduce the amount of timber being harvested in the area. In addition to its own development plans, the Forest Service has been working with the Kaibab Paiutes to coordinate its recreation development plans with the tribe's tourism development efforts (Lund 1992).

9. The report covered thirteen parks, including Grand Canyon.

10. These 24,288 acres of Navajo Reservation lands were the same ones that had been authorized for inclusion in the park in the 1975 enlargement act, subject to tribal concurrence.

11. See, for example, the movie *Grand Canyon* (Twentieth Century Fox, 1991) for an offbeat view of the place of the Grand Canyon in contemporary culture!

Chapter 9

1. Tribal access to park lands has been allowed only on an informal basis to date, although the relationship has been largely satisfactory to the tribe.

2. The centerpiece of the Babbitt ranching operations, the CO Bar Ranch, in recent years has been reduced to a fraction of its former size, encompassing some 850,000 acres north of Flagstaff, extending across half of Kaibab National Forest eastward to include large portions of Wupatki National Monument, stopping on the east at the Little Colorado River. In 1975, this ranch was spun off to shareholders. The other Babbitt Ranch, Cataract Ranch, lies west of the railroad that runs from Williams to the Grand Canyon (Smith 1989).

REFERENCES

Abbey, Edward
   1977   *The Journey Home.* New York: E. P. Dutton.
Adams, Robert W.
   1974   Letter to Morris Udall, November 15, 1974. Morris Udall Archives, Legislative Assistant Files, 93d Congress, Box 25. Special Collections, University of Arizona Library.
Akwesasne Notes
   1975   Havasupai Grand Canyonlands Returned. *Akwesasne Notes* (early spring 1975):36.
Albright, Horace M.
   1985   *The Birth of the National Park Service: The Founding Years, 1913–1933.* Salt Lake City and Chicago: Howe Brothers.
   1930   Telegram to M. R. Tillotson, May 9, 1930. Grand Canyon National Park Archives.
Allen, Mark
   1989   Native American Control of Tribal Natural Resource Development in the Context of the Federal Trust and Tribal Self-Determination. *Boston College Environmental Affairs Law Review* 16:857–895.
Babbitt, Bruce
   1994   Utah Public Television interview with Bruce Babbitt, June 1994. Transcript.
   1991   Public Use and the Future of the Federal Lands. *A Society to Match the Scenery: Personal Visions of the Future of the American West,* ed. Gary Holthaus, Patricia Nelson Limerick, Charles F. Wilkinson, and Eve Stryker Munson, 163–170. Niwot: University Press of Colorado.
Bailey, Vernon
   1929   Memorandum to Mr. Redington, December 5, 1929. Grand Canyon National Park Archives.
   nd   Grand Canyon National Park. Typescript. Grand Canyon National Park Archives.
Balsom, Jan
   1991   Interview with Robert Keller, Grand Canyon National Park, November 25, 1991.
Bashore, H. W.
   1944   Memorandum to Newton B. Drury, September 5, 1944. Grand Canyon National Park Archives.
Basso, Keith H.
   1990   "Speaking with Names": Language and Landscape among the

Western Apache. *Western Apache Language and Culture: Essays in Linguistic Anthropology,* 138–173. Tucson: University of Arizona Press.

Bracey, Terry
1973   Memorandum to Morris Udall, January 3, 1973. Morris Udall Archives, Legislative Assistant Files, 93d Congress, Box 21. Special Collections, University of Arizona Library.

Brew, J. O.
1979   Hopi Prehistory and History to 1850. *Handbook of American Indians,* vol. 9, 514–523. Washington, D.C.: Smithsonian Institution.

Brugge, David M.
1986   Navajo Prehistory and History to 1850. *Handbook of American Indians,* vol. 11, 368–397. Washington, D.C.: Smithsonian Institution.

Brugge, David M., and J. Lee Correll
1971   *The Story of the Navajo Treaties.* Navajo Historical Publications, Documentary Series No. 1. Window Rock: Research Section, Navajo Parks and Recreation.

Bryant, H. C.
1946   Memorandum to the Region Three Director, January 29, 1946. Grand Canyon National Park Archives.

1945   Memorandum to the Region Three Director, May 10, 1945. Grand Canyon National Park Archives.

1944   Memorandum to the Region Three Director, October 31, 1944. Grand Canyon National Park Archives.

1943b   Memorandum to the Director, July 19, 1943. Grand Canyon National Park Archives.

1943a   Memorandum to the Director, April 29, 1943. Grand Canyon National Park Archives.

Bunney, Gary E.
1976   Memorandum to the Western Region Director, June 21, 1976. Grand Canyon National Park Archives.

Bunte, Pamela A., and Robert J. Franklin
1987   *From the Sands to the Mountains: Change and Persistence in a Southern Paiute Community.* Lincoln: University of Nebraska Press.

Buono, Frank
1992   Interview with author, Grand Canyon National Park, February 25, 1992.

1990   Memorandum to Peter Rowlands and Kim Crumbo, October 2, 1990. Grand Canyon National Park Archives.

Bureau of Indian Affairs
1979   The Secretarial Land Use Plan for the Addition to the Havasupai Reservation. Draft Environmental Statement, Report No. INT DES 79–42, United States Department of the Interior, Washington, D.C.

Bureau of Reclamation

1992   Programmatic Agreement among the Bureau of Reclamation, the Advisory Council on Historic Preservation, the National Park Service, and the Arizona State Historic Preservation Office Regarding the Operation of the Glen Canyon Dam. Unpublished document. Page, Arizona: Bureau of Reclamation.

Byler, James H.

1974   Mailgram to Congressman Morris K. Udall, May 17, 1974. Morris Udall Archives, Legislative Correspondence Files, 93d Congress, Box 4. Special Collections, University of Arizona Library.

Byler, William, and MaryLou Byler

1991   Interview with Robert Keller, Washington, D. C., October 17, 1991.

Byrnes, Robert F.

1975   Letter to Sam Steiger, April 24, 1975. Grand Canyon National Park Archives.

Cahn, Robert

1969   How LBJ's national park plan slipped away. *Christian Science Monitor,* January 23, 1969.

Cammerer, Arno B.

1939   Memorandum to the Acting Superintendent, October 30, 1939. Grand Canyon National Park Archives.

1938   Letter to M. R. Tillotson, May 6, 1938. Grand Canyon National Park Archives.

1929   Letter to M. R. Tillotson, May 1, 1929. Grand Canyon National Park Archives.

Canyon Shadows

1974   Sierra Club votes to support Havasupai. *Canyon Shadows* February 3, 1974, 1–4.

Carothers, Steven W., and Bryan T. Brown

1991   *The Colorado River through the Grand Canyon.* Tucson: University of Arizona Press.

Chandler, Robert

1992   Interview with author, Grand Canyon National Park, May 11, 1992.

Collier, John

1943   Letter to Newton B. Drury, April 26, 1943. Grand Canyon National Park Archives.

Conkin, Merle E.

1973   Statement before the U.S. House of Representatives, Committee on Interior and Insular Affairs, Subcommittee on National Parks and Recreation, November 12, 1973. Morris Udall Archives, Legislative Assistant Files, 93d Congress, Box 25. Special Collections, University of Arizona Library.

Conservation Report

1974b   Floor action on expansion held over. *Conservation Report* No. 30, August 23, 1974, 407–408.

1974a   Consideration of Grand Canyon bill delayed by Democratic caucus. *Conservation Report* No. 25, July 19, 1974, 332.

Coordinating Commission on National Parks and Forests
1925   Report of the Coordinating Commission on the National Parks and Forests, October 15, 1925. Grand Canyon National Park Archives.

Cordasco, Billy
1992   Interview with author, Flagstaff, Arizona, April 10, 1992.

Critchfield, H. M.
1943   Letter to John O. Crow, October 21, 1943. Grand Canyon National Park Archives.

Crumbo, Kim
1994   Interim Wilderness Management, Grand Canyon and the Colorado River. Paper presented at the Sixth National Wilderness Conference, Santa Fe, New Mexico, November 14–18, 1994.

1992   Interview with author, Grand Canyon National Park, January 21, 1992.

Deloria, Vine, Jr., and Clifford Lytle
1984   *The Nations Within: The Past and Future of American Indian Sovereignty.* New York: Pantheon Books.

Demaray, A. E.
1937   Letter to M. R. Tillotson, July 3, 1937. Grand Canyon National Park Archives.

Dickinson, Russell E.
1974   Memorandum to the Secretary of the Interior, December 24, 1974. Grand Canyon National Park Archives.

Dobyns, Henry F., and Robert C. Euler
1971   *The Havasupai People.* Phoenix: Indian Tribal Series.

Donovan, Bill
1995   Big Boquillas spread remains a symbol of Navajo corruption. *The Arizona Republic,* February 19, 1995, B1, B3.

Drury, Newton B.
1943b   Memorandum to the Indian Affairs Commissioner, September 13, 1943. Grand Canyon National Park Archives.

1943a   Memorandum to Region Three Director, June 29, 1943. Grand Canyon National Park Archives.

Eakin, J. R.
1926b   Letter to Stephen T. Mather, August 4, 1926. Grand Canyon National Park Archives.

1926a   Letter to Colonel F. S. Breen, March 27, 1926. Grand Canyon National Park Archives.

1925d   Letter to Stephen Mather, September 4, 1925. Grand Canyon National Park Archives.

1925c   Letter to Stephen Mather, May 11, 1925. Grand Canyon National Park Archives.

1925b   Letter to Stephen Mather, May 5, 1925. Grand Canyon National Park Archives.

1925a   Letter to Stephen Mather, April 1, 1925. Grand Canyon National
         Park Archives.
1924b   Letter to Arno Cammerer, August 6, 1924. Grand Canyon Na-
         tional Park Archives.
1924a   Letter to Director, March 5, 1924. Grand Canyon National Park
         Archives.
Eiseman, Fred B., Jr.
1972   Letter to Morris Udall, November 7, 1972. Morris Udall Archives,
         Legislative Assistant Files, 93d Congress, Box 21. Special Collec-
         tions, University of Arizona Library.
Ellis, Florence H.
1974   The Hopi: Their History and Use of Lands. *Hopi Indians.* New
         York: Garland Publishing Company.
Environmental Action
1974   Grand Canyon up for grabs. *Environmental Action* September 28,
         1974, 7.
Evans, R. T.
1925   Letter to Stephen T. Mather, April 8, 1925. Grand Canyon Na-
         tional Park Archives.
1923   Letter to Colonel C. H. Birdseye, December 1, 1923. Grand Can-
         yon National Park Archives.
Everhart, William C.
1983   *The National Park Service.* Boulder, Colo.: Westview Press.
Flagstaff Game Protective Association
1930   Minutes of meeting, June 2, 1930. Grand Canyon National Park
         Archives.
Fletcher, Colin
1967   *The Man Who Walked through Time.* New York: Vintage Books.
Foresta, Ronald A.
1984   *America's National Parks and Their Keepers.* Washington, D.C.:
         Resources for the Future.
Foucault, Michel
1982   The Subject and Power. *Critical Inquiry* 8:777–795.
Fradkin, Philip L.
1981   *A River No More: The Colorado River and the West.* New York:
         Alfred A. Knopf.
Freemuth, John C.
1991   *Islands under Siege: National Parks and the Politics of External
         Threats.* Lawrence: University of Kansas Press.
1975   The History of S. 1296: The Enlargement of Grand Canyon Na-
         tional Park. M. A. thesis, Claremont Graduate School, Clare-
         mont, California.
Frizzell, Kent
1976   Letter to Sterling Mahone, April 22, 1976. Grand Canyon Na-
         tional Park Archives.

Gattrell, Anthony
　1983　*Distance and Space: A Geographical Perspective.* Oxford: Clarendon Press.
Gibbons, George
　1992　Interview with author, Tusayan, Arizona, February 27, 1992.
Goldwater, Barry
　1973　Letter to Morris Udall, April 26, 1973. Morris Udall Archives, Legislative Assistant Files, 93d Congress, Box 25. Special Collections, University of Arizona Library.
Goldwater, Barry, and Morris K. Udall
　1971　Letter to Frank Bracken, February 25, 1971. Grand Canyon National Park Archives.
Gordon-McCutcheon, R. C.
　1991　*The Taos Indians and the Battle for Blue Lake.* Santa Fe: Red Crane Books.
Grand Canyon National Park
　1995　Draft General Management Plan and Environmental Impact Statement. Grand Canyon National Park, March 1995.
　1993b　Preliminary Alternatives Workbook for General Management Plan. Grand Canyon National Park, September 1993.
　1993a　Final Wilderness Recommendation: 1993 Update. Grand Canyon National Park.
　1992　General Management Plan, Environmental Impact Statement, Scoping Summary. Grand Canyon National Park.
　1990　Wayside Plan Outline. Grand Canyon National Park, December 1990.
　1989b　Briefing Statements. Grand Canyon National Park, January 1989.
　1989a　Land Protection Plan. Grand Canyon National Park, November 1989.
　1988　Superintendent's Annual Report for 1988. Grand Canyon National Park.
　1984　Superintendent's Annual Report for 1983. Grand Canyon National Park, February 1984.
　1981b　Anonymous document, May 7, 1981. Grand Canyon National Park Archives.
　1981a　Adjacent Lands Study, public review draft, March 1981. Washington, D.C.: U.S. Department of Interior, National Park Service and Bureau of Land Management, and Department of Agriculture, National Forest Service.
　1978　Final Task Directive: Adjacent Lands Study, Grand Canyon National Park, Arizona. Washington, D.C.: U.S. Department of Interior, National Park Service.
　1976b　Preliminary Wilderness Proposal, July 1976. Washington, D.C.: U.S. Department of the Interior, National Park Service.
　1976a　Park Suitability Study, February 1976. Washington, D.C.: U.S. Department of the Interior, National Park Service.

1973   Grand Canyon National Park Master Plan. Grand Canyon National Park Archives.

1971   Grand Canyon National Park Master Plan, final working draft, August 1971. Grand Canyon National Park Archives.

nd   Discussion with Havasupai Tribe, BIA, and Forest Service. Grand Canyon National Park Archives.

Grand Canyon Trust

1990   The Future of the Colorado Plateau, Preserving Its Natural Wonders while Securing Economic Opportunity for Its Residents: A Progress Report to the Ford Foundation, May 1990. Grand Canyon Trust, Flagstaff, Arizona.

Greenwood, W. Barton

1943   Letter to A. W. Simington, January 30, 1943. Grand Canyon National Park Archives.

Guse, N. G.

1972   Memorandum to Superintendent, April 27, 1972. Grand Canyon National Park Archives.

Hardin, Garrett

1968   The Tragedy of the Commons. *Science* 162:1243–1248.

Havasupai Tribe

1973   Statement by the Havasupai Tribe before the United States House of Representatives, Committee on Interior and Insular Affairs, Subcommittee on National Parks and Recreation, November 12, 1973. Morris Udall Archives, Legislative Assistant Files, 93d Congress, Box 25. Special Collections, University of Arizona Library.

1967   Resolution No. 13–67 of the Governing Body of the Havasupai Reservation, Supai, Arizona, August 19, 1967. Grand Canyon National Park Archives.

Hawkins, Beth

1994   Canyon capitalism. *The Tucson Weekly,* July 6–12, 1994, 4–5, 10–11.

Hayden, Carl

1938b   Letter to H. L. Huffer, March 24, 1938. Grand Canyon National Park Archives.

1938a   Letter to M. R. Tillotson, January 6, 1938. Grand Canyon National Park Archives.

1937   Letter to Arno B. Cammerer, June 24, 1937. Grand Canyon National Park Archives.

Herman, Floyd

1974   Letter to the Arizona Wildlife Federation Club, September 3, 1974. Morris Udall Archives, Legislative Assistant Files, 93d Congress, Box 25. Special Collections, University of Arizona Library.

Hinchliffe, Louise M.

1976   Legislative History of Grand Canyon National Park. Unpublished report, August 1976. Grand Canyon National Park Archives.

Hirst, Stephen
    1976   *Life in a Narrow Place.* New York: David McKay.
Hodapp, Steve
    1987   Record of telephone call. Grand Canyon National Park Archives.
Hough, John
    1991   The Grand Canyon National Park and the Havasupai People: Co-
             operation and Conflict. *Resident Peoples and the National Parks:
             Social Dilemmas and Strategies in International Conservation,* ed.
             Patrick C. West and Steven R. Brechin, 215–230. Tucson: Univer-
             sity of Arizona Press.
Housley, Raymond M.
    1973   Statement of Raymond L. Housley, Associate Deputy Chief, Na-
             tional Forest Service, before the United States House of Represen-
             tatives, Committee on Interior and Insular Affairs, Subcommittee
             on National Parks and Recreation, November 12, 1973. Morris
             Udall Archives, Legislative Assistant Files, 93d Congress, Box 25.
             Special Collections, University of Arizona Library.
Hughes, J. Donald
    1978   *In the House of Stone and Light: A Human History of the Grand
             Canyon.* Grand Canyon, Arizona: Grand Canyon Natural His-
             tory Association.
    1967   *The Story of Man at the Grand Canyon.* Grand Canyon, Arizona:
             Grand Canyon Natural History Association, Bulletin No. 14.
Hulett, Stanley W.
    1973   Memorandum to Director, November 13, 1973. Grand Canyon
             National Park Archives.
Humphrey, Marshall
    1973   Statement of Marshall Humphrey, Chairman, Arizona Power Au-
             thority, before the United States House of Representatives, Com-
             mittee on Interior and Insular Affairs, Subcommittee on National
             Parks and Recreation, November 12, 1973. Morris Udall Ar-
             chives, Legislative Assistant Files, 93d Congress, Box 25. Special
             Collections, University of Arizona Library.
Iliff, Flora Gregg
    1954   *People of the Blue Water: My Adventures among the Walapai and
             Havasupai Indians.* New York: Harper and Brothers.
Indian Affairs
    1975   Havasupai victory. *Indian Affairs* No. 88, 1, 7.
    1974   Havasupai: One step toward freedom. *Indian Affairs* No. 87, 1–4.
Jackson, Elmer
    1945   Letter to Carl Hayden, November 15, 1945. Grand Canyon Na-
             tional Park Archives.
James, Evelyn
    1992   Letter to author, March 25, 1992.
Jenkins, Leigh
    1992   Interview with author, Flagstaff, Arizona, April 9, 1992.

Jones, Stephen B.
  1959   Boundary Concepts in the Setting of Place and Time. *Annals of the Association of American Geographers* 49(3):241–255.

Kauffman, John M.
  1954   Conservation Objectives at Grand Canyon: A History of the Boundaries of Grand Canyon National Park and Monument. Grand Canyon National Park Archives.

Kell, John E.
  1954   Boundary Study Report, Grand Canyon National Park and Grand Canyon National Monument, July 1954. Grand Canyon National Park Archives.

Kelly, Isabel T., and Catherine S. Fowler
  1986   Southern Paiute. *Handbook of American Indians,* vol. 11, 368–397. Washington, D.C.: Smithsonian Institution.

Ketchner, Wayne B.
  1974   Letter to Sam Steiger, May 22, 1974. Morris Udall Archives, Legislative Correspondence Files, 93d Congress, Box 4. Special Collections, University of Arizona Library.

Kreutz, Douglas
  1994   Canyon under siege. *Arizona Daily Star,* July 24, 1994.

Kulosa, Erwin
  1973   Statement of Erwin Kulosa, Manager, Southwestern Forest Resources Affairs for Federal Timber Purchasers Association, before the United States House of Representatives, Committee on Interior and Insular Affairs, Subcommittee on National Parks and Recreation, November 12, 1973. Morris Udall Archives, Legislative Assistant Files, 93d Congress, Box 25. Special Collections, University of Arizona Library.

Law, Mark
  1992   Interview with author, Grand Canyon National Park, February 25, 1992.

LeFebvre, Henri
  1991   *The Production of Space,* trans. David Nicholson-Smith. Oxford: Basil Blackwell.

Lindquist, Leonard A.
  1989   Letter to Jack Davis, February 1, 1989. Grand Canyon National Park Archives.

Lippman, Robert
  1987   Memorandum to Laura Loomis, July 13, 1987. Grand Canyon National Park Archives.

Lloyd, J. V.
  1938   Letter to M. R. Tillotson, January 14, 1938. Grand Canyon National Park Archives.

Lopez, Rick
  1994   Development proposal threatens canyon. *Arizona Daily Star,* August 22, 1994, A11.

Lovegren, Robert R.
   1972b   "Blue envelope" memorandum to Western Region Director, May
            8, 1972. Grand Canyon National Park Archives.
   1972a   Letter to J. R. Babbitt, May 8, 1972. Grand Canyon National
            Park Archives.
Lund, R. Dennis
   1994   Tusayan Land Exchange: Summary of Purpose and Need, Issues,
            and Alternatives. Kaibab National Forest, Recreation and Lands
            mailer.
   1992   Interview with author, Williams, Arizona, April 8, 1992.
MacDonald, Peter
   nd   Letter to Roy A. Taylor. Morris Udall Archives, Legislative Assis-
            tant Files, 93d Congress, Box 25. Special Collections, University
            of Arizona Library.
Mahone, Sterling
   1973   Statement of Sterling Mahone, Chairman, Hualapai Tribe, before
            House Subcommittee on National Parks and Recreation, House
            Committee on Interior and Insular Affairs, November 12, 1973.
            Morris Udall Archives, Legislative Assistant Files, 93d Congress,
            Box 25. Special Collections, University of Arizona Library.
Malach, Roman
   1975   *The Arizona Strip in Mohave County.* Kingman: Arizona Bicen-
            tennial Commission.
Manges, Gayle E.
   1969   Memorandum to Southwest Region Director, June 16, 1969.
            Grand Canyon National Park Archives.
Marks, Richard
   1985b   Letter to T. L. Britt, August 28, 1985. Grand Canyon National
            Park Archives.
   1985a   Statement for Management, Grand Canyon National Park, May
            10, 1985. Grand Canyon National Park Archives.
   1984   Briefing Statements, January 1984. Grand Canyon National Park
            Archives.
Martin, John F.
   1985   From Judgment to Land Restoration: The Havasupai Land Claims
            Case. *Irredeemable America,* ed. Imre Sutton, 271–300. Albuquer-
            que: University of New Mexico Press.
Mather, Stephen T.
   1925   Letter to Henry W. Temple, May 14, 1925. Grand Canyon Na-
            tional Park Archives.
   1923   Letter to Philip J. Smith, September 10, 1923. Grand Canyon Na-
            tional Park Archives.
McArdle, Richard E.
   1956   Letter to Conrad L. Wirth, April 10, 1956. Grand Canyon Na-
            tional Park Archives.

McClure, Beaumont C.

1991   Letter to John Lancaster, November 29, 1991. Grand Canyon National Park Archives.

McComb, John A.

1975   *Southwest Wildlands* 5(6), November 5, 1975. Grand Canyon National Park Archives.

1973   Testimony of John A. McComb, Southwest Representative, Sierra Club, before House Subcommittee on National Parks and Recreation, Committee on Interior and Insular Affairs, November 12, 1973. Morris Udall Archives, Legislative Assistant Files, 93d Congress, Box 25. Special Collections, University of Arizona Library.

1971   Memorandum to Terry Emerson and Terry Bracey, February 22, 1971. Morris Udall Archives, Legislative Assistant Files, 93d Congress, Box 21. Special Collections, University of Arizona Library.

McCullough, T. E.

1930   Letter to Henry Ashurst, June 16, 1930. Grand Canyon National Park Archives.

McGuire, Thomas R.

1988   Illusions of Choice in the Indian Irrigation Service: The Ak-Chin Project and an Epilogue. *Journal of the Southwest* 30(2):200–221.

McLaughlin, John S.

1955   Memorandum to Director, November 17, 1955. Grand Canyon National Park Archives.

McPhee, John

1971   *Encounters with the Archdruid.* New York: Farrar, Straus and Giroux.

Metzger, Jack

1992   Interview with author, Flagstaff, Arizona, April 10, 1992.

Moskey, G. A.

1937   Letter to Director, August 4, 1937. Grand Canyon National Park Archives.

Mott, William

1985   Letter to John McCain, October 9, 1985. Grand Canyon National Park Archives.

Nash, Roderick

1982   *Wilderness and the American Mind.* 3d ed. New Haven: Yale University Press.

National Parks and Conservation Association

1988   Selected Boundary Adjustments: Arches, Bandelier, Canyonlands, Carlsbad Caverns, Guadalupe Mountains, Congaree Swamp, Curecanti National Recreation Area, Custer Battlefield, Dinosaur, Everglades/Big Cypress, Grand Canyon, Olympic, Yosemite National Parks. February 1988. Washington, D.C.: National Parks and Conservation Association.

National Park Service

1991   Authorities for Water Resources Decision Making on the Colorado River. Draft report, April 1991. Fort Collins, Colo.: U.S.

Department of the Interior, National Park Service, Water Resources Division.

1973b Memorandum to Regional Directors, September 14, 1973. Grand Canyon National Park Archives.

1973a Memorandum to Associate Director for Legislation, February 6, 1973. Grand Canyon National Park Archives.

1937   Letter to William B. Bankhead, March 19, 1937. Grand Canyon National Park Archives.

New York Times

1974   Grand Canyon raid. *New York Times,* July 10, 1974.

Nielson, E. G.

1957   Memorandum to Legislative Counsel, May 10, 1957. Grand Canyon National Park Archives.

Nixon, Richard

1974   Statement by the President, May 3, 1974. Morris Udall Archives, Legislative Assistant Files, 93d Congress, Box 25. Special Collections, University of Arizona Library.

O'Brien, Jack

1981   Memorandum (no addressee indicated), May 11, 1981. Grand Canyon National Park Archives.

Olmsted, Frederick Law, H. C. Bryant, and Harold Ratcliff

1943   Report on Indian Service Proposal for Transfer of Grand Canyon National Park and Monument Lands to Indian Service as Reservation for Havasupai Indians, May 4, 1943. Grand Canyon National Park Archives.

Olsen, Russ

1985   Administrative History: Organizational Structures of the National Park Service, 1917 to 1985. Washington, D.C.: National Park Service.

Paya, Oscar

1974   Telegram to Morris Udall, March 4, 1974. Morris Udall Archives, Legislative Correspondence Files, 93d Congress, Box 4. Special Collections, University of Arizona Library.

1973   Letter to Juel Rodack, March 4, 1973. Morris Udall Archives, Legislative Assistant Files, 93d Congress, Box 21. Special Collections, University of Arizona Library.

Perlin, John

1989   *A Forest Journey: The Role of Wood in the Development of Civilization.* New York: W. W. Norton.

Person, G. W., and James A. Diffin

1930   Letter to W.E.S. Thompson, April 19, 1930. Grand Canyon National Park Archives.

Phelps, Glenn A.

1991   Mr. Gerry Goes to Arizona: Electoral Geography and Voting Rights in Navajo Country. *American Indian Culture and Research Journal* 15(2):63–92.

Pontius, Dale
  1974   Memorandum to Morris K. Udall, October 30, 1974. Morris
          Udall Archives, Legislative Assistant Files, 93d Congress, Box 25.
          Special Collections, University of Arizona Library.
Pooler, Frank C. W.
  1940   Letter to Chief Forester, May 1940. Grand Canyon National
          Park Archives.
Powell, John Wesley
  1962   *Report on the Lands of the Arid Region of the United States with
          a More Detailed Account of the Lands of Utah,* 2d ed. Cambridge,
          Mass.: Belknap Press.
Pratt, E. B.
  1937   Letter to Carl Hayden, December 30, 1937. Grand Canyon Na-
          tional Park Archives.
Pratt, Elwin
  1937   Letter to Carl Hayden, December 31, 1937. Grand Canyon Na-
          tional Park Archives.
Prescott, J.V.R.
  1987   *Political Frontiers and Boundaries.* London: Hutchinson.
Putt, Patrick John
  1991   *South Kaibab National Forest: A Historical Overview.* Williams,
          Arizona: Kaibab National Forest Office.
Pyne, Stephen J.
  1989   *Fire on the Rim.* New York: Weidenfeld and Nicolson.
  1982   *Dutton's Point: An Intellectual History of the Grand Canyon.*
          Grand Canyon Village: Grand Canyon Natural History Associa-
          tion, Monograph No. 5.
Qua'Toqti
  1974b   Kennedy joins supporters in Havasupai land return. *Qua'Toqti,*
          May 30, 1974, 1.
  1974a   Senator Humphrey supports Havasupai. *Qua'Toqti,* April 4,
          1974, 1.
Ray, John
  1992   Interview with author, Grand Canyon National Park, February
          25, 1992.
Redington, Paul G., and R. Y. Stuart
  1930   Letter to Horace M. Albright, February 19, 1930. Grand Canyon
          National Park Archives.
Reed, John
  1992   Interview with author, Grand Canyon National Park, January
          23, 1992.
Robinson, Bestor
  1950   Letter to Frederick Law Olmsted, March 3, 1950. Grand Canyon
          National Park Archives.
Robinson, Glen O.
  1975   *The Forest Service.* Baltimore: Johns Hopkins University Press, for
          Resources for the Future.

Rodack, Juel
  1973   Letter to Oscar Paya, March 8, 1973. Morris Udall Archives, Leg-
            islative Assistant Files, 93d Congress, Box 25. Special Collections,
            University of Arizona Library.

Rose, Carol M.
  1985   Possession as the Origin of Property. *The University of Chicago
            Law Review* 52(73):73–88.

Rosenthal, Harvey D.
  1985   Indian Claims and the American Conscience. *Irredeemable
            America,* ed. Imre Sutton, 35–70. Albuquerque: University of New
            Mexico Press.

Ruch, Jim
  1992   Interview with author, Flagstaff, Arizona, March 9, 1992.

Runte, Alfred
  1979   *National Parks: The American Experience.* Lincoln: University of
            Nebraska Press.

Russo, John
  1964   The Kaibab North Deer Herd—Its History, Problems, and Man-
            agement. State of Arizona Fish and Game Department, *Wildlife
            Bulletin* No. 7, July 1964.

Sahlins, Peter
  1989   *Boundaries: The Making of France and Spain in the Pyrenees.*
            Berkeley: University of California Press.

Saux, Curt
  1983   Memorandum to Chief of Resources, July 20, 1983. Grand Can-
            yon National Park Archives.

Sax, Joseph
  1976   Helpless Giants: The National Parks and the Regulation of Private
            Lands. *Michigan Law Review* 75:239–274.

Schrepfer, Susan R.
  1983   *The Fight to Save the Redwoods: A History of Environmental Re-
            form, 1917–1978.* Madison: University of Wisconsin Press.

Scoyen, E. T.
  1957   Memorandum to Legislative Counsel, February 25, 1957. Grand
            Canyon National Park Archives.

Searle, R. Newell
  1977   *Saving Quetico-Superior: A Land Set Apart.* St. Paul: Minnesota
            Historical Society Press.

Seaton, Fred A.
  1961   Covering Brief to the President, January 13, 1961. Grand Canyon
            National Park Archives.

Seavey, Charles A.
  1994   "The Most Sublime of All Earthly Spectacles": Exploration and
            Mapping of the Grand Canyon. *Exploration and Mapping of the
            National Parks,* ed. Jenny Marie Johnson, 148–181. Occasional
            Paper No. 4, Map and Geography Round Table of the American
            Library Association. Winnetka, Ill.: Speculum Orbis Press.

Seymour, Edmund
1930   Letter to Horace M. Albright, August 18, 1930. Grand Canyon National Park Archives.

Shadegg, Stephen C.
1986   *Arizona Politics: The Struggle to End One-Party Rule.* Tempe: Arizona State University.

Shankland, Robert
1951   *Steve Mather of the National Parks.* New York: Alfred A. Knopf.

Sierra Club
1974   Statement of Position of the National Native American Issues Committee of the Sierra Club—Havasupai and the Grand Canyon National Park Bill (S. 1296, H. R. 5900), March 30, 1974. Morris Udall Archives, Legislative Assistant Files, 93d Congress, Box 25. Special Collections, University of Arizona Library.

Simington, A. W.
1943   Letter to Allan G. Harper, March 20, 1943. Grand Canyon National Park Archives.

Skeels, Alfred
1926   Letter to J. R. Eakin, March 30, 1926. Grand Canyon National Park Archives.

Smith, Dean
1989   *Brothers Five: The Babbitts of Arizona.* Tempe: Arizona Historical Foundation.

Smith, Henry Nash
1970   *Virgin Land: The American West as Symbol and Myth.* Cambridge: Harvard University Press.

Smith, Melvin T.
1972   The Colorado River: Its History in the Lower Canyons Area. Ph.D. dissertation, Brigham Young University, Salt Lake City, Utah.

Soja, Edward W.
1989   *Postmodern Geographies: The Reassertion of Space in Critical Social Theory.* London: Verso.

Sparks, Joe
nd   Havasupai: Justice or Questions of Precedent. Morris Udall Archives, Legislative Assistant Files, 93d Congress, Box 25. Special Collections, University of Arizona Library.

Stegner, Wallace
1954   *Beyond the 100th Meridian: John Wesley Powell and the Second Opening of the West.* Boston: Houghton Mifflin Company.

Steiger, Sam
1975   Letter to John Kyl, April 30, 1975. Grand Canyon National Park Archives.

Stoffle, Richard W., and Michael J. Evans
1978   *Kaibab Paiute History: The Early Years.* Fredonia, Arizona: Kaibab Paiute Tribe.

Stoffle, Richard W., David B. Halmo, Michael J. Evans, and Diane E. Austin
1993   Piapaxa 'Uipi (Big River Canyon): Ethnographic Resource Inven-

tory and Assessment for Colorado River Corridor, Glen Canyon National Recreation Area, Utah and Arizona, and Grand Canyon National Park, Arizona. Draft final report, November 1993. Bureau of Applied Research in Anthropology, University of Arizona, Tucson.

Stuart, R. Y.
1930   Letter to Carl Hayden, June 9, 1930. Grand Canyon National Park Archives.

Suazo, Pedro A.
1972   Memorandum to Western Region Director, August 2, 1972. Grand Canyon National Park Archives.

Sutphen, Debra L.
1991   Grandview, Hermit, and South Kaibab Trails: Linking the Past, Present and Future at the Grand Canyon of the Colorado, 1890–1990. M. A. thesis, Flagstaff, Northern Arizona University.

Thompson, Ben H.
1955   Memorandum to Region Three Director, December 19, 1955. Grand Canyon National Park Archives.
1945   Report to M. R. Tillotson, January 31, 1945. Grand Canyon National Park Archives.

Thompson, Richard A.
1972   Letter to Fred B. Eiseman, Jr., January 8, 1972. Grand Canyon National Park Archives.

Tillotson, M. R.
1949   Memorandum to Director, January 10, 1949. Grand Canyon National Park Archives.
1945   Memorandum to Director, April 6, 1945. Grand Canyon National Park Archives.
1938b   Letter to J. D. Walkup, March 16, 1938. Grand Canyon National Park Archives.
1938a   Letter to Mohave County Board of Supervisors, March 16, 1938. Grand Canyon National Park Archives.
1937   Letter to Carl Hayden, July 5, 1937. Grand Canyon National Park Archives.
1936   Letter to Director, June 10, 1936. Grand Canyon National Park Archives.
1935   Letter to Director, September 25, 1935. Grand Canyon National Park Archives.
1930b   Letter to Director, May 8, 1930. Grand Canyon National Park Archives.
1930a   Letter to Director, April 29, 1930. Grand Canyon National Park Archives.

Tillotson, M. R., and Frank J. Taylor
1935   *Grand Canyon Country.* Stanford, Calif.: Stanford University Press.

Travers, Brad
  1992   Interview with author, Grand Canyon National Park, January
          22, 1992.
Twight, Ben W.
  1983   *Organizational Values and Political Power: The Forest Service
          Versus the Olympic National Park*. University Park: Pennsylvania
          State University Press.
Udall, Morris K.
  1974b   Letter to Edward B. Danson, June 7, 1974. Morris Udall Archives,
          Legislative Correspondence Files, 93d Congress, Box 4. Special
          Collections, University of Arizona Library.
  1974a   Letter to Oscar Paya, March 6, 1974. Morris Udall Archives, Leg-
          islative Correspondence Files, 93d Congress, Box 4. Special Col-
          lections, University of Arizona Library.
Udall, Stewart L.
  1966   Letter to John J. Rhodes, May 23, 1966. Grand Canyon National
          Park Archives.
  1963   *The Quiet Crisis*. New York: Holt, Rinehart and Winston.
U.S. Congress
  1974   Committee on Interior and Insular Affairs Report and Dissenting
          Views to Accompany S. 1296, Further Protecting the Outstanding
          Scenic, Natural and Scientific Values of the Grand Canyon by En-
          larging the Grand Canyon National Park in the State of Arizona,
          and for Other Purposes. Report No. 93–1374, U.S. Congress,
          House of Representatives, 93d Congress, 2d Session, September
          25, 1974.
U.S. Department of Agriculture
  1988   Tools to Manage the Past: Research Priorities for Cultural Re-
          sources Management in the Southwest. General Technical Report
          RM–164. U.S. Department of Agriculture, Rocky Mountain For-
          est and Range Experiment Station, Fort Collins, Colo.
U.S. Department of the Interior
  1989   Analysis of the Operating Criteria and Alternatives of Glen Can-
          yon Dam, AZ, Colorado River Storage Project. *Federal Register*
          54(207):43870–43871.
  1976b   Memorandum to the Associate Solicitor, February 6, 1976. Grand
          Canyon National Park Archives.
  1976a   Letter to Carl Albert, January 23, 1976. Grand Canyon National
          Park Archives.
  1925   Memorandum for the press, October 31, 1925. Grand Canyon
          National Park Archives.
U.S. Forest Service
  1987   Kaibab National Forest Plan, October 1987. Washington, D.C.:
          Department of Agriculture, U.S. Forest Service.
U.S. House of Representatives
  1974b   Enlarging the Grand Canyon National Park, Conference Report

No. 93-1611 to Accompany S. 1296. House of Representatives, 93d Congress, 2d Session, December 17, 1974.

1974a   *Congressional Record.* House of Representatives, 93d Congress, 2d Session, October 11, 1974. Copy on file in Grand Canyon National Park Archives.

U.S. Senate

1973b   Enlarging the Grand Canyon National Park in the State of Arizona. Report No. 93-406, Senate Miscellaneous Reports on Public Bills, September 21, 1973, vol. 13017-6, 93d Congress, 1st Session.

1973a   Hearing before the Subcommittee on Parks and Recreation of the Committee on Interior and Insular Affairs, June 20, 1973, 93d Congress, 1st Session. Washington, D.C.: U.S. Government Printing Office.

Verkamp, Margaret M.

1940   History of Grand Canyon National Park. M. A. thesis, Flagstaff, Northern Arizona University.

Walema, Edgar

1991   Interview with Robert Keller, Peach Springs, Arizona, November 14, 1991.

Walker, Henry P., and Don Bufkin

1986   *Historical Atlas of Arizona.* 2d ed. Norman: University of Oklahoma Press.

Walkup, J. D.

1938b   Letter to John R. Murdock, March 18, 1938. Grand Canyon National Park Archives.

1938a   Letter to Henry F. Ashurst, March 18, 1938. Grand Canyon National Park Archives.

Walkup, J. D., and H. L. Huffer

1938   Resolution of the Flagstaff Chamber of Commerce, March 4, 1938. Grand Canyon National Park Archives.

Whitney, Stephen

1982   *A Field Guide to the Grand Canyon.* New York: Quill.

Wirth, Conrad L.

1957   Memorandum to Legislative Counsel, May 27, 1957. Grand Canyon National Park Archives.

1956   Letter to Barry Goldwater, November 1956. Grand Canyon National Park Archives.

1954   Memorandum to Regional Director, Region Three, June 22, 1954. Grand Canyon National Park Archives.

Witherspoon, Gary

1986   Navajo Social Organization. *Handbook of North American Indians,* vol. 11, 368–397. Washington, D.C.: Smithsonian Institution.

Witzig, Fred T.

1983   The Crane Lake Issue in the Establishment of Voyageurs National Park. *Upper Midwest History* 3:41–53.

Worster, Donald

    1985   *Rivers of Empire: Water, Aridity, and the Growth of the American West.* New York: Pantheon Books.

    1979   *Nature's Economy: The Roots of Ecology.* Garden City, New York: Anchor Press/Doubleday.

Wray, Jacilee

    1990   Havasupai Ethnohistory on the South Rim of Grand Canyon National Park: A Case Study for Cultural Resource Management in the National Park Service. M. A. thesis, Flagstaff, Northern Arizona University.

Yard, Sterling

    1919   *The New Grand Canyon National Park: An Analysis of Its Scenic Features with Suggestions for Its Better Comprehension and Enjoyment.* Washington, D.C.: National Parks Association.

Yazhe, Herbert

    1992   Interview with author, Tucson, Arizona, May 8, 1992.

Young, James L.

    1973   Statement of James L. Young, President, Kaibab Industries, before the United States House of Representatives, Subcommittee on National Parks and Recreation, Committee on Interior and Insular Affairs, November 12, 1973. Morris Udall Archives, Legislative Assistant Files, 93d Congress, Box 25. Special Collections, University of Arizona Library.

INDEX

ABOUT THE AUTHOR

Barbara Morehouse has a long-standing interest in natural resource management and in the interplay of ideas and personalities that underpin the ways we understand and use those resources. A geographer by training, she combines a lively interest in politics, culture, and environmental science with a curiosity about how America's landscapes have evolved into highly distinctive forms. Barbara Morehouse holds a Ph.D. in geography from the University of Arizona and has taught both there and at the University of Minnesota—Duluth.